IMAGES of America

DETROIT'S DEAF HERITAGE

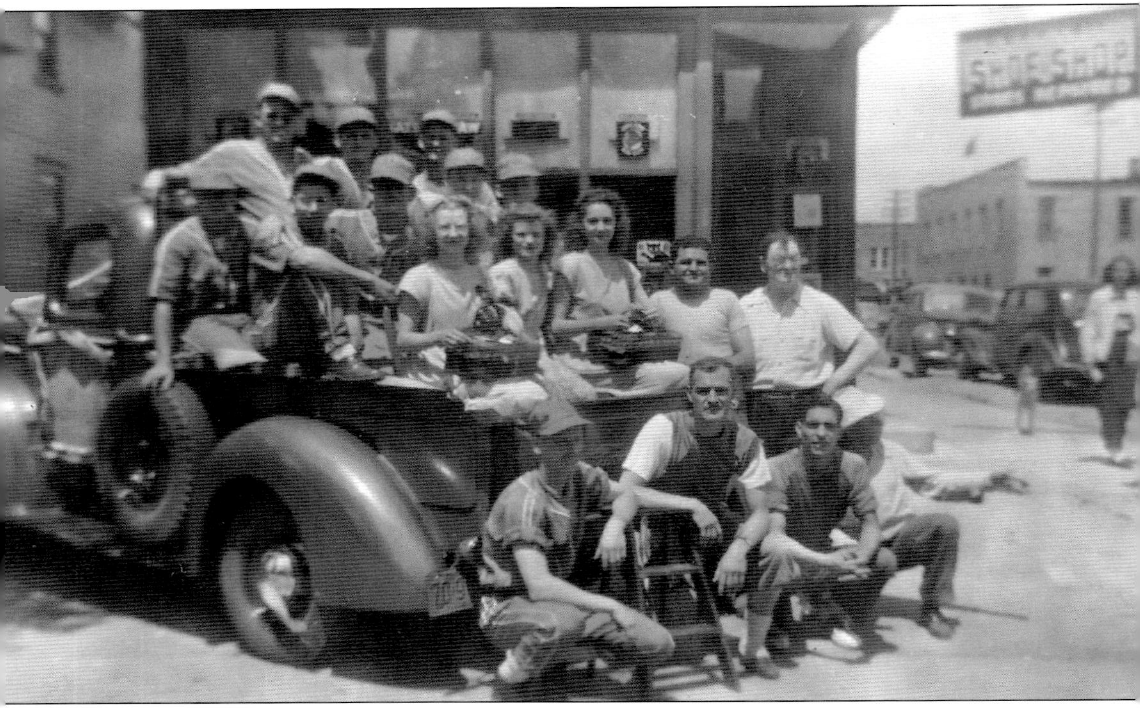

ON THE COVER: A group of Detroit Association of the Deaf members and the Wahowiak deaf family are excited to be part of the Fourth of July parade in the Upper Peninsula town of Gladstone around 1945. From left to right are (first row) Frederick McCall, Raymond Wahowiak, Frank Friday Jr., and unidentified; (second row) Germaine "Joan" Wahowiak, Helen Friday, Melvina Wahowiak McCall, Joseph Nuchs, and John Wahowiak, the Shoe Hospital's deaf owner. Everyone in the third row is unidentified. The Shoe Hospital was located at 901 Minnesota Avenue in Gladstone. John and his wife, Georgianna, ran the shop since the early 1920s. Their deaf son Raymond and his wife, Joan, took over in 1957. The business is no longer running and the structure has been converted into an apartment building. Melvina McCall died in 2015, leaving Helen Friday and Germaine Wahowiak as the only ones in this photograph known to still be alive. (Courtesy of Anson and Kathy McCall Mitchell.)

IMAGES
of America

DETROIT'S DEAF HERITAGE

Kathleen Brockway on behalf of the
Detroit Association of the Deaf

ARCADIA
PUBLISHING

ISBN 978-1-4671-1601-5

Published by Arcadia Publishing
Charleston, South Carolina

Printed in the United States of America

Library of Congress Control Number: 2015958047

For all general information, please contact Arcadia Publishing:
Telephone 843-853-2070
Fax 843-853-0044
E-mail sales@arcadiapublishing.com
For customer service and orders:
Toll-Free 1-888-313-2665

Visit us on the Internet at www.arcadiapublishing.com

We, Kathleen Brockway and the Detroit Association of the Deaf, dedicate this book to the Deaf Community.

Contents

ACKNOWLEDGMENTS

As the primary author, I am grateful for everybody's help, including, in no particular order, Patricia Strandell Schultz and David Croll, both DAD members who answered my questions and made referrals with great patience; Ashley and Maureen Aiple, my daughters, for their patience; DAD members who were very great in communicating; Nancy Capek McCall; Clare Cassidy Photography; Ronald Rood Sr. and Rose Russell; Carole Wood Mair; Grace Beaver Wood Cherniaski; the Deaf News group in Michigan; Ray McCall; Arlyn and Hester Meyerson; Judy and Larry Vardon; Glenn and Susan Stewart; Dr. Glenn Anderson; Dr. Ernest Hairston; Istvan "Steve" Kovacs; Donna Delikta Klarr; Robert and Diane Strandell Snider; Paul and Carol Kuplicki; Paul Kuplicki Jr.; Fr. Michael Depcik and the SJDC volunteers; FAD, MDA, and MSD staff; MSD Alumni Association; Charles and Diane Cutshaw McKittrick; Anson and Kathleen McCall Mitchell; Abram Powell; Diane Knight; Helen Booker; Rosalyn and Jack Gannon; and more whom I have not named—they have provided wonderful help sharing these stories with the public, especially showing that there are more unknown deaf role models out there.

Key to abbreviations:

AAAD	American Athletics Association of the Deaf
ASL	American Sign Language
BSL	British Sign Language
CAAD	Central Athletics Association of the Deaf
DAD	Detroit Association of the Deaf
DDSD	Detroit Day Deaf School
FAD	Flint Association of the Deaf
LSD	Lutheran School for the Deaf
MAD	Michigan Association of the Deaf (later Michigan Deaf Association)
MCAD	Motor City Association of the Deaf
MDA	Michigan Deaf Association
MSD	Michigan School for the Deaf
SJDC	St. John's Deaf Center

Introduction

In the early 1900s, Detroit, known as the "Motor City," welcomed many, including prominent transplanted figures, to work and interact in the Deaf Community. Detroit attracted Benjamin Beaver along with his brother, Ralph Beaver, both of whom moved from Illinois to the booming city and became active in the newly founded Detroit Association of the Deaf (DAD), one of the oldest deaf clubs in America. They were not the only ones who came from Illinois; Ivor Friday and Henry Furman followed Ralph and Benjamin. The Illinois deaf men joined Emanuel Jacobs, the early Detroit deaf leader, to establish the Rosedale Club at Benjamin and Ralph Beaver's home on Rosedale Court in Detroit around 1916. Soon their home became a known social site for the deaf athletes who longed for a permanent club. The main purpose of any deaf club is to be a gathering place in which deaf people can feel free to mingle and enjoy the company of their own kind. Emanuel Jacobs and Ivor Friday soon moved "the Rosedalers" to Monroe Avenue. According to the 1941 *Silver Jubilee Program and Year Book* celebrating the 25th-anniversary banquet, everybody agreed that Emanuel Jacobs was the founder and first president of the club. Jacobs was also often the one who took responsibility for completing the details. Friday was known to deserve half of the credit for the establishment. Benjamin Beaver was also honored for the many things he did to push the club into a long-running establishment. He was a longtime member and the oldest at the time of his death.

The Beaver family today runs to five deaf generations on Ralph Beaver's side. The Beavers use American Sign Language (ASL) as their primary communication method. Some attended college and had good jobs to support their families and themselves. Tragically, one member of the Beaver family, Carroll C. Wood, was killed in a terrible car collision crossing a Toledo bridge during extremely icy weather on the way to an invitational basketball tournament in Pittsburgh in 1962. Carroll was killed instantly along with fellow Motor City Association of the Deaf (MCAD) basketball players William W. Knight III and Marvin R. Pierce and coach Valerio DiFalco. Carroll was the son of Grace Beaver Cherniawski, and was Ralph Beaver's grandson. After graduating from the Michigan School for the Deaf (MSD), Carroll's twin deaf sister, Carole, left to attend Gallaudet College (now University) while Carroll stayed behind and chose to work a stable job as the linotype machine operator for the *Wayne Dispatch* in Wayne, Michigan.

Not many in the Deaf Community participated in religion; those who did were mostly Catholic or Lutheran. There is a long history of Catholic deaf organizations being active in services to help the Deaf Community. The only known Protestant school for deaf children in America was the Lutheran School for the Deaf. Some students remembered leaving either Detroit Day Deaf School (DDSD) or MSD to attend two years at Lutheran School for the Deaf (LSD) for their confirmation studies, after which some returned to their own schools to remain as students. There were Jewish deaf residents here; some did not practice the Jewish faith in the Deaf Community, despite the fact that one of the first deaf rabbis in America, David Rabinowitz, lived in Michigan. Rabinowitz, a native of New York City, was ordained in 1962 and died in 2007, when his widow moved back to New York. In my interviews, not many knew about him or attended the Jewish services he provided, and no one could find a photograph of him in time for this book.

Sports were my favorite subject of all in researching this book, though I could not share all of the stories here. The most popular sport in the adult Deaf Community in Michigan has long been bowling. There was even a short-lived newsletter, the *Great Lakes News*, founded in 1934 by Morris Purviance and Alexander Lobsinger, both strong DAD members, that specialized in current events and gossip among bowling organizations in the Great Lakes states. Eventually, that newsletter became popular across America and included news of marriages, events, and gossip. The memory most kept talking about was the best football years at MSD in the 1960s. Istvan "Steve" Kovacs, Anson Mitchell, Dominic "Junior" Zito, and Abram Powell played the school's best years with their deaf coach, Earl Roberts. The most unique sport I found at MSD was the fencing club in the early 20th century, which included both boys and girls.

The buildings pictured in this book are important to the Deaf Community. These schools, businesses, and other buildings hold sentimental memories for the community to hold onto. The MSD superintendent's cottage is the most heartbreaking memory for the Deaf Community, as the State of Michigan sold that building to a developer along with the entire MSD campus. The state is now renting the land from the developer for MSD. The dream is to have it back in the Deaf Community, as the early MSD students built it with their own hands, greatly saving the state labor costs. In the memories chapter, I wanted to share some good and valued memories that can be kept here forever for readers.

With my research and interviews throughout the nation, much communication was through ASL, which is currently recognized as a natural language and is used in bilingual education in state deaf schools across America. In Michigan, deaf-oral individuals went through changes, and presently, sign language is preferred over the oral method.

One

One of the Earliest Deaf Families

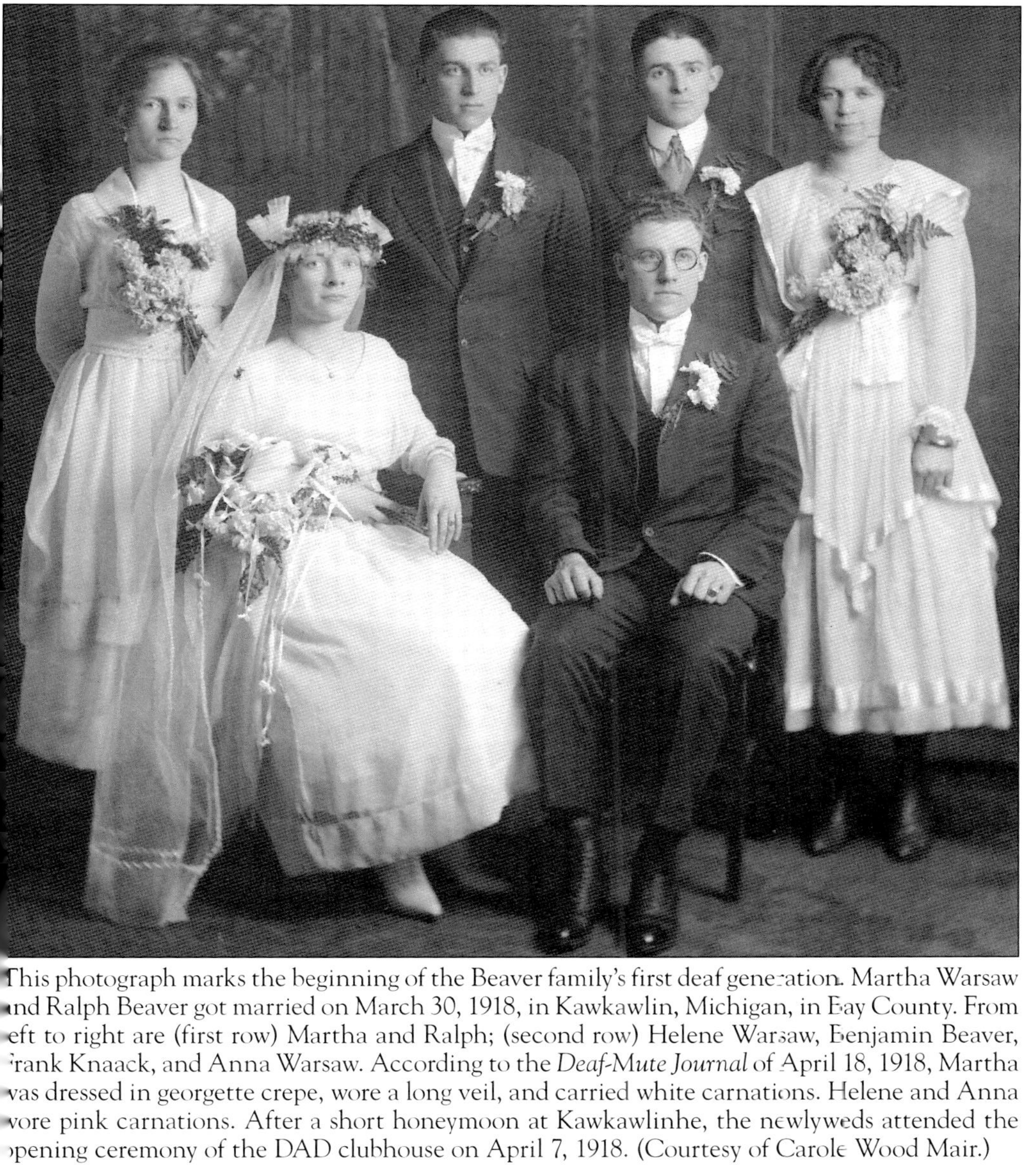

This photograph marks the beginning of the Beaver family's first deaf generation. Martha Warsaw and Ralph Beaver got married on March 30, 1918, in Kawkawlin, Michigan, in Bay County. From left to right are (first row) Martha and Ralph; (second row) Helene Warsaw, Benjamin Beaver, Frank Knaack, and Anna Warsaw. According to the *Deaf-Mute Journal* of April 18, 1918, Martha was dressed in georgette crepe, wore a long veil, and carried white carnations. Helene and Anna wore pink carnations. After a short honeymoon at Kawkawlinhe, the newlyweds attended the opening ceremony of the DAD clubhouse on April 7, 1918. (Courtesy of Carole Wood Mair.)

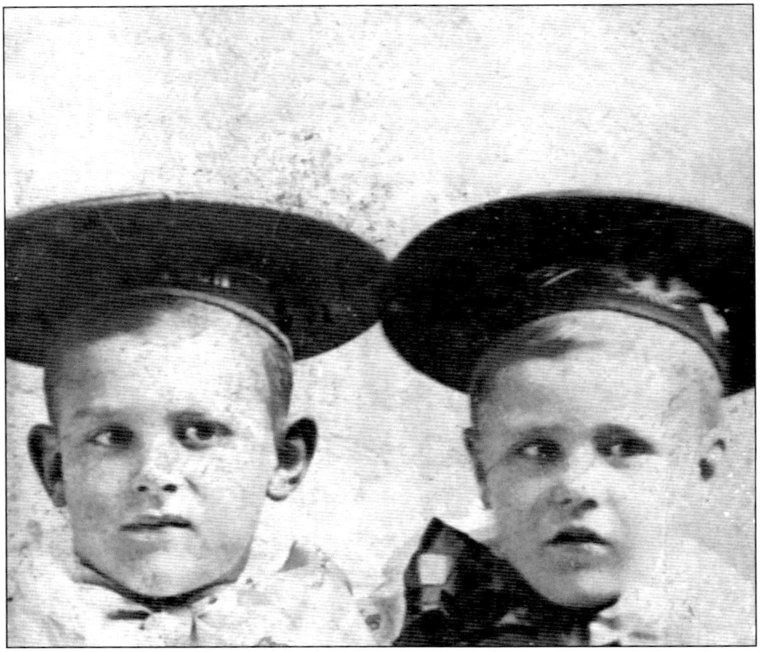

The deaf Beaver brothers are pictured in 1901. At left is Benjamin Jordan Beaver, and at right is Ralph Franklin Beaver. Benjamin was born on May 8, 1892, and Ralph was born on December 18, 1895, in Iuka, Illinois. Their father, Benjamin Newton Beaver, ran a pharmacy and was also a local politician associated with state senator Dr. Walter L. Finn, who was part of Benjamin and Ralph's early lives. The brothers chauffeured for Dr. Finn and others. (Courtesy of Carole Wood Mair.)

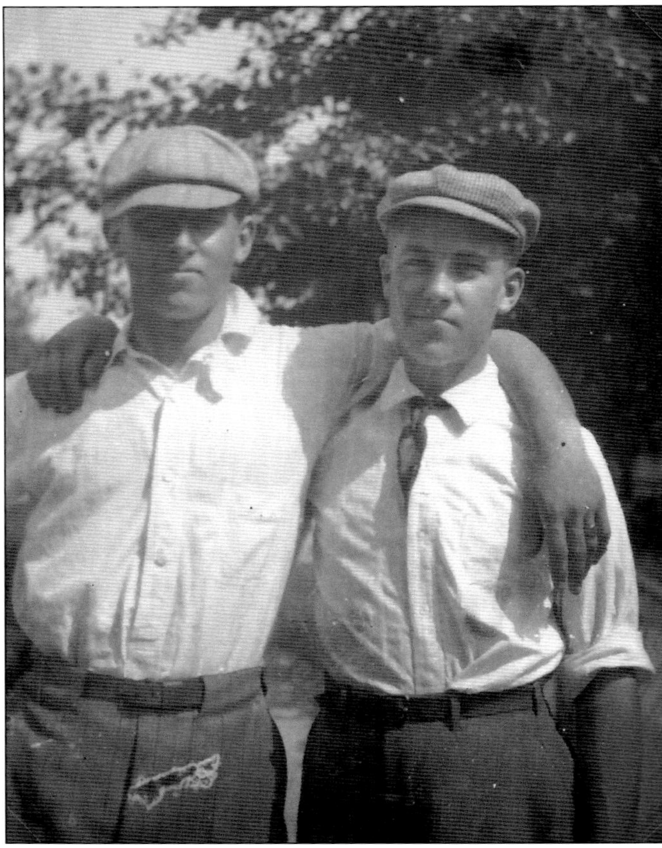

The Beaver brothers are seen here dressed up with pride during their late teen years in 1911. They were already driving around Iuka and Marion Counties. Shortly afterwards, Benjamin moved to Detroit with his mother, Elizabeth, at 21 years old. Ralph joined them later on. Benjamin got his official driver's license in 1918. After the Michigan legislature voted to forbid deaf drivers in 1919, Elizabeth Beaver summoned Dr. Walter Finn to come and give his testimony before the legislature to persuade it to allow deaf residents to drive. (Courtesy of Carole Wood Mair.)

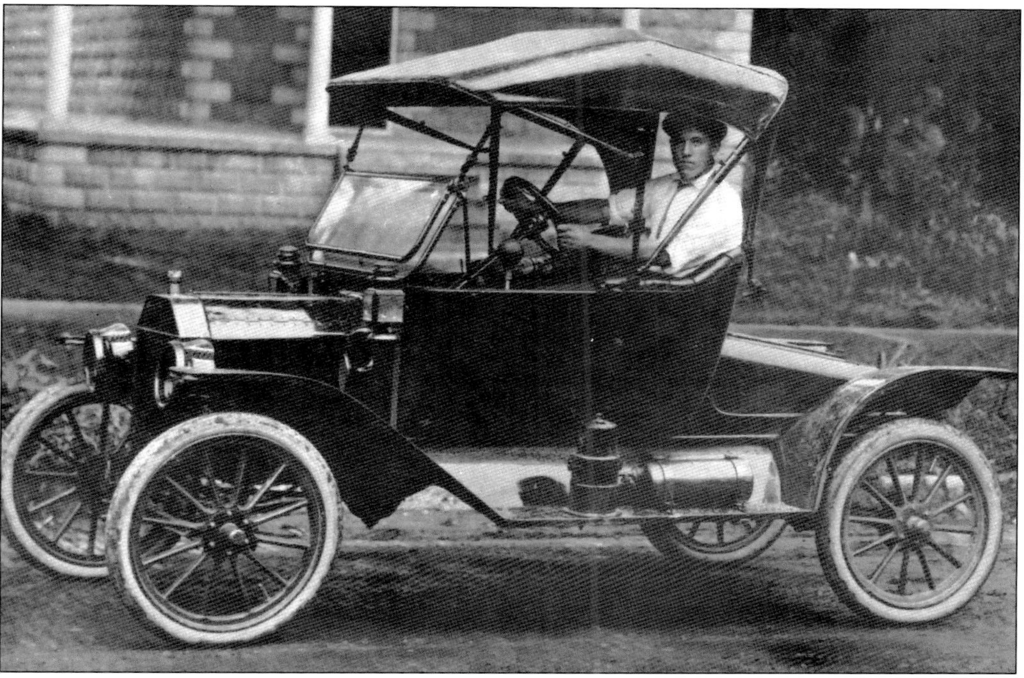

This car is believed to be one of first vehicles the Beaver brothers drove with the help of Dr. Walter Finn. Benjamin drove the 1910 Overland for Dr. Finn in Iuka, a small town near Salem, Illinois. Benjamin and Ralph were still students at the Illinois School for the Deaf. (Courtesy of Carole Wood Mair.)

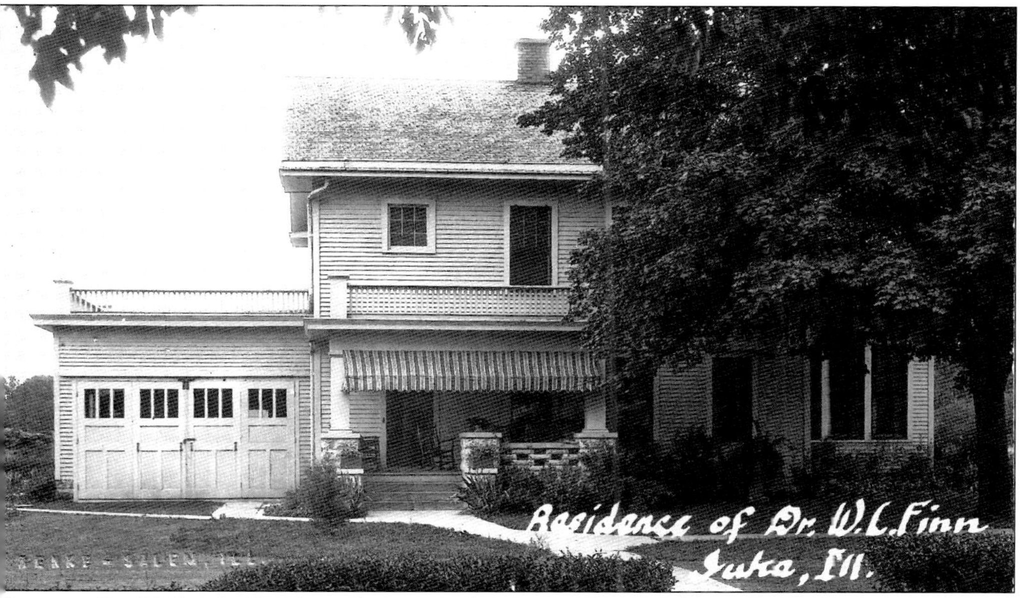

Shown is Dr. Walter L. Finn's residence in Iuka. Dr. Finn was a physician, farmer, and the mayor of Iuka. He also served as a member of the Illinois State Senate from 1929 to 1936. He befriended Benjamin Newton Beaver, Benjamin J. and Ralph's father, who was a small-time politician and a local pharmacist. (Courtesy of Carole Wood Mair.)

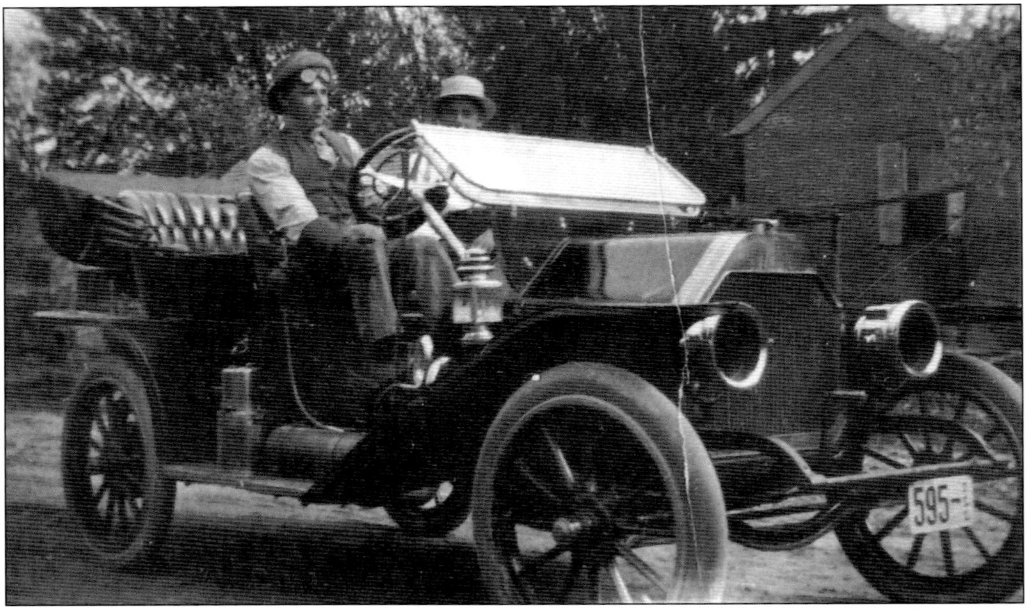

A beautiful 1911 Ford Model T is shown here with Ralph Beaver sitting on the left, driving the vehicle; the person on the right is unidentified. The back of the photograph notes that the Beaver brothers drove the vehicle for the president of the Iuka State Bank, Daniel Wilshire Holstlaw, and his son, Herschel, a cashier. Daniel served as the bank's president from 1908 until he passed away in 1940, when Herschel took over as president. Herschel served until 1954 and passed away in 1955. (Courtesy of Carole Wood Mair.)

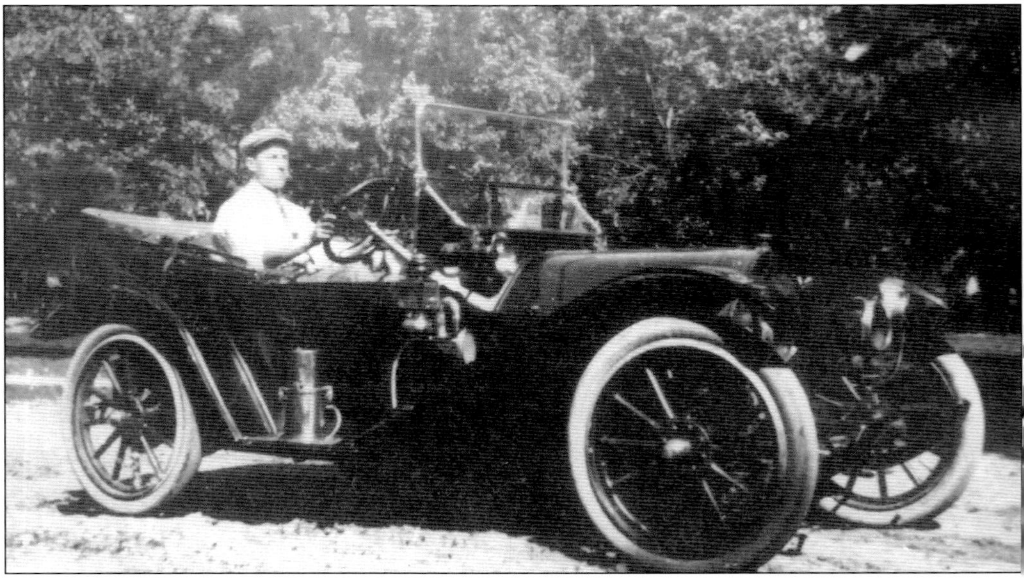

A 1911 Regal is shown here with Ralph Beaver. He enjoyed driving along with his brother. The back of the photograph mentions that both Beaver brothers drove for Dr. Spencer, a dentist, in Iuka. According to the State of Illinois Board of Administration Annual Report, dated October 1, 1910, to September 30, 1912, Benjamin and Ralph were students at the Illinois School for the Deaf from 1910 to 1912 as teenagers. (Courtesy of Carole Wood Mair.)

Benjamin J. Beaver arrived in Michigan from Illinois and first worked for Dodge, then the Ford plant, rising from a coal keeper to an inspector before he retired. He married Etta Mae Evans, who passed away on November 17, 1942. They had three hearing children together. Benjamin then married his second wife, Helen Amelia Warsaw. Benjamin died on September 8, 1992, in Elwyn, Pennsylvania, at 100 years old. His last driver's license, from Florida, expired when he was 95 years old. (Courtesy of Carole Wood Mair.)

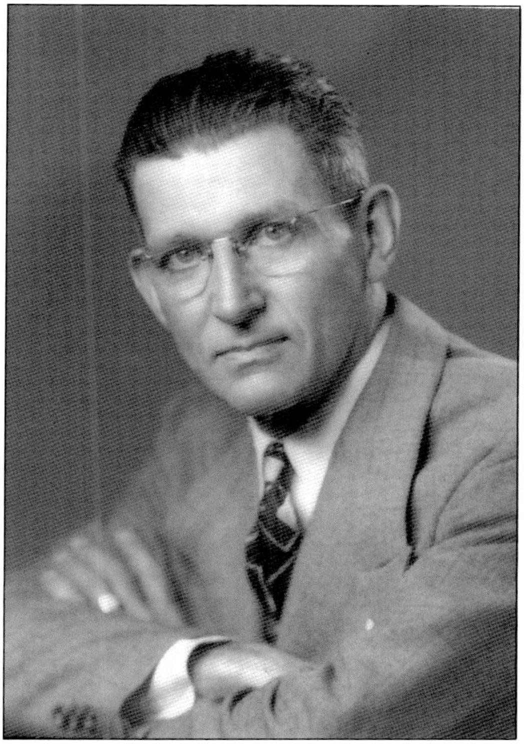

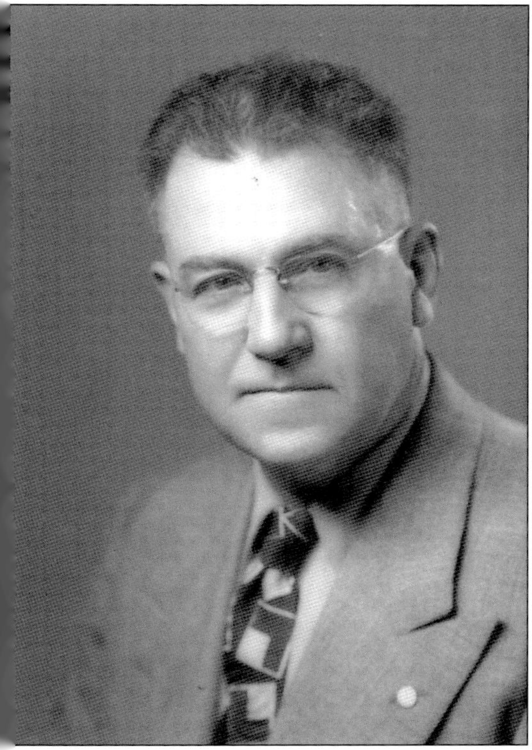

Ralph F. Beaver first worked in a bakery near Highland Park, Michigan. Later, he worked in a Ford assembly plant, rising from a machinist to a mail clerk before he retired. Ralph and Martha were family-oriented people who gave birth to four deaf children. Currently, there are five deaf generations in the family. Ralph passed away at 81 on May 12, 1975, in Bradenton, Florida, and was buried in Livonia, Michigan. (Courtesy of Carole Wood Mair.)

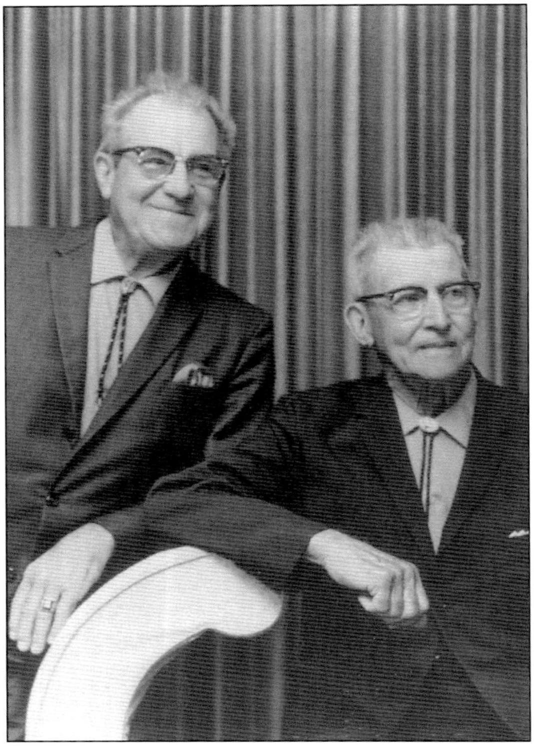

Benjamin (right), pictured with his brother, Ralph, was supposed to drive an experimental car across America from New York City to San Francisco. The trip was mentioned in the *Santa Ana Register* and *Chicago Livestock World* newspapers and *Motor Age* magazine. The *Santa Ana Register* of December 2, 1915, noted: "Benjamin J. Beaver, a deaf mute will drive a 8 cylinder King on a transcontinental trip from New York City to San Francisco. Driving a motor car for past 3 years and feels confident that his ability to feel any noise would allow him to make the journey without mishaps." It is not known if he completed the trip. (Courtesy of Carole Wood Mair.)

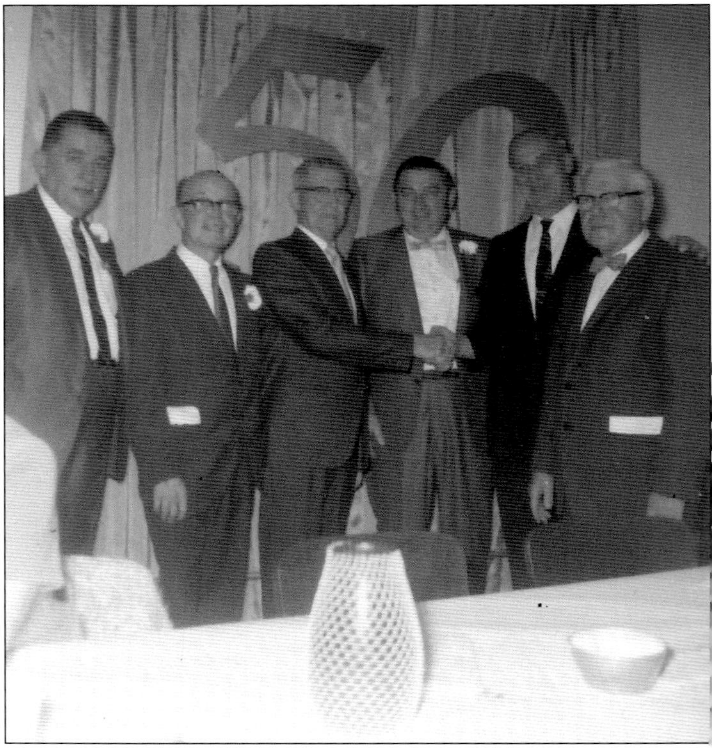

This group of activists celebrating the belated 50th anniversary of DAD includes, from left to right, Dudley M. Cutshaw, Paul Coffey, Benjamin J. Beaver, William Staszczak, lawyer Harold Ryan, and Adalbert Furmann. Cutshaw was a long-time editor then with the *Sign Post*, Beaver had broken the record for continuous membership without interruption since 1916, and Staszczak was frequently elected president of DAD. A new building was being constructed during the actual 50th anniversary in 1966; it was completed in 1968, and the anniversary was celebrated late in 1969. (Courtesy of DAD.)

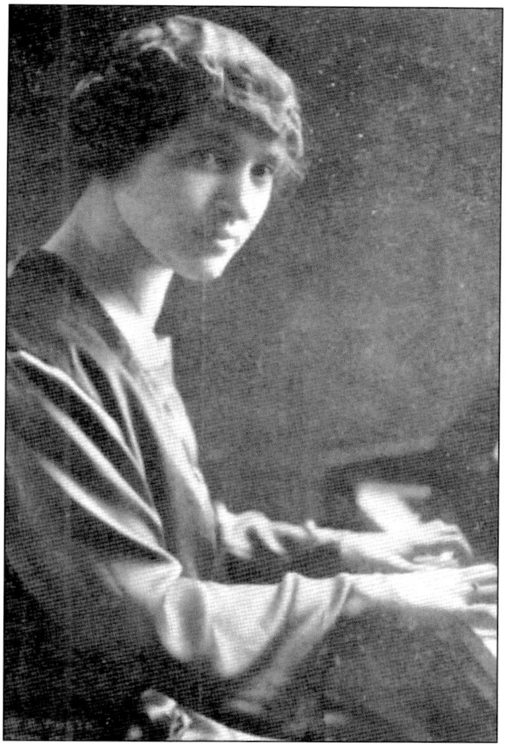

Etta Mae Evans Beaver, the first wife of Benjamin Beaver, was very active in the Ladies Auxiliary and played the piano for Anetta Lobsinger's performance as the Indian princess Lelawala. An interesting note in the August 8, 1922, *Deaf-Mute Journal* reports that Benjamin had a collision on his motorcycle in July 1922. He settled out of court for the damage to the motorcycle and decided to buy Etta a piano with the money. Etta remarked that it was all right, according to the article. (Both, courtesy of DAD.)

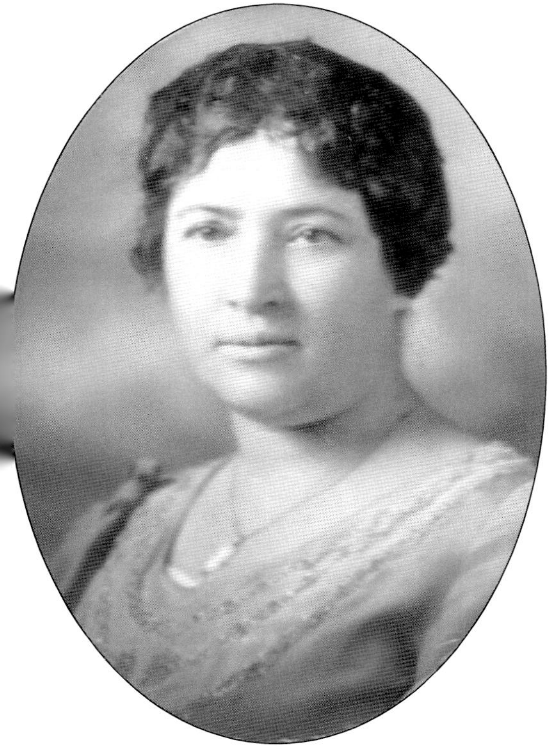

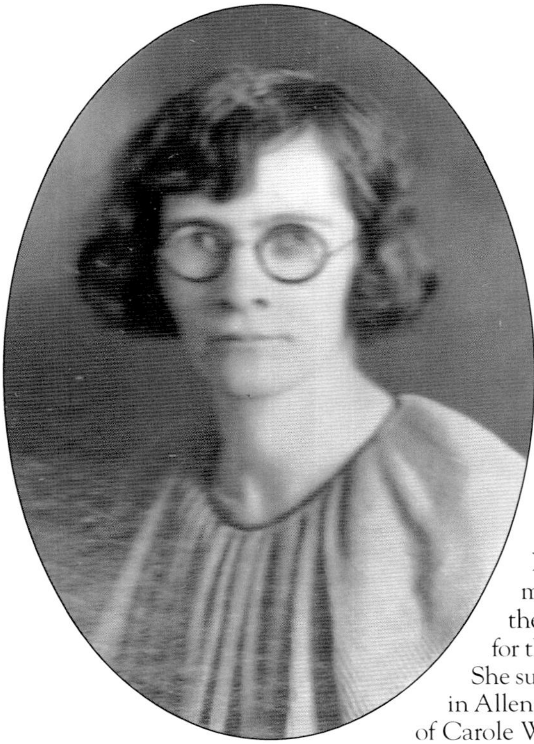

Martha Emma Elizabeth Warsaw Beaver was born in Kawkawlin, Michigan, on January 4, 1898. She attended MSD but left, then met and married Ralph F. Beaver on March 30, 1918, in Bay City, Michigan. She was a longtime DAD member and officer and often wrote articles in the *American Deaf Citizen*, a nationwide newspaper for the deaf. She and Ralph raised four deaf children. She succumbed to liver cancer on December 15, 1982, in Allen Park, Michigan, at 84 years old. (Both, courtesy of Carole Wood Mair.)

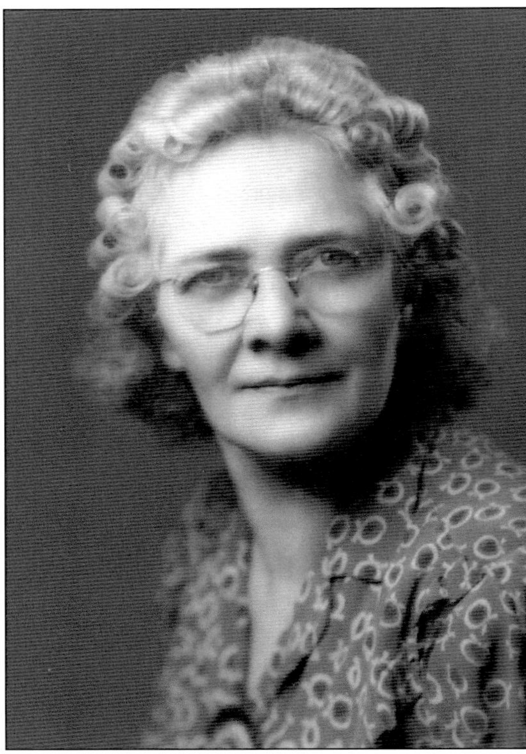

Helene Amelia Warsaw Beaver was born in St. Helen, Michigan, on January 11, 1889, to Herman L. and Augusta Warsaw. She attended MSD but did not graduate there. She joined Martha as a member of DAD. Helene was Benjamin Beaver's sweetheart before he married Etta. After Etta passed away, Benjamin rekindled their romance and married Helene. Helene passed away at 94 in September 1983. (Courtesy of Carole Wood Mair.)

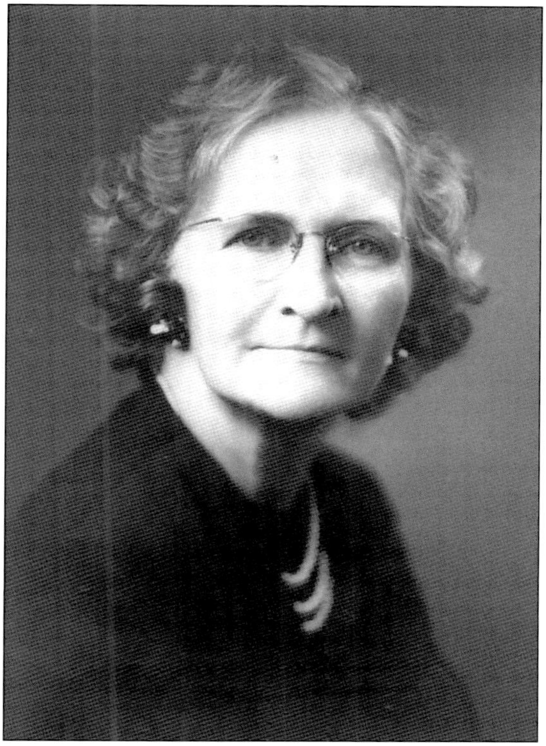

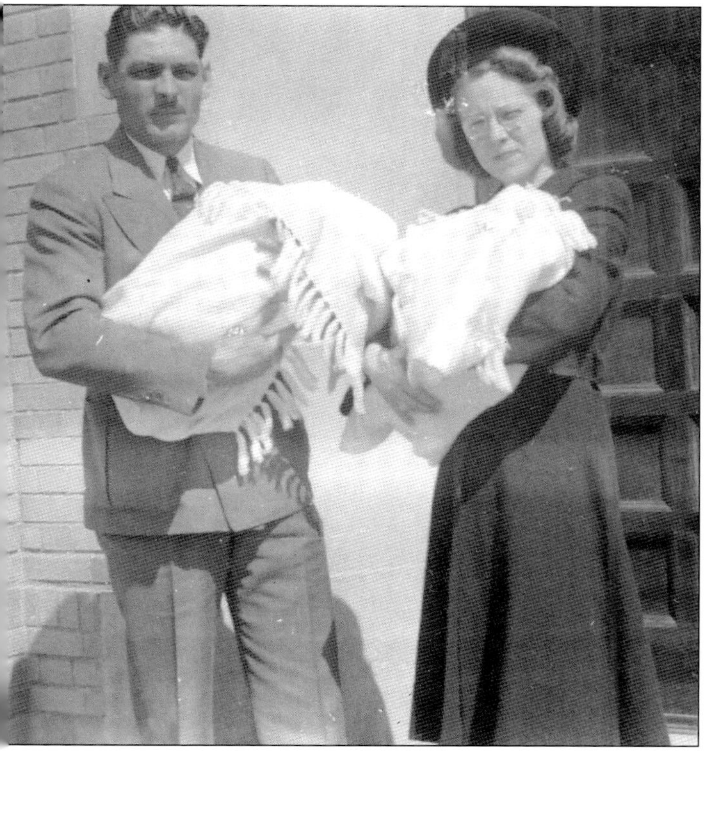

Shown here are Carroll Wood, a proud deaf father, and his wife, Grace, at a family baptism held at the Lutheran Church for the Deaf in 1941. Carroll attended Missouri School for the Deaf. Grace, the daughter of Ralph Beaver, left Michigan School for the Deaf during her high school years. Here, they proudly show off their twin deaf babies, Carole and Carroll Jr. Around 14 months later, daughter Mary joined the twins. All three deaf children attended Michigan School for the Deaf. (Courtesy of Carole Wood Mair.)

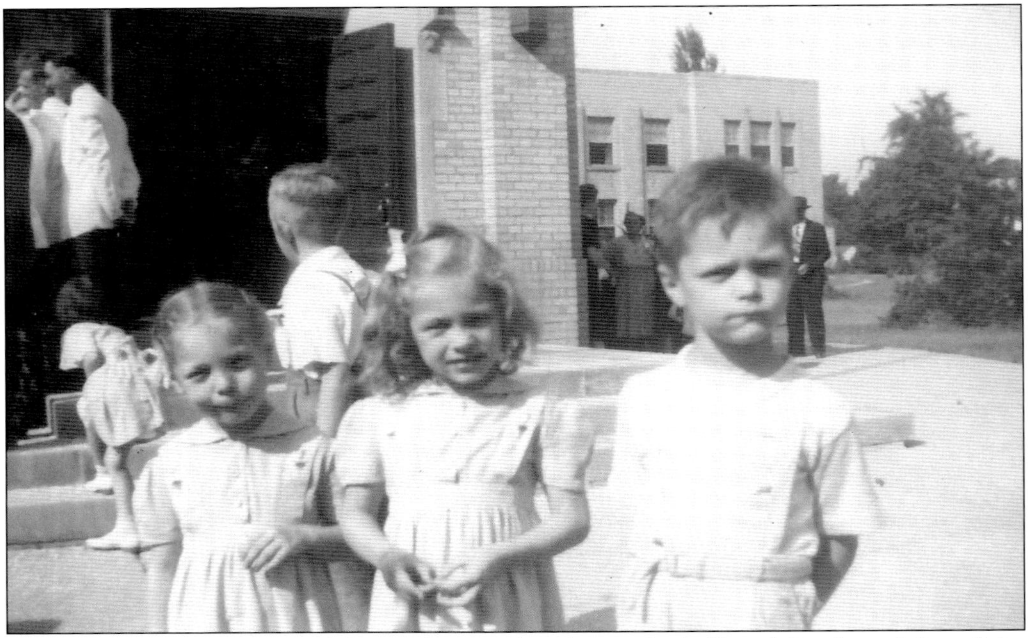

The Wood siblings are, from left to right, Marilyn, four and a half; and Carole and Carroll Jr., both six and a half. They are shown attending the Lutheran Church for the Deaf around August 1947. Grace was a devoted mother who focused on the family, taking them to events to keep them busy. She remembered taking them to family activities like the annual deaf picnic in the field behind the LSD school building for years. (Courtesy of Carole Wood Mair.)

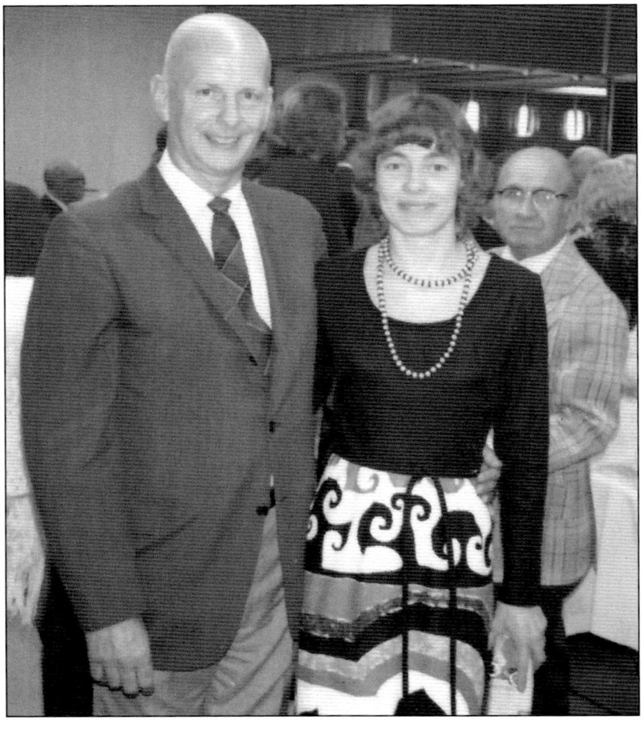

Carole is seen here next to her husband, Frank Mair, in October 1975. Frank traveled to Detroit with the other Gallaudet boys. Carole was visiting Detroit from MSD to attend the American Athletics Association of the Deaf (AAAD) tournament in April 1960 and was introduced to Frank by her stepfather, Mike Cherniawski. They reunited at Gallaudet and married in August 1964. The newlyweds lived in Virginia so Carole could complete her studies at Gallaudet, then moved back to Michigan. (Courtesy of Carole Wood Mair.)

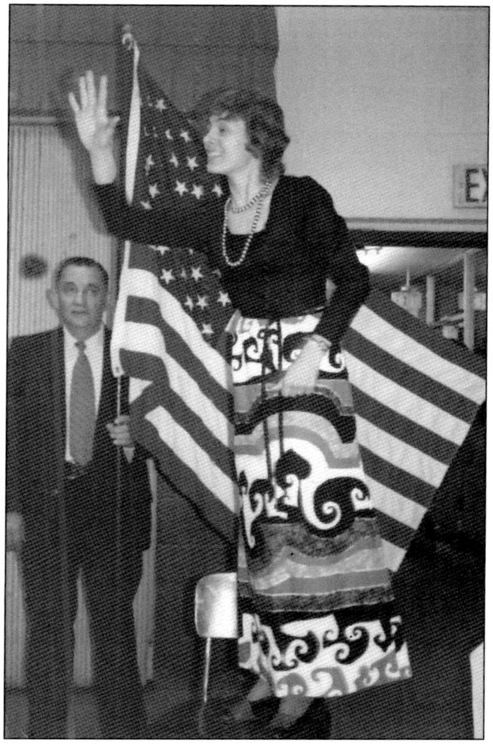

On October 11, 1975, Carole Mair wrote a poem and gave a special, surprise signing at the 59th DAD banquet honoring her uncle Benjamin Beaver. Dudley Cutshaw looks on holding onto the American flag behind Carole. The DAD officers, except for Frank Mair, her husband, had no idea Carole had planned this. Frank started the campaign by making requests to the president of the United States, Gerald Ford, and others to send congratulatory letters. She determined that her uncle deserved the honors when he was never officially recognized as the only living founder of DAD. When she completed the signing, the members had tears in their eyes. (Both, courtesy of Carole Wood Mair.)

AN ODE TO UNCLE BEN

My dear Uncle Ben,
I wonder when you will start to rest,
Seems your good deeds never stop
Because you do not know how
To stop your busy toil.
Since when you were a young man,
You have so much desires in your heart,
That has been to help other deaf people
In different groups.
I see no other deaf person like you.

DAD was first founded 59 years ago
By 38 strong-believing young men,
Who first met at your mother's house.
As the years passed,
You still support DAD with full heart.
You, too are a strong supporter
Of different groups
Like Ill.AD, NFSD, Mich.AD, NAD,
Lutheran group and are the treasurer of
The Senior Citizens group.
I see no other deaf person like you.

Not only thanks to you,
But to your wife, Helene, too
For what she has been doing
That is to see you eat your apple a day
To keep the doctor away
And that you keep your good health
To continue on your relentless goal
To improve the lives of the deaf.
Not only of the DAD, but also elsewhere, everywhere.
If it was not for your part in the beginning,
DAD would have no home like here.
This night all honors are yours,
We all love you!

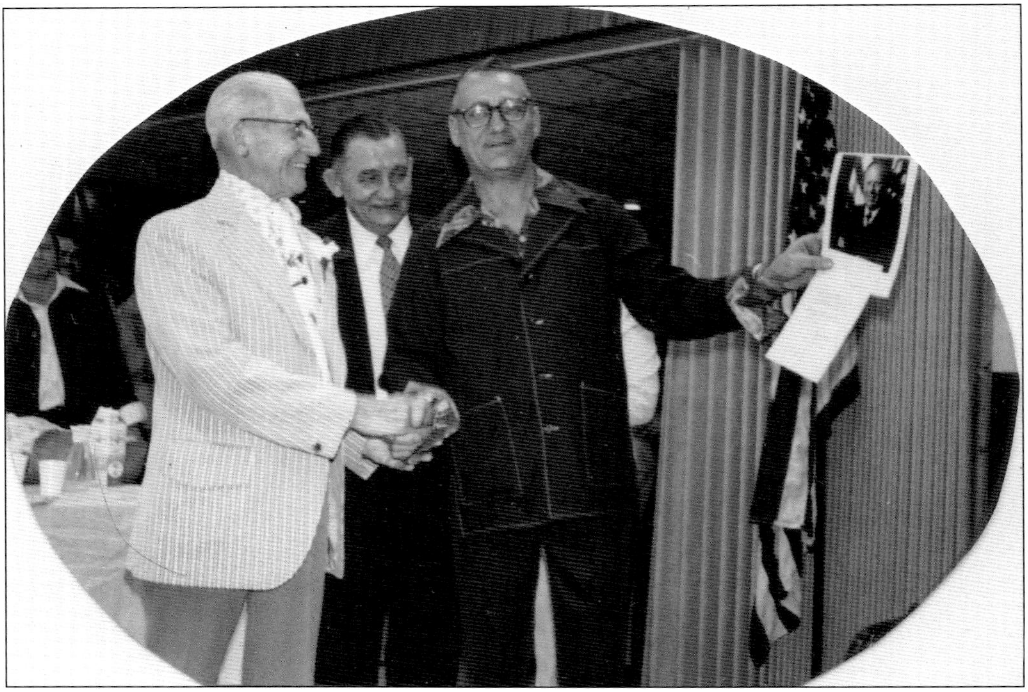

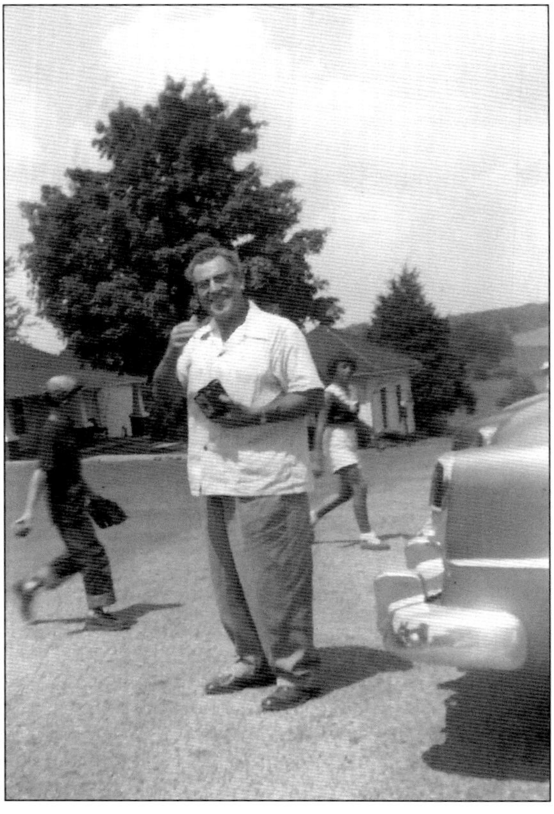

Shown here from left to right are Benjamin Beaver, Dudley Cutshaw, and Alexander Radanovich, DAD president in 1975. Cutshaw and Radanovich were unaware when they opened the letter that it contained congratulations from Pres. Gerald Ford, a native of Michigan. Beaver is beaming with pride. (Courtesy of Carole Wood Mair.)

Ralph Beaver is shown at an annual deaf picnic with his family. Grace, his daughter, recalled that he was a very family-oriented man and always took them out to the picnic to interact with others. Grace followed in his footsteps and only attended picnics and outings that allowed family to be involved. Others remembered Ralph as a cheery and comical guy. (Courtesy of Carole Wood Mair.)

From left to right are Deena Dunn, Lysle Dunn, and Virginia Stevenson, Benjamin Beaver's granddaughter, her husband, and his daughter. They enjoyed the 59th annual banquet. Only absent was Benjamin's son Bruce. Benjamin has two sons and a daughter, all hearing, from his first marriage to Etta. Helene, his second wife, married Benjamin in 1943, a year after his first wife passed away. (Courtesy of Carole Wood Mair.)

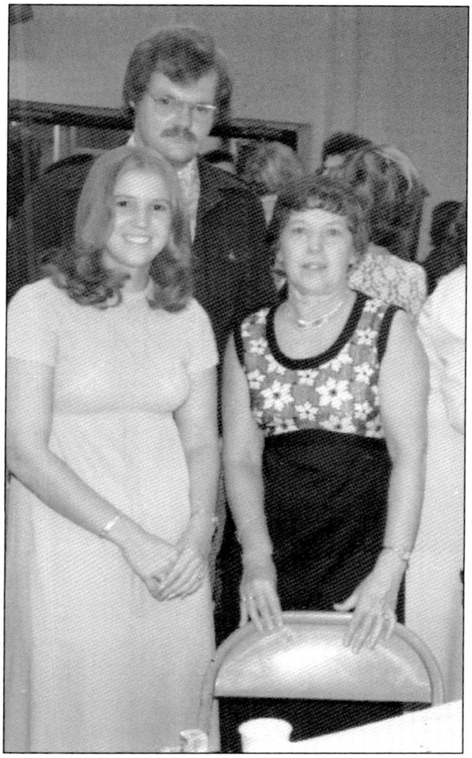

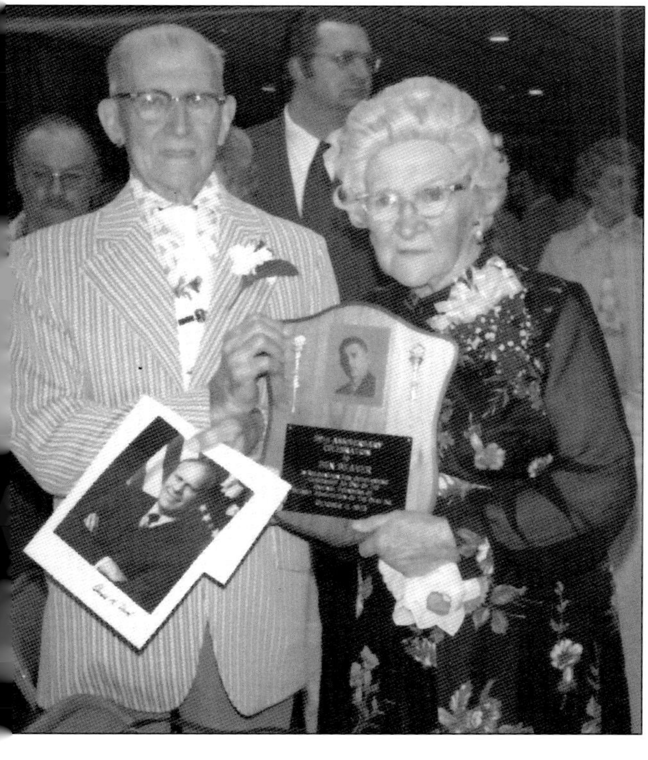

Benjamin is pictured with his wife, Helene. Helene was Ralph Beaver's wife's deaf sister and Benjamin's sweetheart before he married his first wife, Etta. Helene was an activist with DAD for years. After Etta died, Benjamin courted Helene, and they married in 1943 when Helene was 54. She passed away at 94 years old. (Courtesy of Carole Wood Mair.)

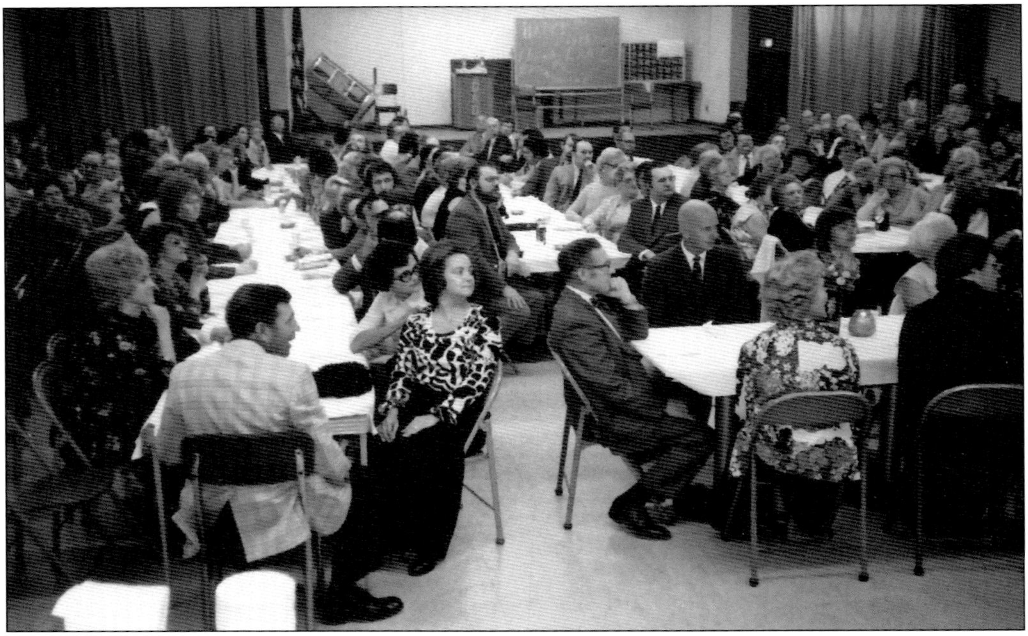

The 59th annual banquet was celebrated on Third Avenue. No one had any idea what was coming from Carole Wood Mair and her husband, Frank Mair. Carole worked hard for three weeks before the banquet planning the surprise. She practically begged Benjamin Beaver's children to attend without telling them why. One son, Bruce, did not come, but Benjamin's other son, Howard, and daughter, Virginia, did come. (Courtesy of Carole Wood Mair.)

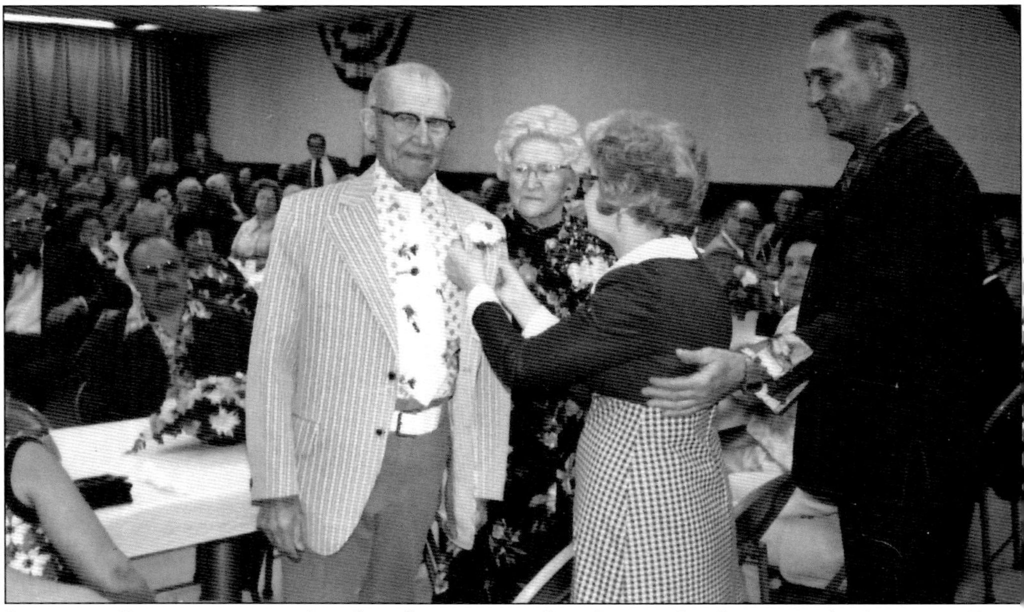

Benjamin Beaver is pictured with a flower pinned on him in his honor at the banquet. From from left to right are Robert Beaver (behind Benjamin), Benjamin Beaver, Helene Warsaw Beaver, unidentified, and Alexander Radanovich, then the DAD president. (Courtesy of Carole Wood Mair.)

Two

Recognized Individuals

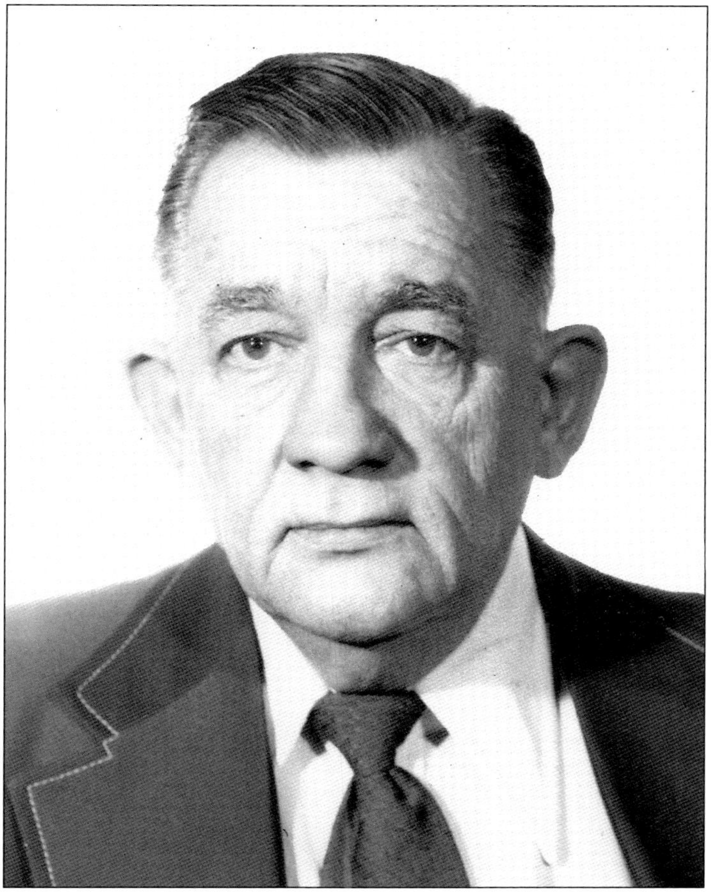

Dudley Cutshaw was born deaf in Knoxville, Tennessee, in 1922 and was raised in a deaf family; in order from oldest to youngest are Theodore, Emily, Mildred, Dudley, Dorothy, and Christine. He was known to be an expert at negotiations and saved lots of money for DAD, and was also a great entertainer. Dudley married Elizabeth and had children Dudley Cutshaw Jr. and Diana Cutshaw McKittrick. (Courtesy of Charles and Diana Cutshaw McKittrick.)

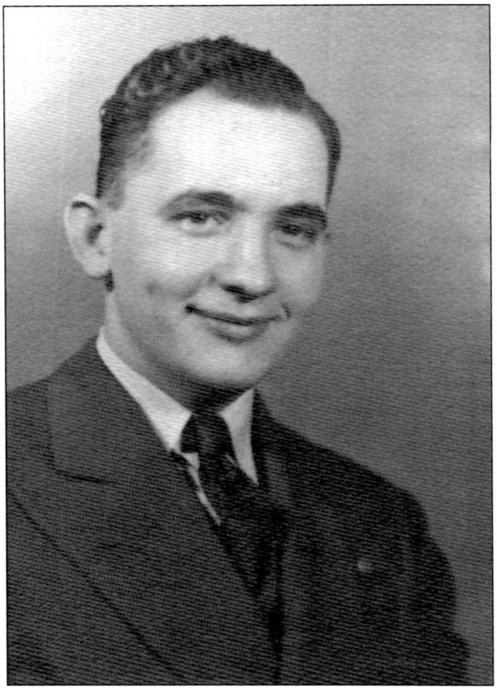

A young Dudley Cutshaw attended the Tennessee School for the Deaf in his late teens; he left to travel with a group of salesmen with his deaf parents' permission. Dudley's father found a job in Detroit, and the deaf family moved there, where Dudley joined them. He became an avid reader during his travels with the salesmen, which led him to become the editor of the *Sign Post* with DAD. He succeeded Marion J. Allen in the position. (Courtesy of Charles and Diana Cutshaw McKittrick.)

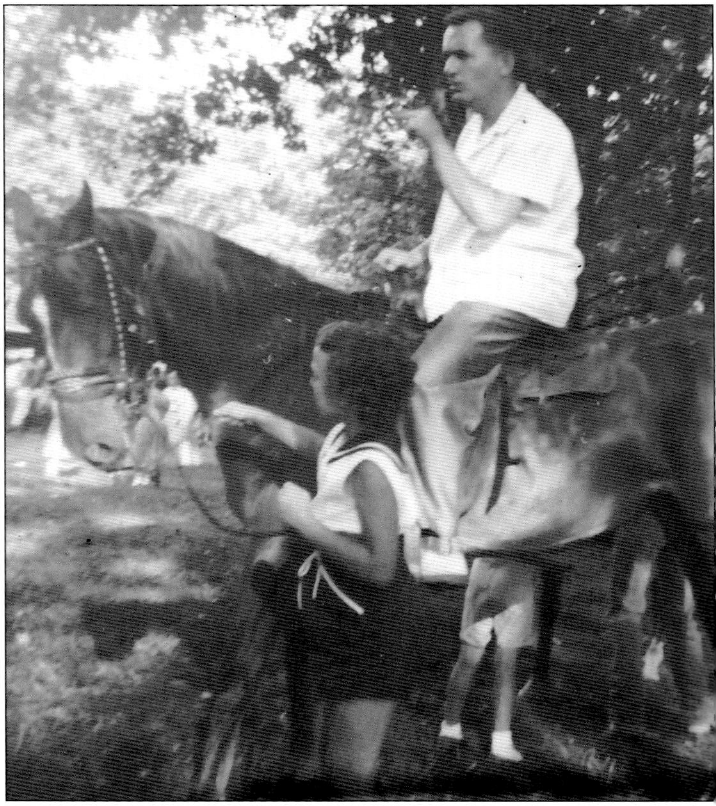

In the early 1950s, a young Diana, Dudley's daughter, is holding the reins of a horse while her father rides. This was at one of the annual deaf gatherings at the New Liberty Park on Bredow Road in the vicinity of the Detroit–Wayne County Airport, between Middle Belt and Inkster Roads. The memorable annual event included field races for adults, a softball game, volleyball, comedy acts, and cash prizes. Often, the admission would be $1 per adult and free for children. (Courtesy of Charles and Diana Cutshaw McKittrick.)

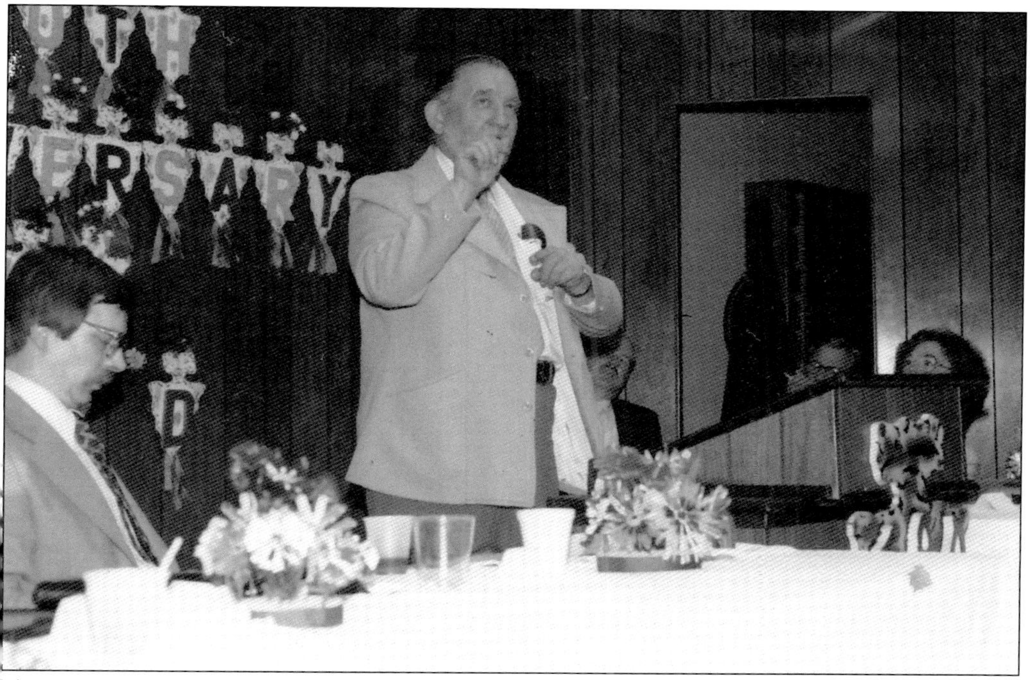

Flint Association of the Deaf (FAD) celebrated its 60th anniversary with a banquet and invited Dudley Cutshaw as the keynote speaker from Detroit. He was a popular and frequent visitor to FAD. The only rivalry between FAD and DAD is in sports. Cutshaw is pictured here speaking. (Courtesy of Charles and Diana Cutshaw McKittrick.)

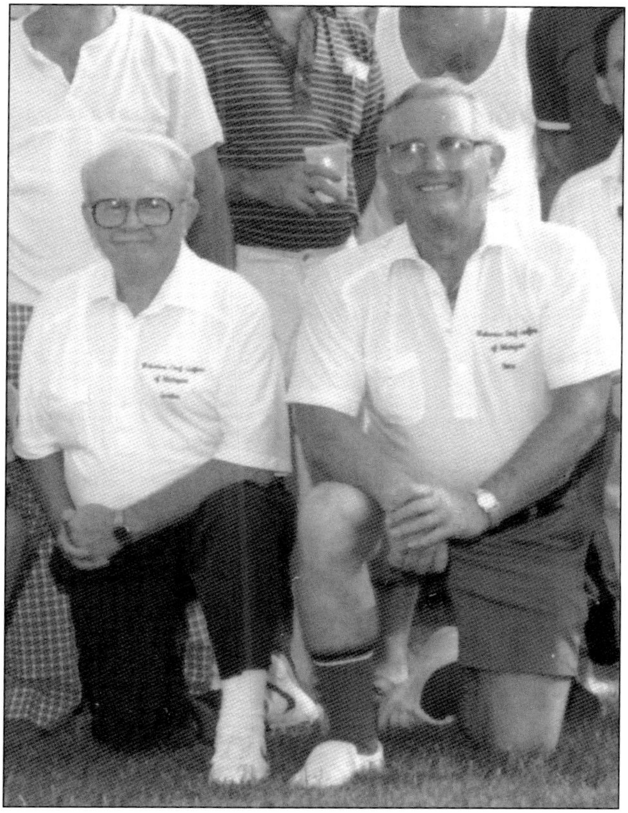

On the left is Gordon Bachman, and on the right is Steven Popp, who passed away in 2015. Bachman was one of the founders of Wolverine Deaf Golfers of Michigan, established on September 14, 1957, by Bachman, Bill Knight, Billy Ray Curry, David Croll, Harry Petrowske, Frank Lytle, D. Halford, Clarence Schulz, Glen Robertson, Michael Tyler, Blodie Virkstis, and Pat Garman. In September 2017, the group will celebrate its 60th anniversary. (Courtesy of Wolverine Deaf Golfers of Michigan.)

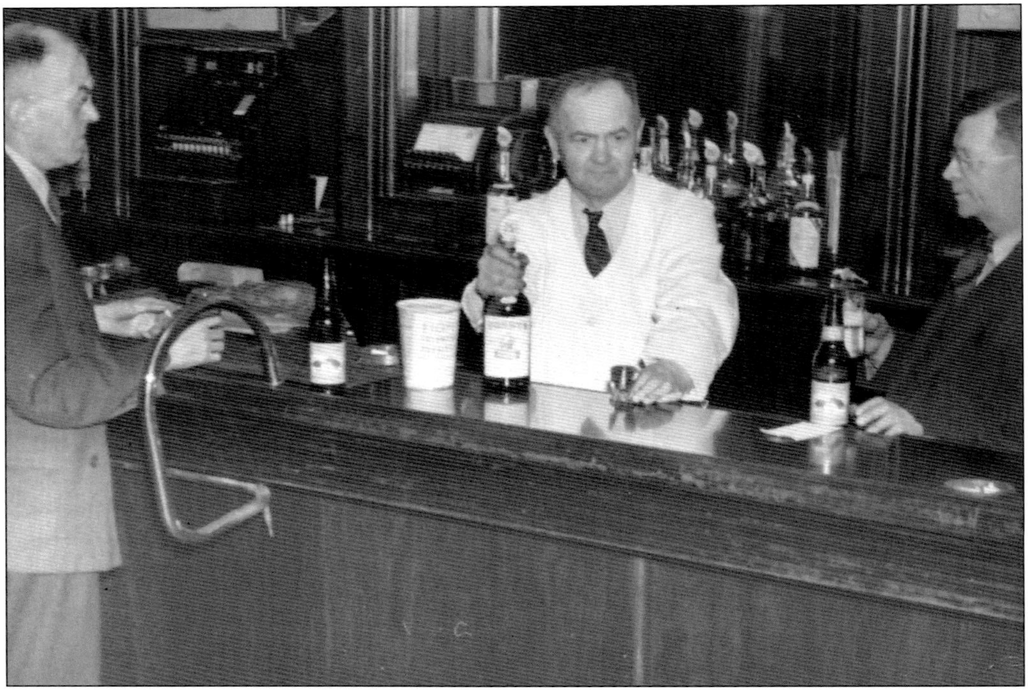

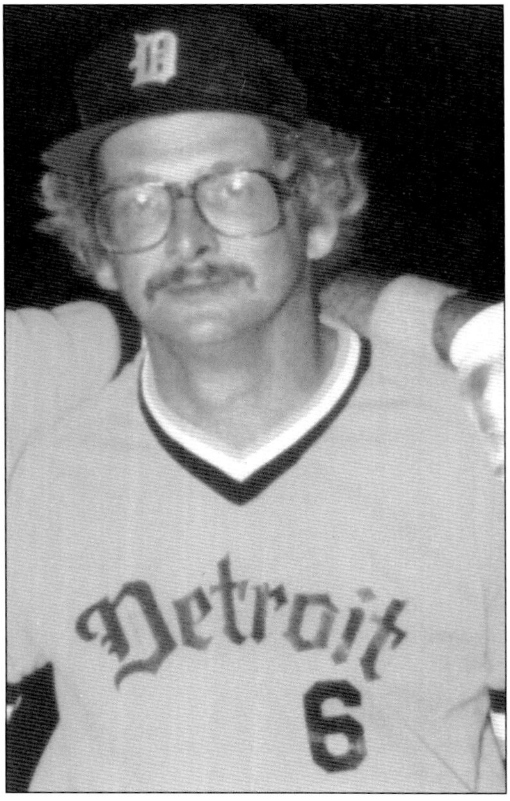

This early 1950s photograph shows the 105 Davenport Street location of DAD. On the left is Morris Purviance, the father of the *Sign Post* and the *Great Lakes News*; at center is Fred Engler, a paid steward who managed the bar room; the man at right is unidentified. According to a March 1954 edition of the *Sign Post*, Engler worked for DAD for years and when he retired, he handed the job over to his successors, Charles Newman and Victor Novinski. (Courtesy of DAD.)

Dominic Zito Jr. played in the softball tournaments and was involved with DAD for many years, participating as an officer. Zito Jr. became ill after returning from a cruise and shared his hospital room with his father, Dominic Zito Sr. Zito Sr., who was ill for a time. Zito Jr. died of cancer on January 17, 2000, three days before his father. (Courtesy of Dominic and Dorothy Etkie Zito.)

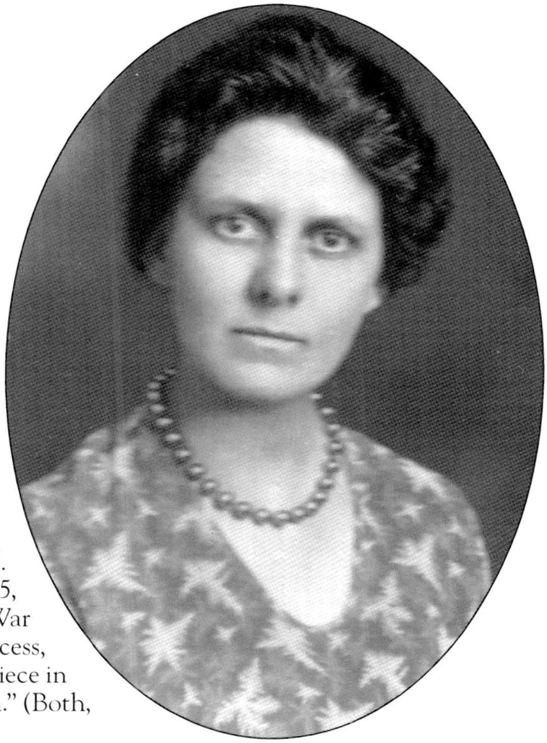

Anetta Lyllavett Johnston Lobsinger was a DAD activist for years since 1920. She came from Canada with her husband, Alexander Lobsinger. She was also active in the St. Joseph Ephpheta Society and in the DAD Ladies Auxiliary and played in many entertaining performances, including as an Indian princess, Lelawala. Etta Beaver played the piano while Anetta Lobsinger performed. A *Deaf-Mute Journal* article dated October 25, 1928, notes: "Mr. Leon Laporte as the Indian War Chief, and Mrs. Alexander Lobsinger the Princess, made a great hit as they reeled off piece after piece in the traditional legendary way of the Red Men." (Both, courtesy of DAD.)

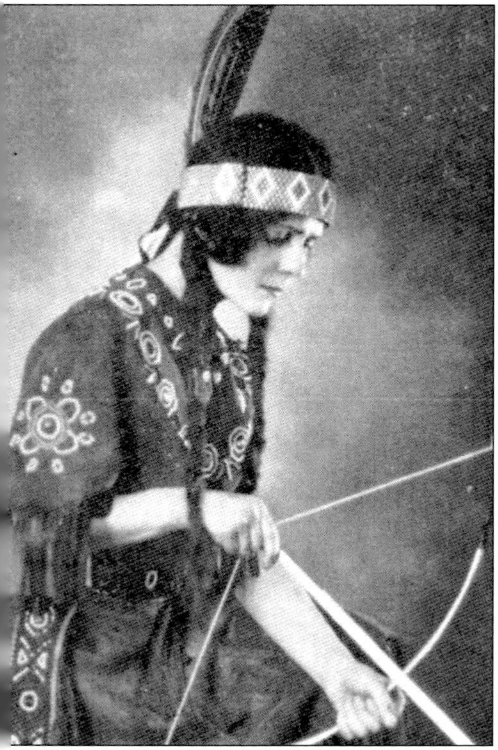

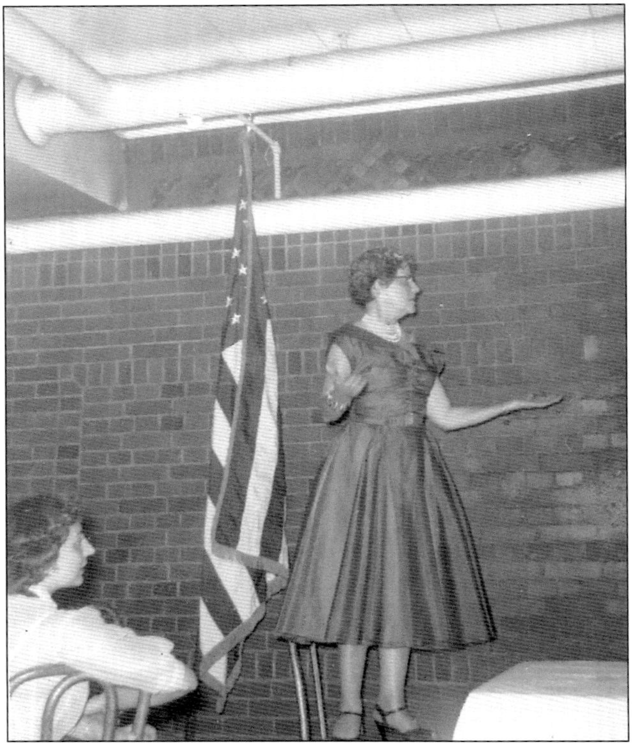

Anetta Lobsinger is shown in the late 1940s. She and her husband were induced as members of the St. Joseph Ephpheta Society in March 1920, according to a preserved journal. Noted in the journal on May 16, 1920, members surprised Msgr. Henry J. Kaufmann with a "fine Ford" car. Someone wrote in the journal on November 15, 1942, that "Ford Motor Company wants more Deaf workers, because they know the Deaf don't have to go to the war." (Courtesy of SJDC.)

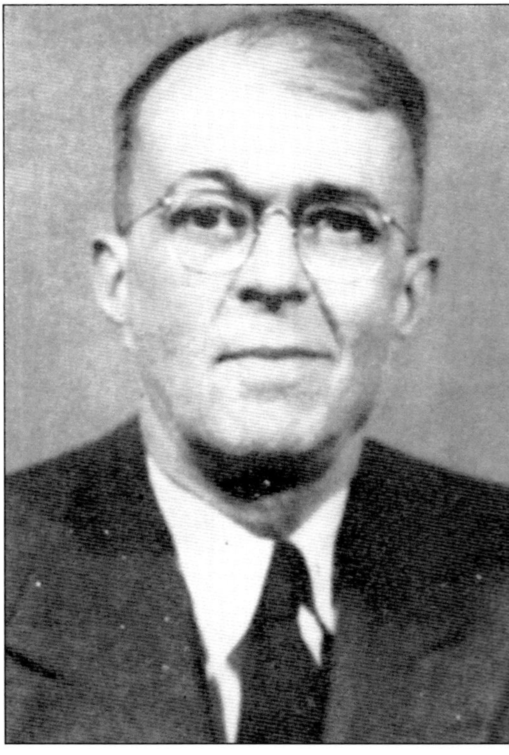

Without Morris Purviance, the *Sign Post* newsletter and the *Great Lakes News*, the *Sign Post*'s predecessor, would not have happened. Since 1921, the *Detroit News* had employed him as a printer. He began printing the newsletters with the cooperation of Alexander Lobsinger. Morris's wife, Ruth, sometimes contributed a column and was an activist for the DAD Ladies Auxiliary. Morris passed away on January 12, 1953, succumbing to asthma complications. (Courtesy of DAD.)

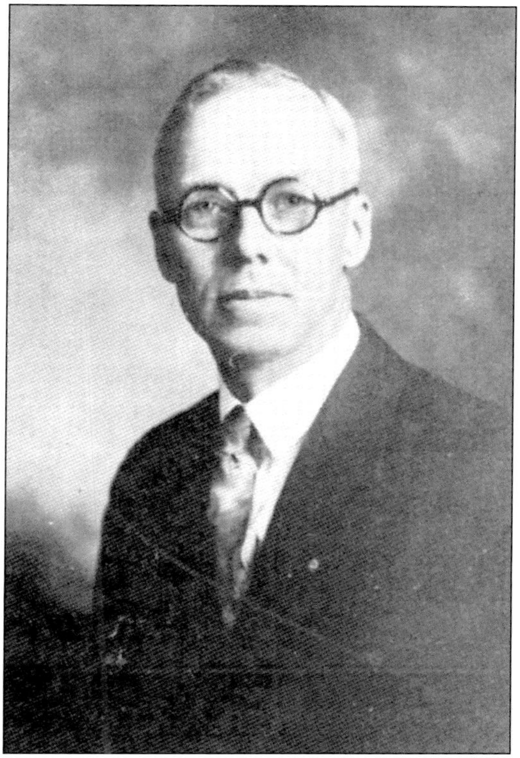

Alexander Lobsinger is pictured at right in a DAD member photograph and below at 21 years old in 1914 in his British Columbia Boundary League hockey uniform; he was nicknamed "Moose." According to Gerry Foster in "Boundary Hockey History," Lobsinger played in Saskatchewan for two seasons before coming to Grand Forks and was probably the highest paid player in the area, turning down two professional contracts with the Pacific Coast League. A member of a Grand Forks championship team, Lobsinger moved to Ottawa after one season in Grand Forks and never played again. He was a longtime activist in DAD and Catholic deaf organizations. (Right, courtesy of DAD; below, courtesy of Boundary Museum Society.)

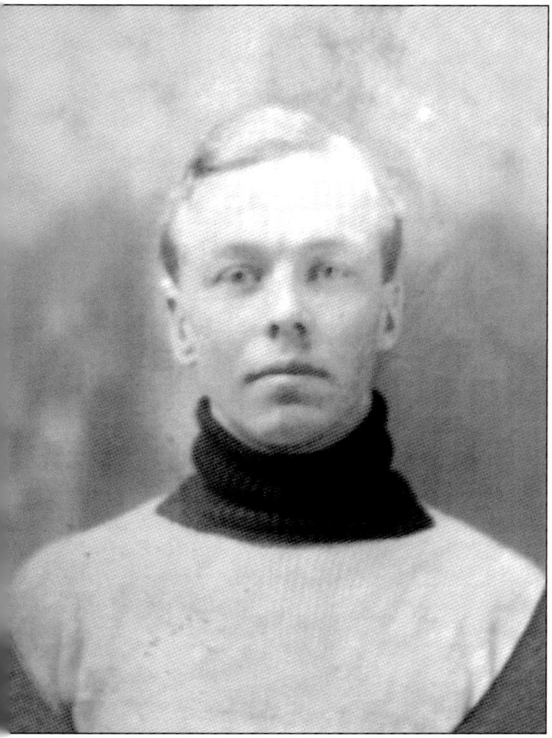

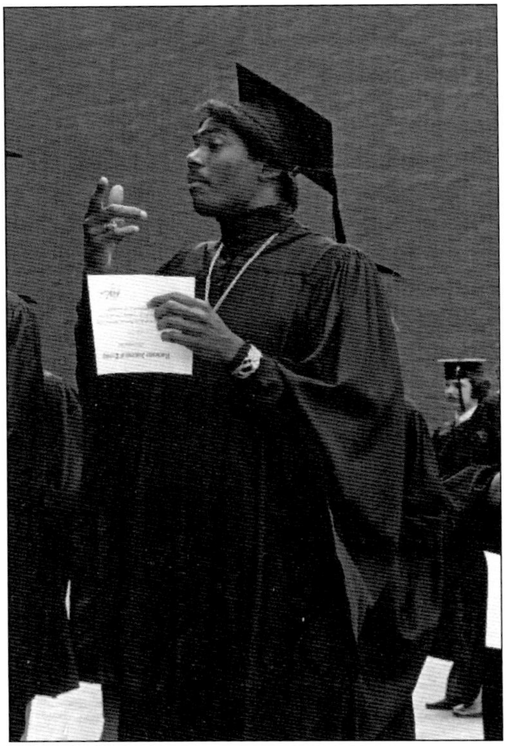

In June 1974, Glenn Stewart graduated as the first deaf black man from Rochester Institute of Technology (RIT) with a bachelor's degree in fine arts. He became active with the Detroit Silent Club, then with the National Black Deaf Advocates' Detroit chapter for a long time. He is married to Susan Stewart, who met Glenn while he was a student at RIT and later joined him in Detroit after her graduation from St. Mary School for the Deaf in Buffalo, New York. (Courtesy of Glenn and Susan Stewart.)

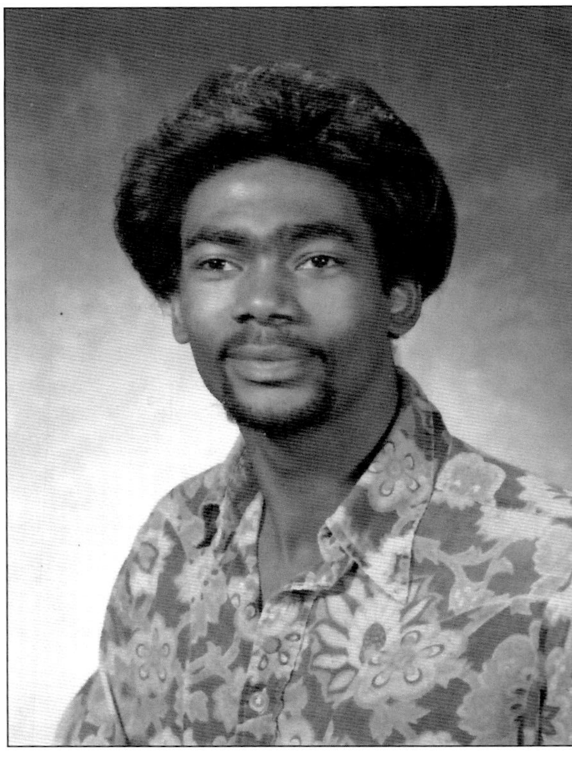

Glenn Stewart was involved in choir, his dance company, and church activities. He also worked for the post office in the Detroit area. (Courtesy of Glenn and Susan Stewart.)

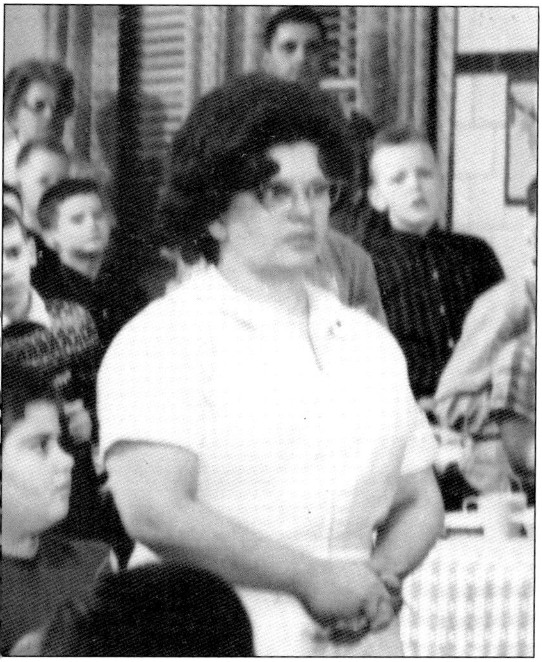

Sandra Evans was the first deaf woman to work at LSD. She graduated from MSD and was very supportive of ASL. As a houseparent at LSD, she secretly taught the signing ABC's to girls in the dormitory since the school banned signing at the time. Judy Manik Vardon, one of the students, remembered that she was delighted to learn from Evans. This blurry c. 1960s image shows Evans standing in the dining room with students and staff. (Courtesy of Judy and Larry Vardon.)

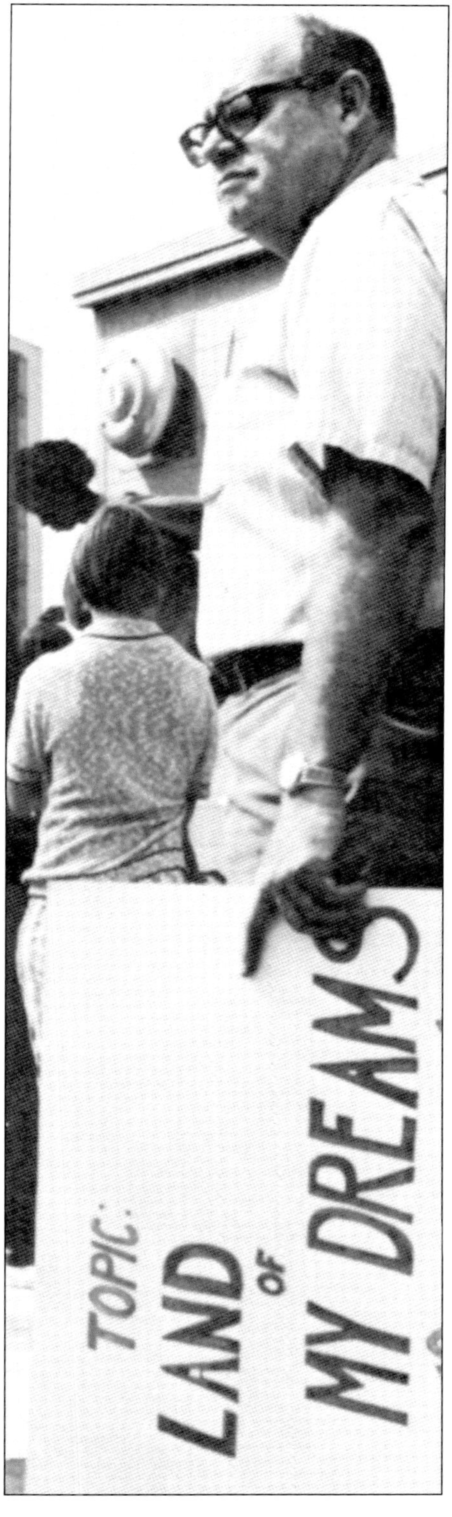

Eric "Malz" Malzkuhn was a recognized DAD sports editor with the *Sign Post* in the early days, an entertainer and comedy performer at some DAD events, and on several committees, especially for advertising sports tournaments. He taught at MSD and had a family with his wife, Mary. Later, Malzkuhn and his family moved to the Washington, DC, area, and he taught at Model Secondary School for the Deaf until retirement. He died on January 23, 2008. (Courtesy of MSSD.)

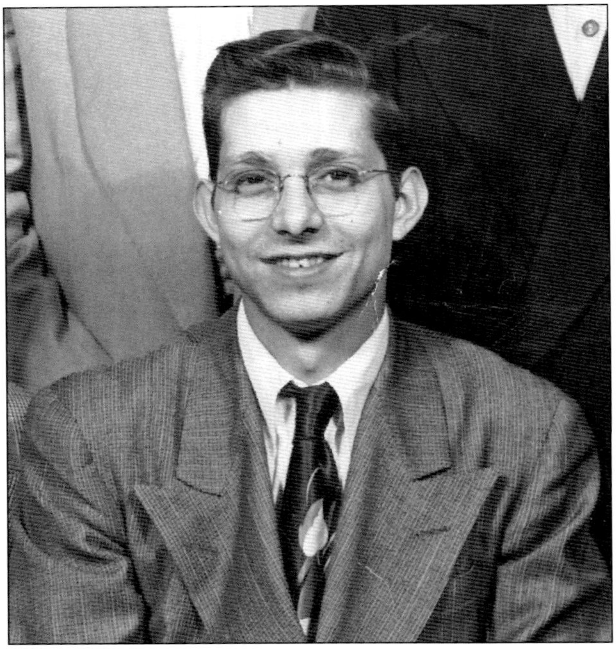

Harvey L. Ellerhorst graduated in 1947 from MSD, then played basketball and softball and bowled with DAD. He founded and chaired some sports tournaments in the Detroit area, especially with the Great Lake Deaf Bowling Association, for which he was secretary-treasurer until his retirement in 2001. He passed away on November 9, 2006. After his death, the DAD bowling league he had managed for a long time ceased, then bowlers joined the Michigan Deaf League. (Courtesy of DAD.)

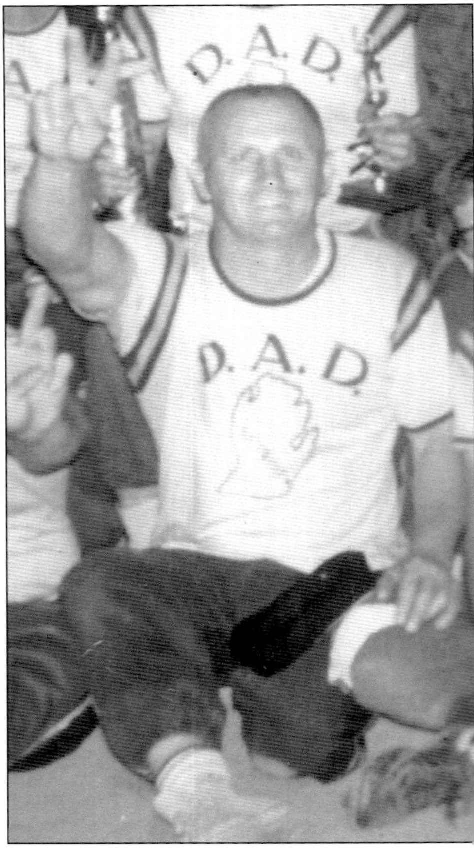

Stephen Popp Jr. was a DAD member for 69 years before he died on June 17, 2015. He was an all-around loyal DAD player, a golfer, and a longtime manager for both men's and women's softball teams until the 1980s. Some remembered that he brought DAD some championships for the softball team. (Courtesy of DAD.)

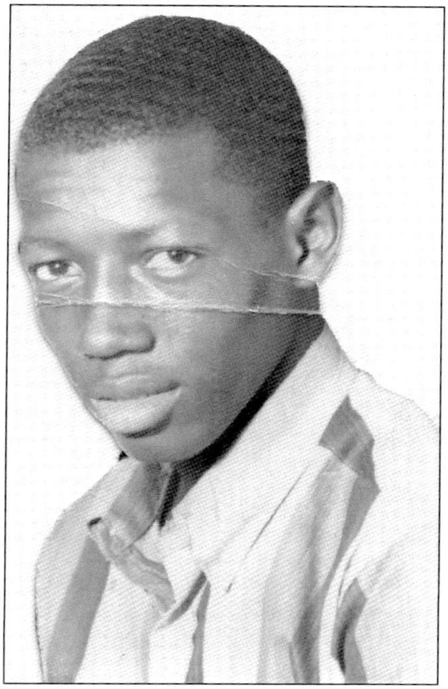

Abram Powell enrolled at MSD in 1950 and graduated in 1964. Abram's all-time favorite activities were sports. Below, Powell is pictured participating in the Deaflympics tryouts as a finalist at the University of Maryland track in 1965. Although he was invited to participate in the International Deaf Olympics games, Powell chose to stay behind and worked for the General Motors Company for 39 years until his retirement on January 1, 2004. After retirement, he established the Abram Powell Foundation to raise money for scholarships for underprivileged children. (Both, courtesy of Abram Powell.)

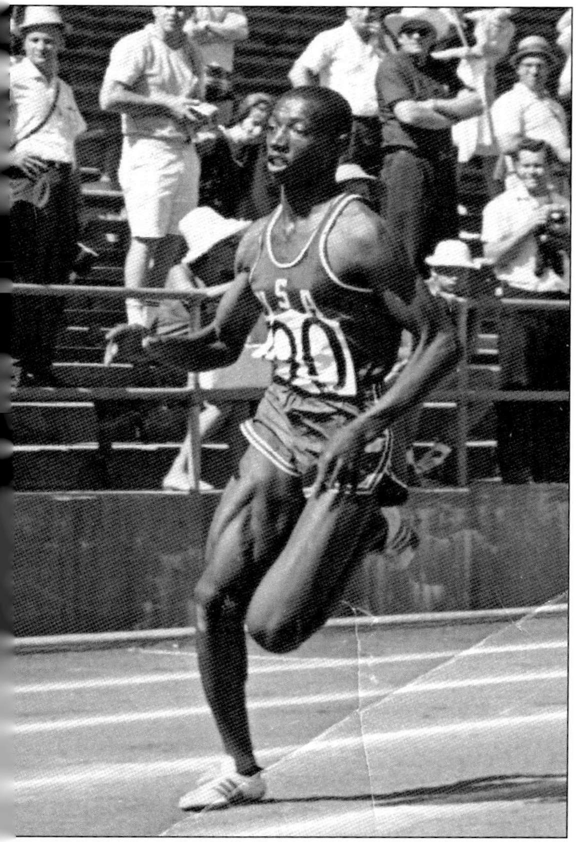

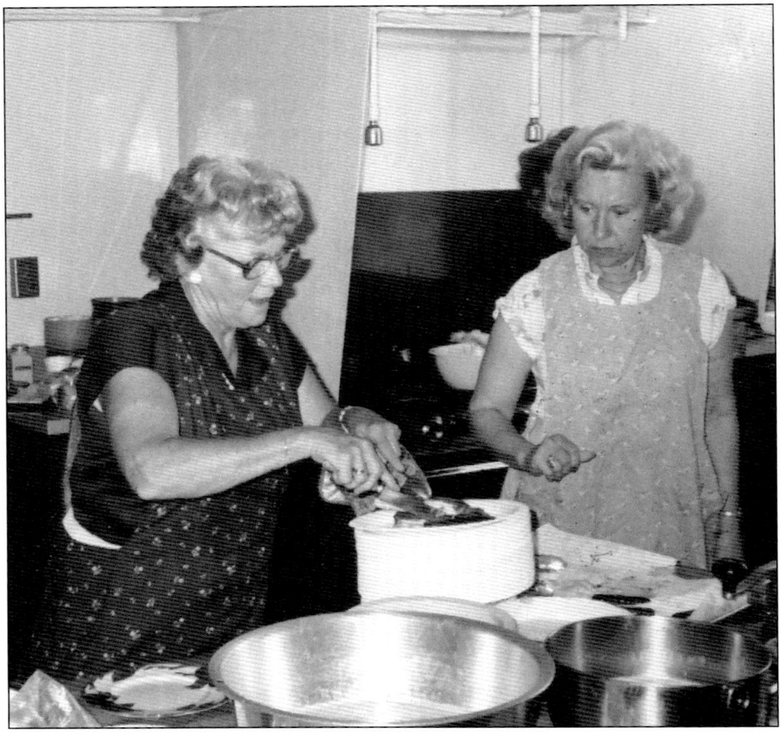

Helen Booker (left) is pictured with Helen Deska. Booker has been a very active member of the Catholic deaf church since she joined in the late 1930s. When St. John's Deaf Center opened up in 1974, Booker was always willing to cook in the kitchen. She also contributed her time with Camp Mark Seven in New York until she had a quadruple bypass and had to stay in Detroit. She still volunteers at 95. (Courtesy of SJDC.)

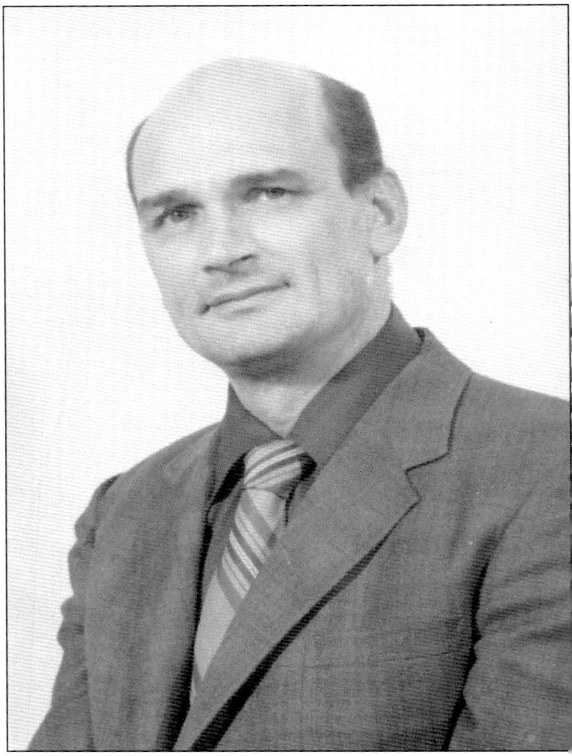

Arlon Dennison was very active with the Flint Association of the Deaf in the 1960s and 1970s. In 1969 and 1970, he was president when FAD's new clubhouse was set up. At the time, there were 225 members, and they all, including Dennison, pledged one percent of their salaries during 1968 to finance the building. At that time, Arlon's wife also was president of the Ladies Auxiliary. (Courtesy of FAD.)

Three

Religion

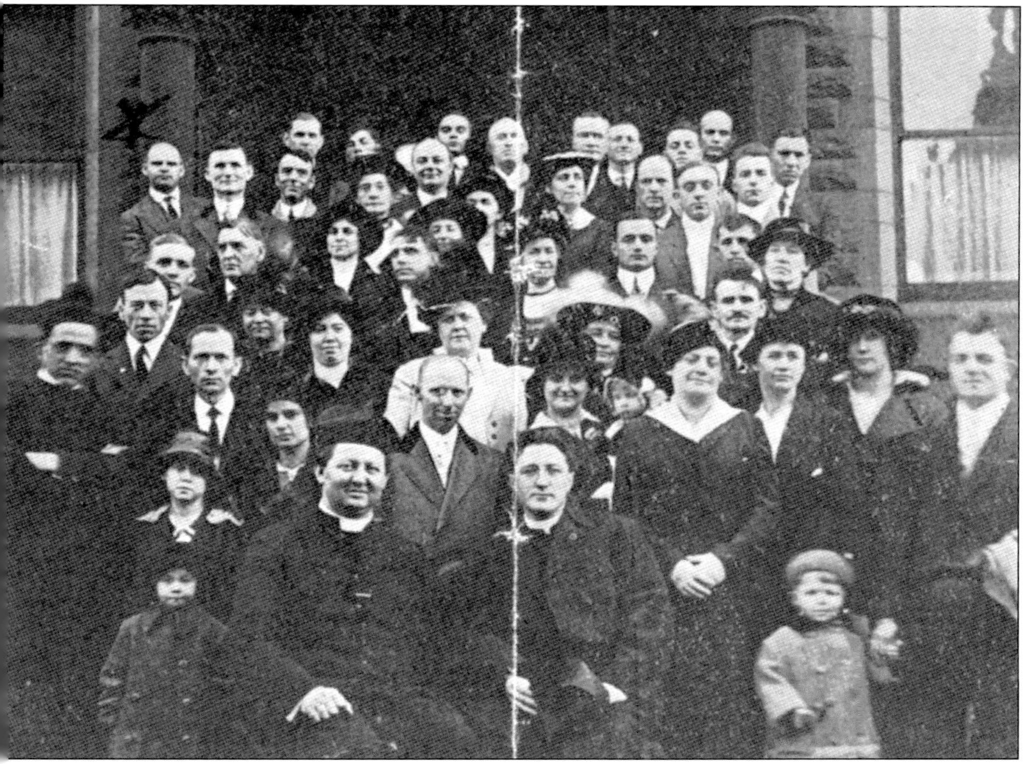

n 1914, a proud group of Catholic deaf church members are shown at the St. Mary's Hospital
Chapel with Monsignor Kaufmann standing at far left. The group first established the St. Joseph
Ephpheta Society on October 11, 1914, with around 37 people. The location was at the St. Joseph
Commercial College at 41 Jay Street in Detroit. (Courtesy of SJDC.)

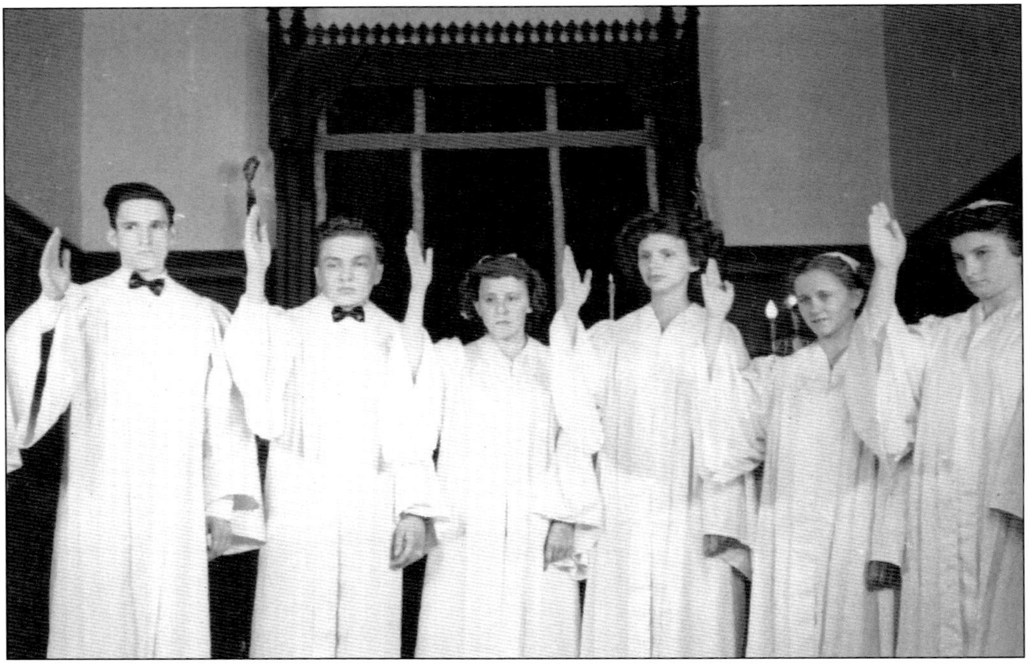

This is the LSD 1946 confirmation class signing the word "God." Pictured are Jean Armour, Vivian Moeller, Ralph Reedy, Robert Gordon, Richard Tuccinardi, Doris Krist, and Jacqueline Bylander. During that time, Rev. N.E. Borchardt and Dr. J.A. Klein managed the school and church activities. From 1895 to the late 1940s, total communication was allowed. Former students remembered that after 1946, they were only allowed to sign in the dormitory or at recess, though they were required to use their voices while signing. (Courtesy of Judy and Larry Vardon.)

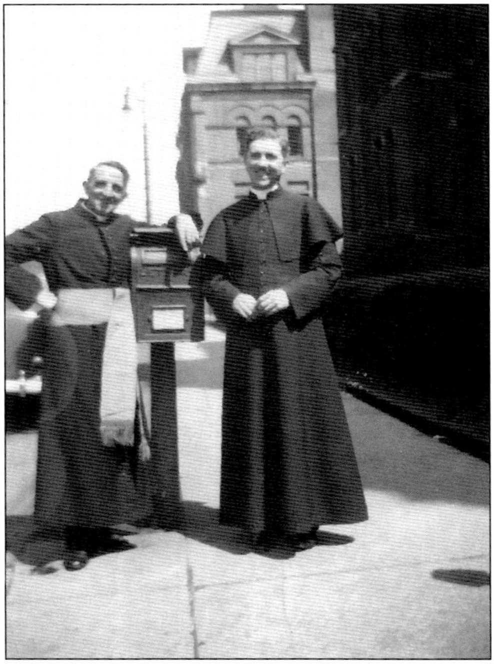

Msgr. Henry J. Kaufmann stands at left next to Fr. Basil Eallard of Ontario, Canada. This photograph was taken on May 23, 1937. According to the *History of the Catholic Deaf* by Sr. Dolores Beere, Kaufmann's association with deaf individuals before he entered the priesthood led him to help by learning sign language around 1909. (Courtesy of SJDC.)

Fr. Daniel Higgins was a well-known missionary to the deaf in the United States and Canada. He established a mission at the St. Mary's Hospital Chapel in 1921. He also wrote a sign-language book called *How to Talk to the Deaf*. Later, he became a pastor at the Holy Redeemer Church in Detroit from 1933 to 1936. (Courtesy of SJDC.)

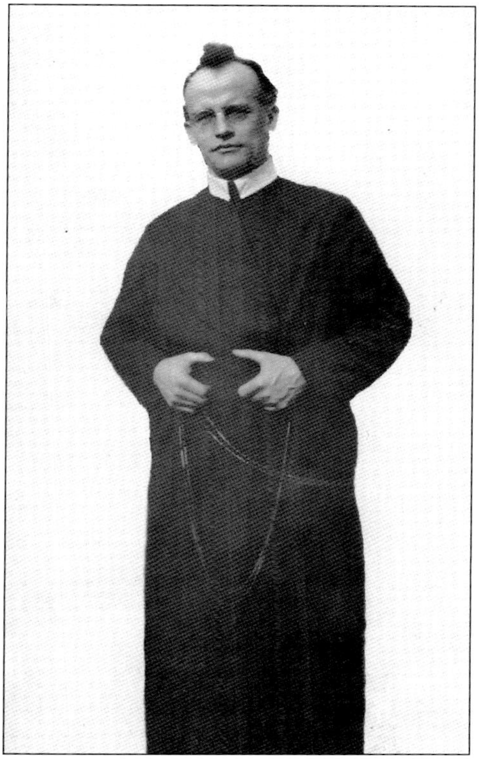

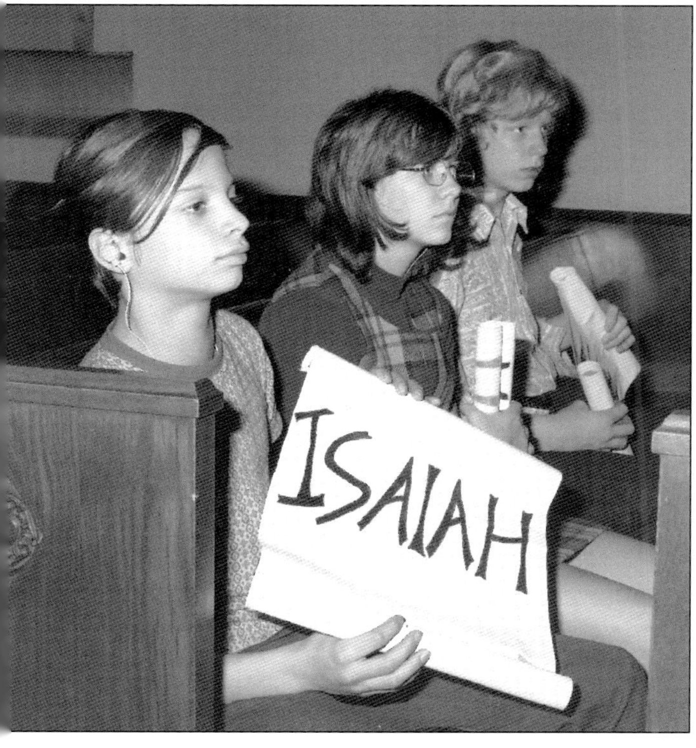

LSD provided a children's Christmas program before the students went home for the holidays. In this 1971 photograph are, from left to right, Tom Futris, Wendy Lewis, and Larry Vardon. Tom got to play as Isaiah, Wendy as Micah, and Larry as Balaam. After every program, the DAD Ladies Auxiliary served tea; afterwards, the parents took the children home or pupils were sent home by other means. (Courtesy of Judy and Larry Vardon.)

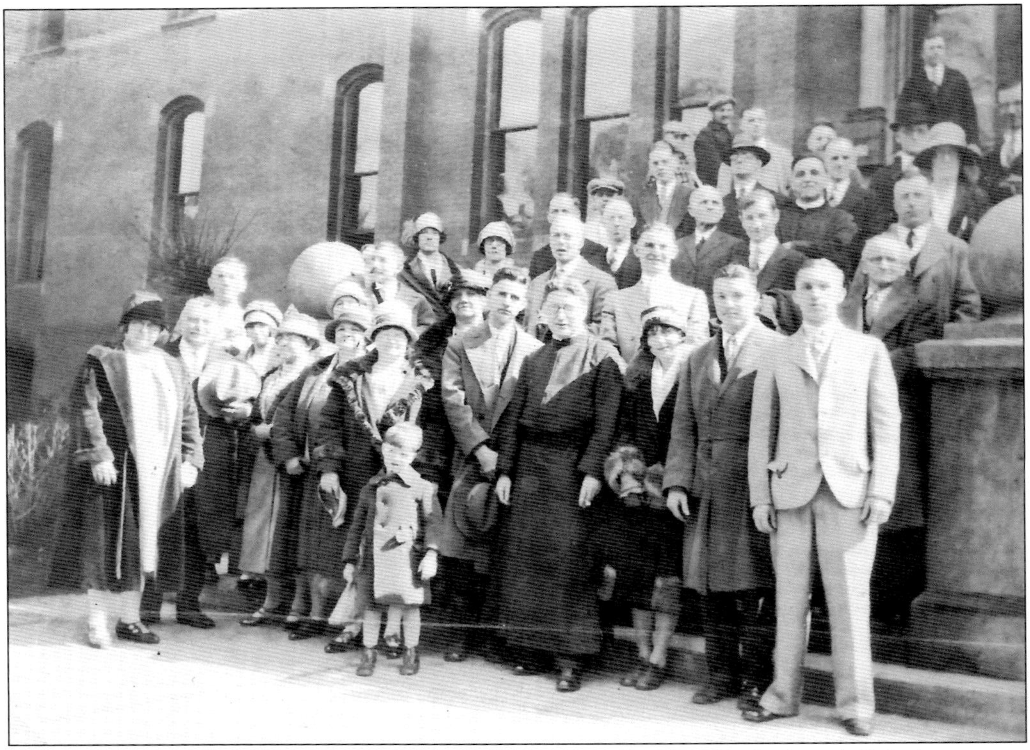

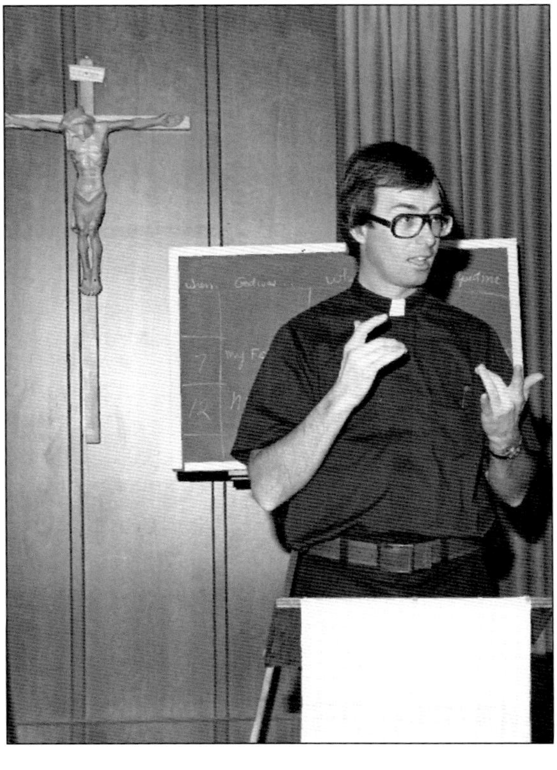

Pictured is the St. Joseph Ephpheta Society at the St. Mary's Hospital after 1922 with Fr. H. Kaufmann standing second from right in the third row. The name "Detroit Association of Catholic Deaf" was adopted on November 12, 1923. Fourth and fifth from the right in the second row are Alexander and Anette Lobsinger, DAD members. Kaufmann received the title of monsignor in 1934 and retired in 1941. He died on January 18, 1958. (Courtesy of SJDC.)

Thomas Coughlin is the first known culturally deaf Catholic priest to be ordained in the nation. According to the *History of the Catholic Deaf*, on May 7, 1977, Coughlin was ordained a Trinitarian priest in the oldest cathedral church in America, the Basilica of the Assumption in Baltimore, Maryland. He came to Detroit in April 1978 to talk at the St. John's Deaf Center. (Courtesy of SJDC.)

According to the Lutheran Deaf Mission Society, the sainted pastor George Speckhard was a teacher for the deaf in Germany before he moved to Michigan as a parish pastor. He was the first superintendent for LSD and the first pastor for the St. Paul's Lutheran Church of Royal Oak, Michigan, and served both starting in 1873. LSD used German from 1883 to 1895. Signs were added to the oral method in 1895, but were dropped several years later in favor of full oral method. (Courtesy of Judy and Larry Vardon.)

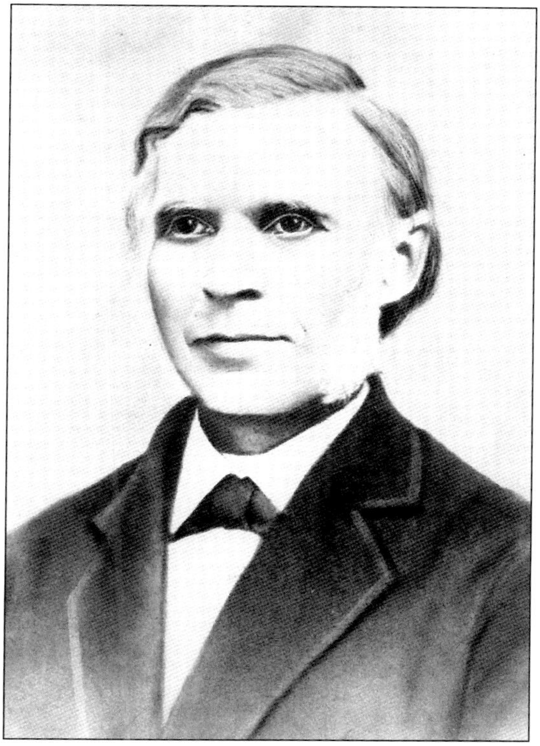

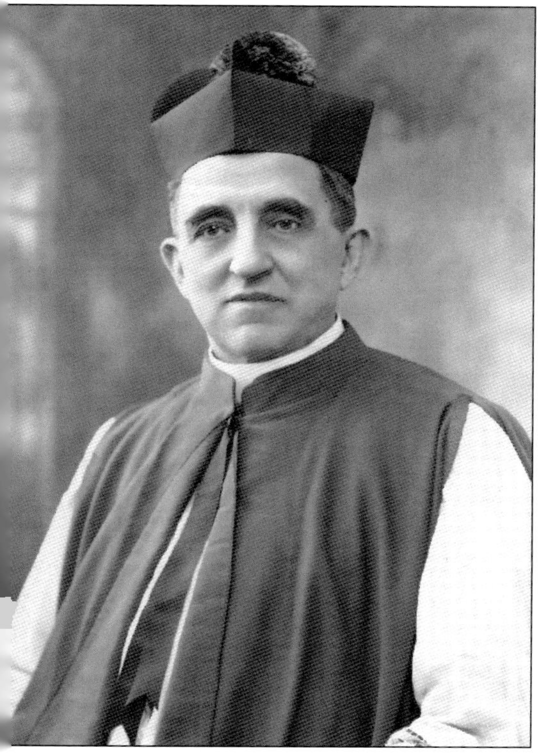

Henry J. Kaufmann was born in Wuerdinghausen, Germany, on April 25, 1871. He arrived in the United States at 14 with his family and made Detroit his hometown. He met some deaf fellows when he was involved in the grocery business before he went off to study for the priesthood. After Kaufmann was ordained in the summer of 1899, he became a hearing liaison for the Deaf Community and devoted his time to help the deaf. (Courtesy of SJDC.)

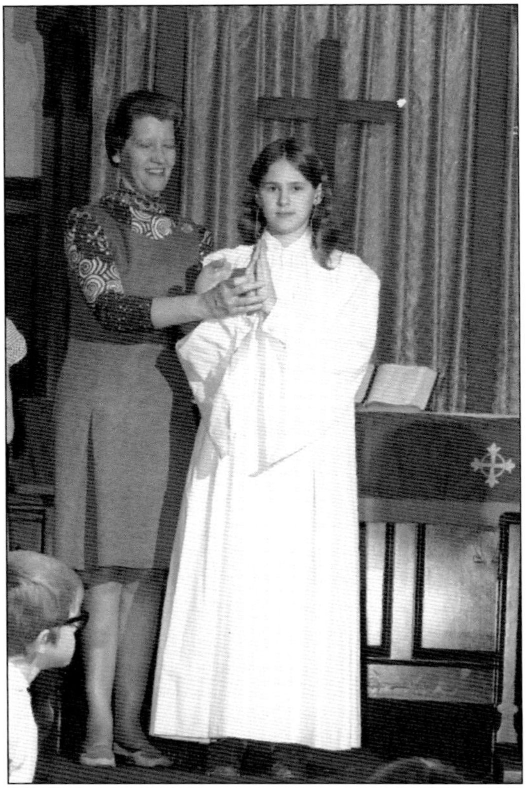

Judy Manik Vardon (right) is shown in 1971 preparing for the Christmas play, practicing as an angel with her teacher, Jane Daniels. Judy graduated from the 1974 confirmation class. Later, she converted from Lutheranism to Catholicism, and is currently very active with the St. John Deaf Center. She directed the film *100th Anniversary of Detroit Catholic Deaf Ministry* in the fall of 2014, which was entered in the Toronto International Deaf Film & Arts Festival. (Courtesy of Judy and Larry Vardon.)

A confirmation class at LSD is shown in 1938. From left to right are (seated) Alberta Moore, director Dr. John A. Klein, Rev. N.E. Borchardt, and Loretta Kling; (standing) Anna Nissen, Norwin Last, Clifford Schaeg, Mearl Kutzner, and Bernidean Berkey. Not pictured is Wilbur Burns. During that time, LSD allowed total communication, including signing. (Courtesy of Judy and Larry Vardon.)

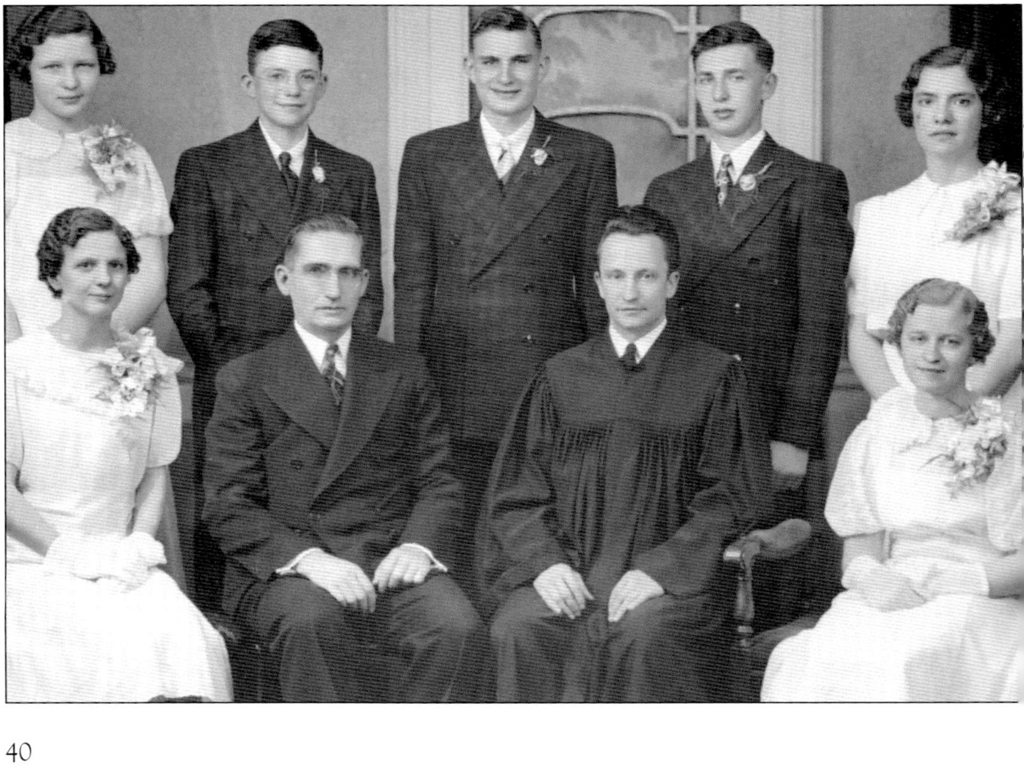

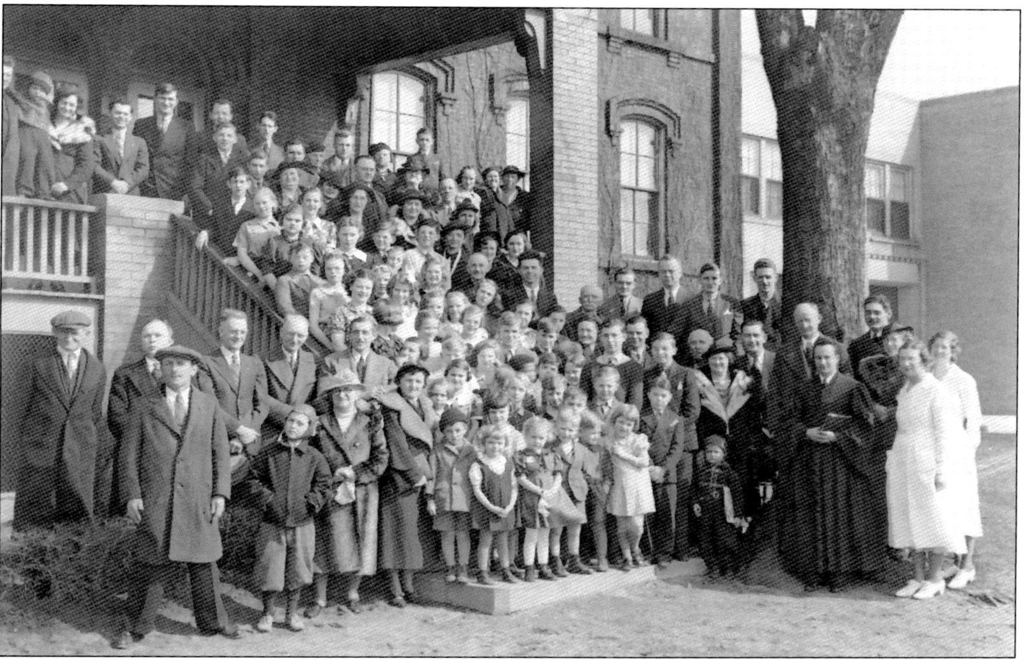

Shown standing second from the right in front around the 1930s is Rev. N.E. Borchardt, who was a pastor of Our Savior Evangelical Lutheran Church for the deaf. Although he was not deaf, he conducted his entire service in sign language. He was a graduate of Concordia Seminary in St. Louis, Missouri. Students from LSD stand on the stairs surrounded by parents and staff. (Courtesy of Judy and Larry Vardon.)

Chapel services were part of the daily program at LSD. Every morning, devotion was provided with the city missionary, who made regular visits to the chapel on the premises. The writing on the back of this March 1952 photograph reads, "Conquest for Christ!" (Courtesy of Judy and Larry Vardon.)

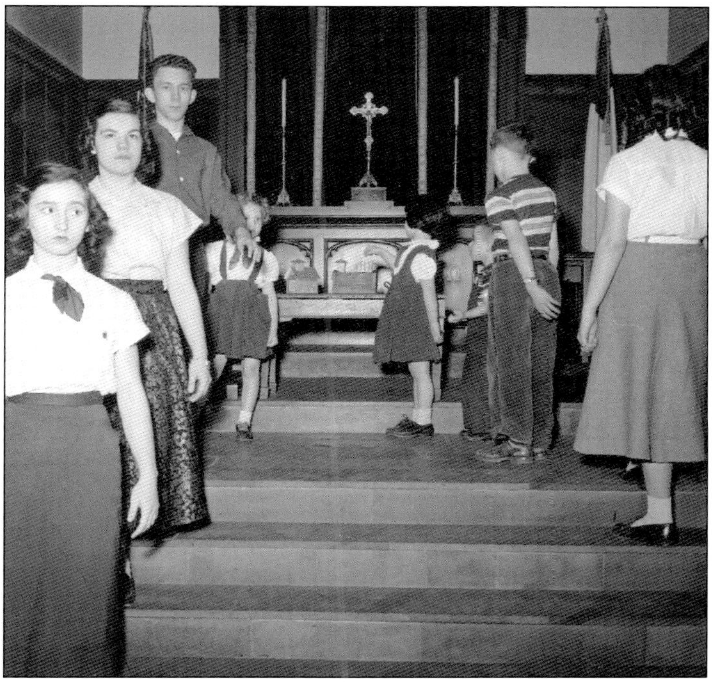

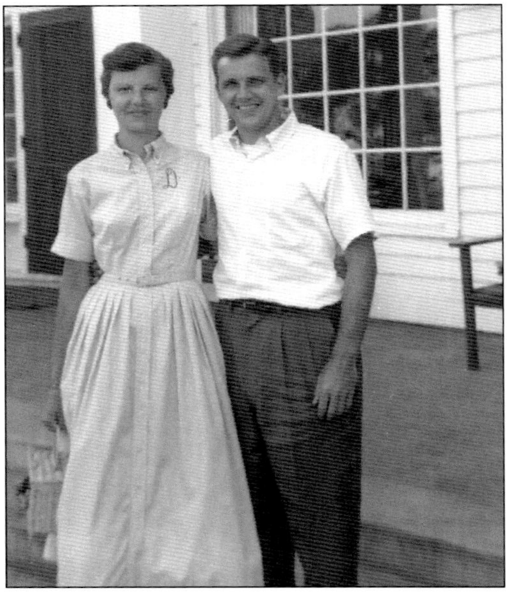

Diane Huyghebaert met William "Bill" Knight III at DDSD before they parted to different high schools. Later, they reunited, got engaged (left), and got married on June 7, 1958, in a Lutheran church (below). They gave birth to a son in 1959, and three years later, Diane was five months pregnant with her daughter when Bill was killed in a car accident with two other deaf players and a deaf coach en route to Pittsburgh for a basketball tournament. Instead of Bill, Diane gave her daughter away at her wedding in 1979, and she now has seven grandchildren. (Both, courtesy of Bill and Diane Huyghebaert Knight.)

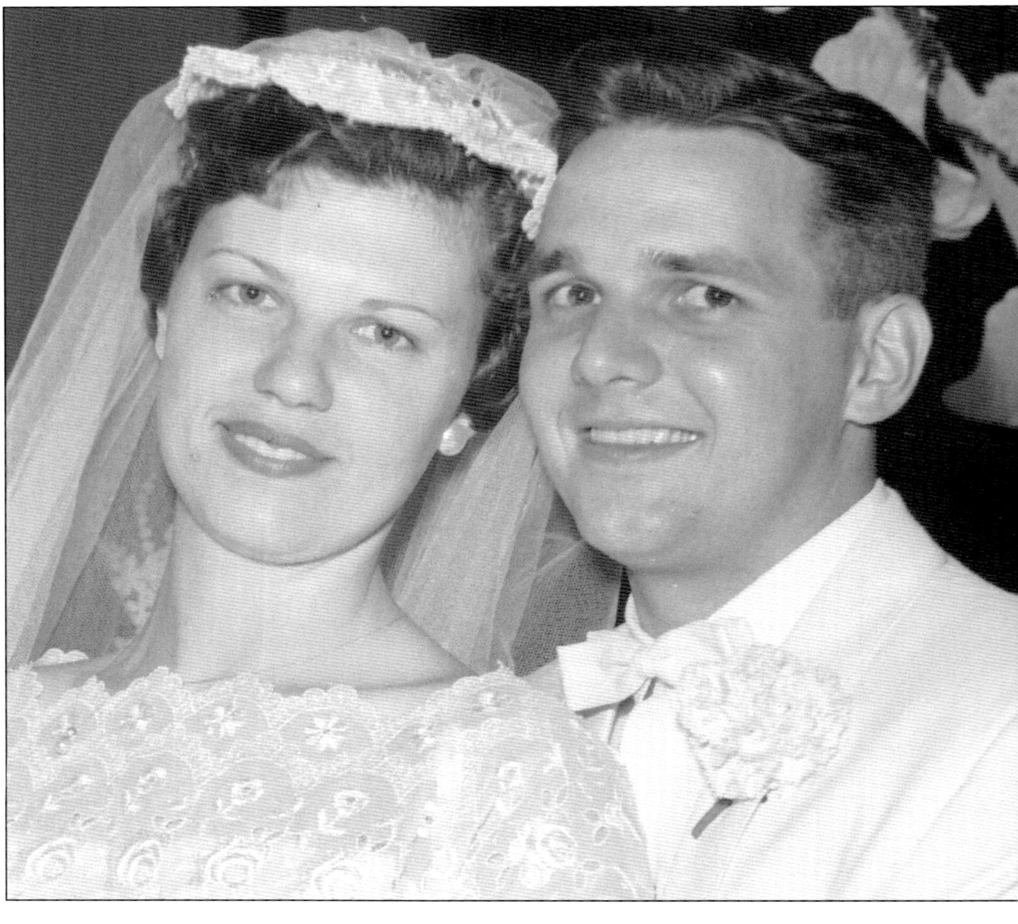

Four

Education

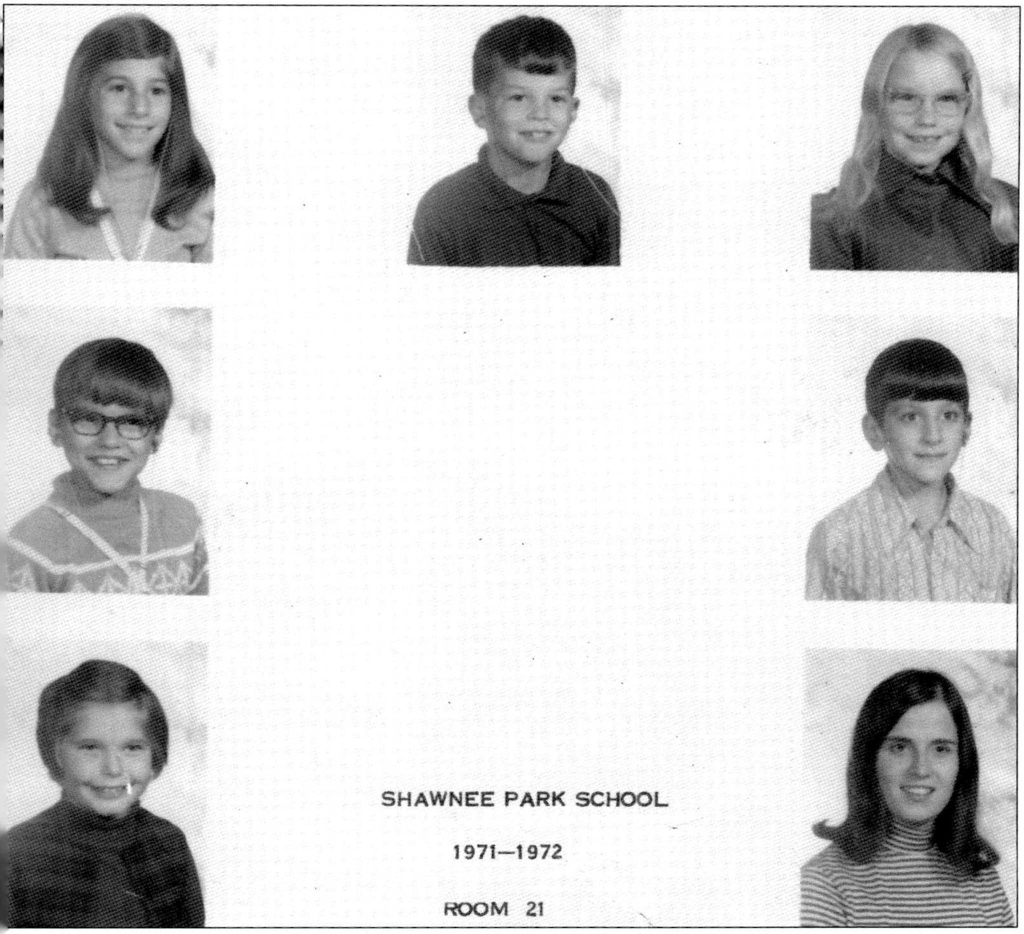

This class attended the Shawnee Park Oral-Deaf School, which did not permit use of sign language. The photograph was taken in 1971 or 1972. Most of the classmates shown grew up together and still get together on special occasions. Today, some use some sign language and some prefer total communication. A mother of one deaf student remembered how the school staff told her that she should not learn sign language to communicate with her child at home. (Courtesy of Nancy Capek McCall.)

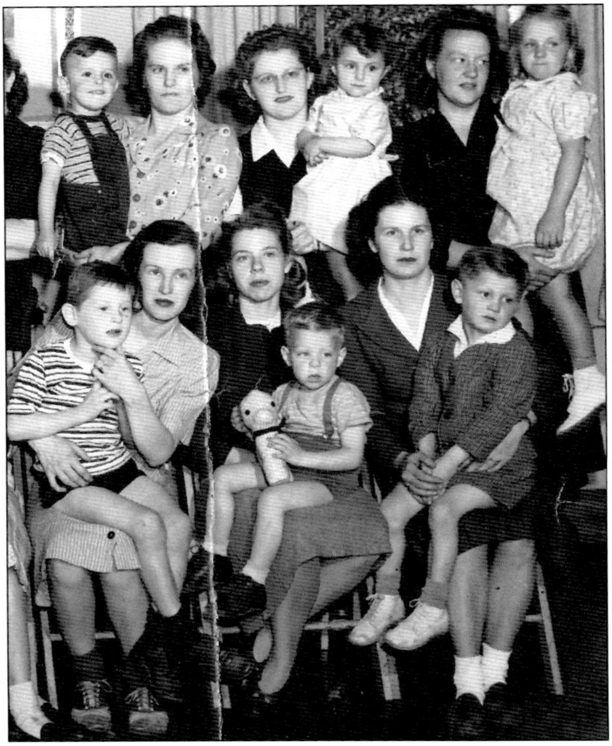

This group of mothers and children stayed together during two days of training at MSD in 1945. Robert Snider is seated at far right with his mother, Myrtle Snider. MSD believed mothers being present helped children feel comfortable as new students in their kindergarten year by staying for two days in the dormitory. Robert recalled that he was already comfortable by the second day and enjoyed the rest of the year. (Courtesy of Robert and Diane Snider.)

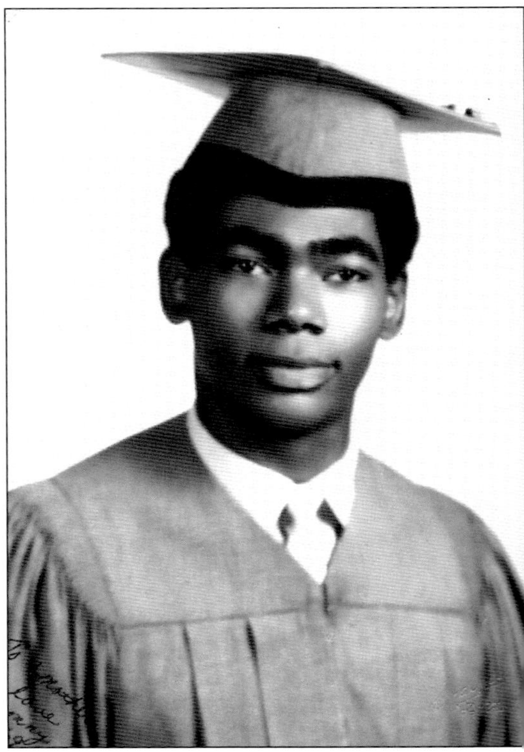

After Glenn Stewart completed ninth grade at Detroit Day Deaf School, he transferred to the Charles E. Chadsey High School. In the early summer of 1969, he graduated from high school along with some deaf students. Chadsey High School was qualified for those who were able to lip read well without interpreters, and all deaf students had to sit in the front row of their classes. Stewart grew up dancing and making art. (Courtesy of Glenn and Susan Stewart.)

Glenn Stewart is pictured in the fall of 1969 at RIT doing algebra work on the blackboard. He remembered very well how he disliked the subject; however, it was a general requirement for the fine arts major. He was a freshman at that time. He later met Susan, who attended St. Mary School for the Deaf nearby, and they got married a few years later, after his graduation. Susan remembered how she noticed him as a nice young gentleman when she made a visit with friends from her high school class. (Courtesy of Glenn and Susan Stewart.)

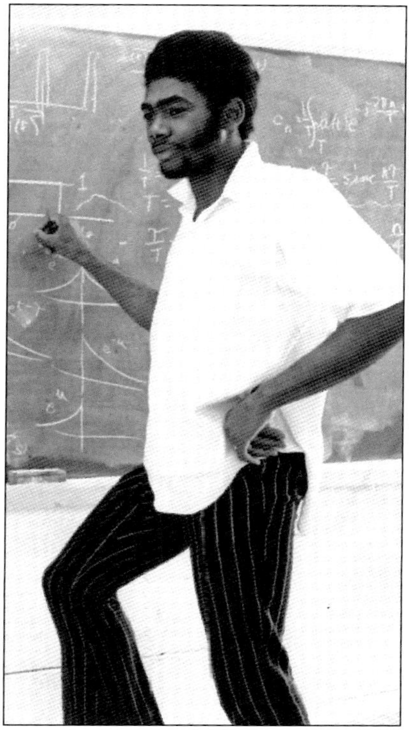

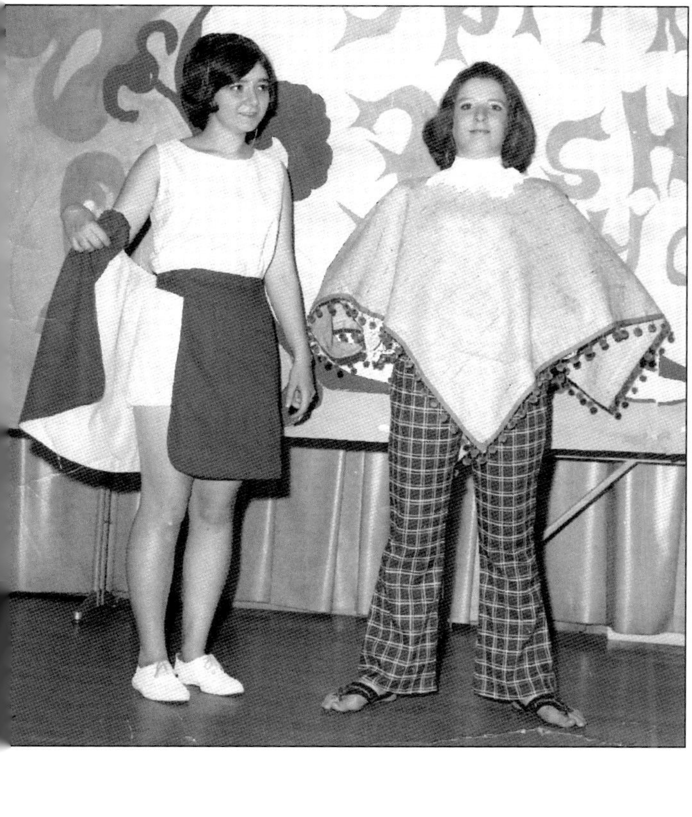

This fashion show was an event at the Detroit Day Deaf School in May 1969. Shown are Melissa Black Ison (left) and Maureen Williams dressed in the clothes they made for the outdoor sports theme. There were 68 entries in the Fashion Parade coordinated by Mabel Jacobs, the sewing teacher. The school provided only oral communication during school hours until after around 1970, when total communication was introduced. (Courtesy of Melissa Black Ison.)

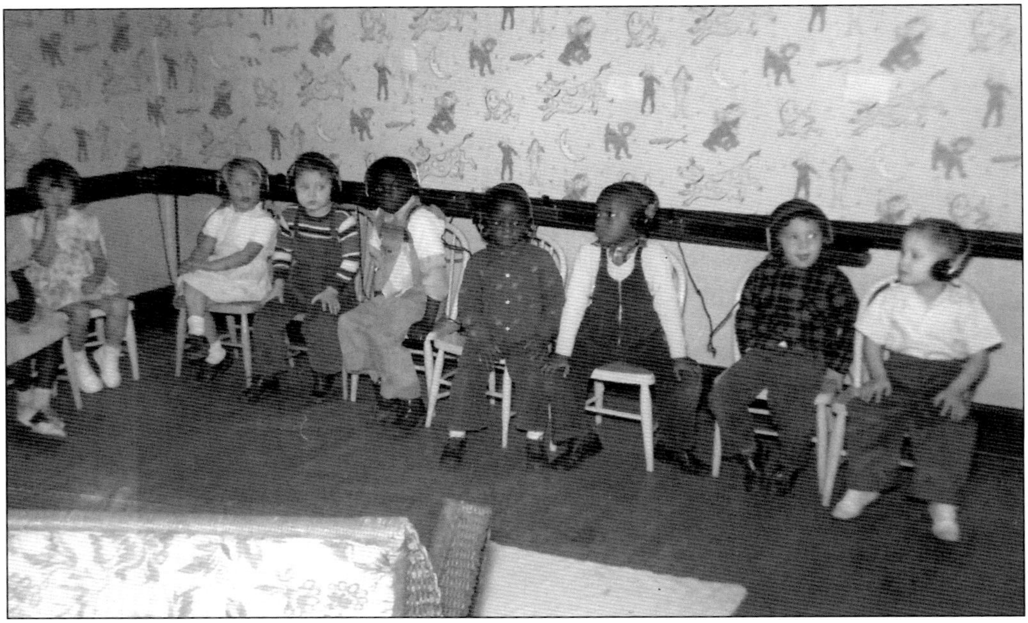

At DDSD, the class learned using the oral method. From left to right are Charlotte Grant, Sue Gore, Mary ?, David Bayones, Albert Thomas, Ricky Martin, Carthon Moorer, Philip Nuccio, and Paul Kuplicki. The photograph was taken in 1956. Paul Kuplicki recalled that one teacher who supported signing closed the door on a daily basis and secretly communicated with the class by signing. During that time, the principal was Harriet Kopp; her husband invented the voice box. (Courtesy of Carol and Paul Kuplicki Sr.)

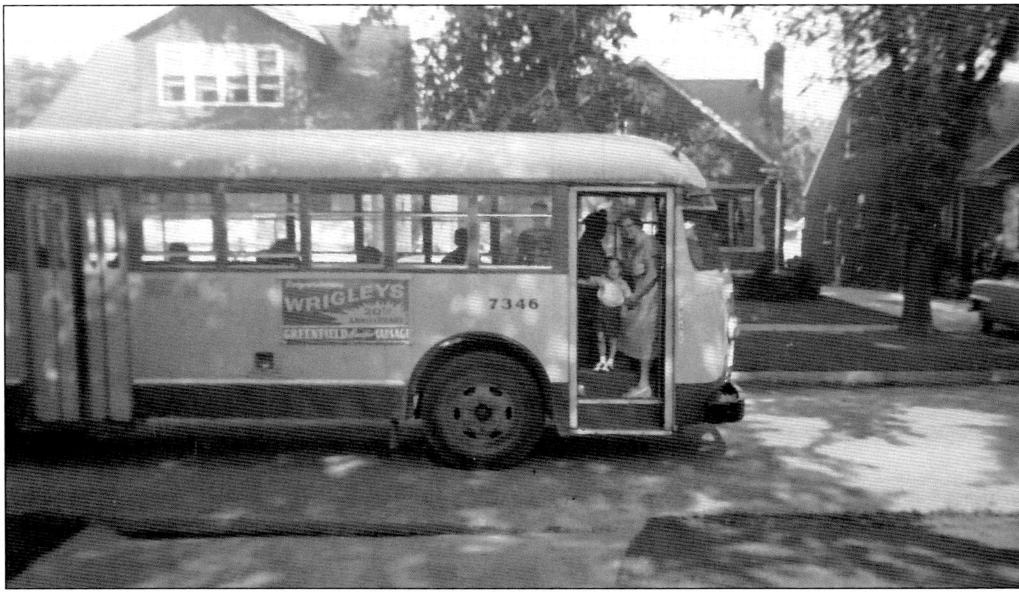

Shown in 1956, under the city's contractual agreement with DDSD, this city bus picked up children from their houses in the mornings and brought them home after school Monday through Friday. In between, the city buses resumed their routes on schedule every day. (Courtesy of Carol and Paul Kuplicki Sr..)

Diane Helene Huyghebaert, daughter of Victor and Marie Huyghebaert, attended DDSD and grew up using the oral method. She was a devout Lutheran who later converted to Catholicism. Shown here is her graduation photograph with the class of 1951, of which she was secretary. (Courtesy of Bill and Diane Huyghebaert Knight.)

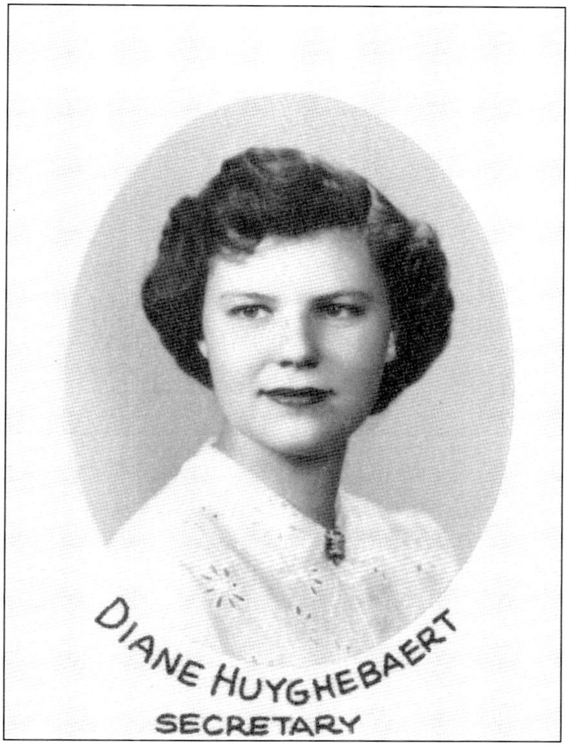

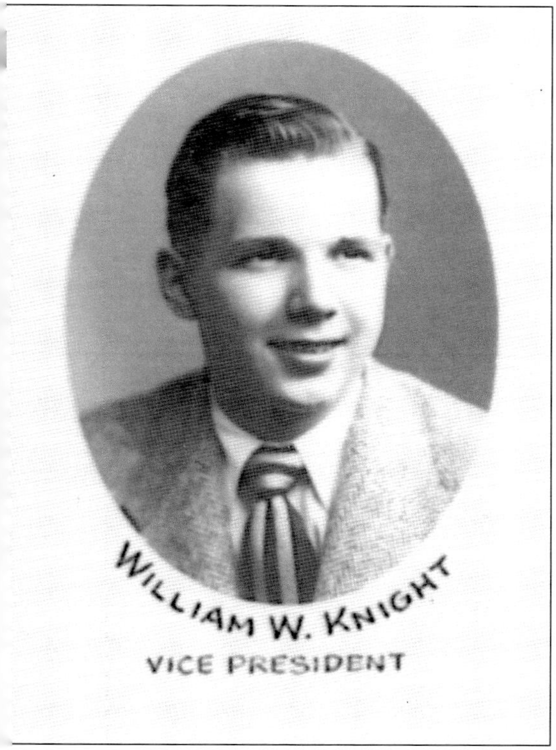

William W. Knight III attended DDSD and graduated in 1950. He continued his education at the Cass Tech High School and completed his education in 1952. He never actively participated in high school sports, but he did participate in the local YMCA league. MCAD discovered his talents and recruited him to join the basketball and softball teams. He was also one of the original members of the Wolverine Deaf Golfers of Michigan. (Courtesy of Bill and Diane Huyghebaert Knight.)

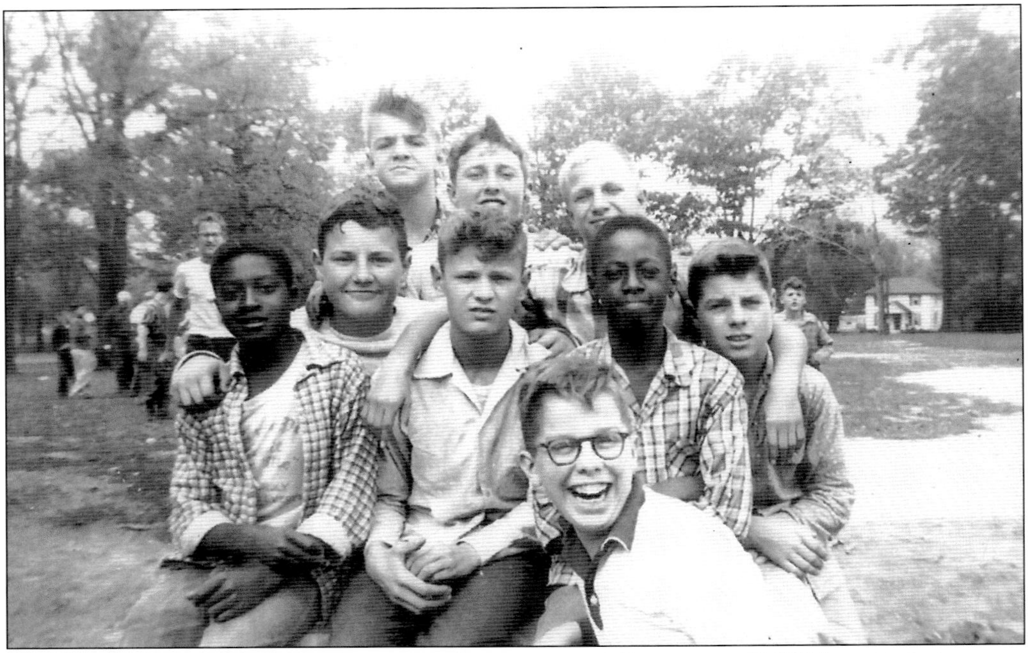

This group of MSD boys includes Robert Snider, second from left in the middle row. The favorite activities at the school were recess and sports, including basketball. (Courtesy of Robert and Diane Snider.)

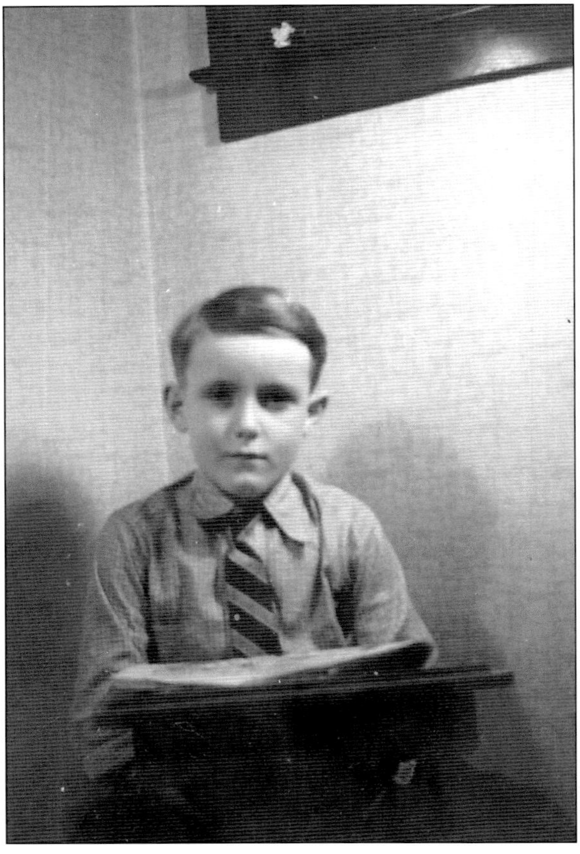

At age six, John E. Klarr stayed for a few months in the hospital with spinal meningitis, which caused him to be deaf. Before he came to the hospital, he attended the St. John Berchmans School as a hearing student. He was transferred to DDSD when he became deaf. His uncle loved to take pictures of him, including this one from 1936. (Courtesy of John and Donna Delikta Klarr.)

A young Paul Kuplicki is shown in July 1965 with a trophy for being a good helper to other deaf children through the Boysville Camp for the Deaf at Macon, Michigan. Paul recalled that he enjoyed attending every summer. The Mission Helpers of Sacred Heart used the land for the four-week camp for the deaf: two weeks for the girls and two weeks for the boys. Signing was allowed freely at the camp every summer from the 1940s to the 1970s. (Courtesy of Carol and Paul Kuplicki Sr.)

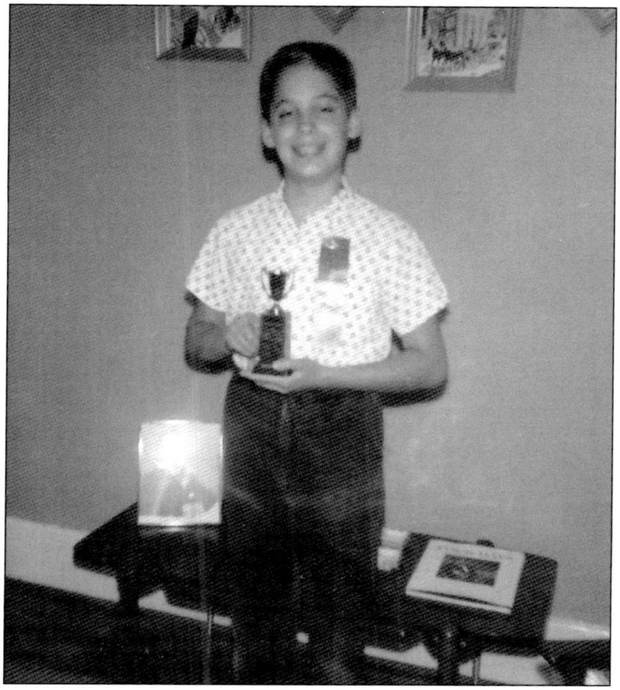

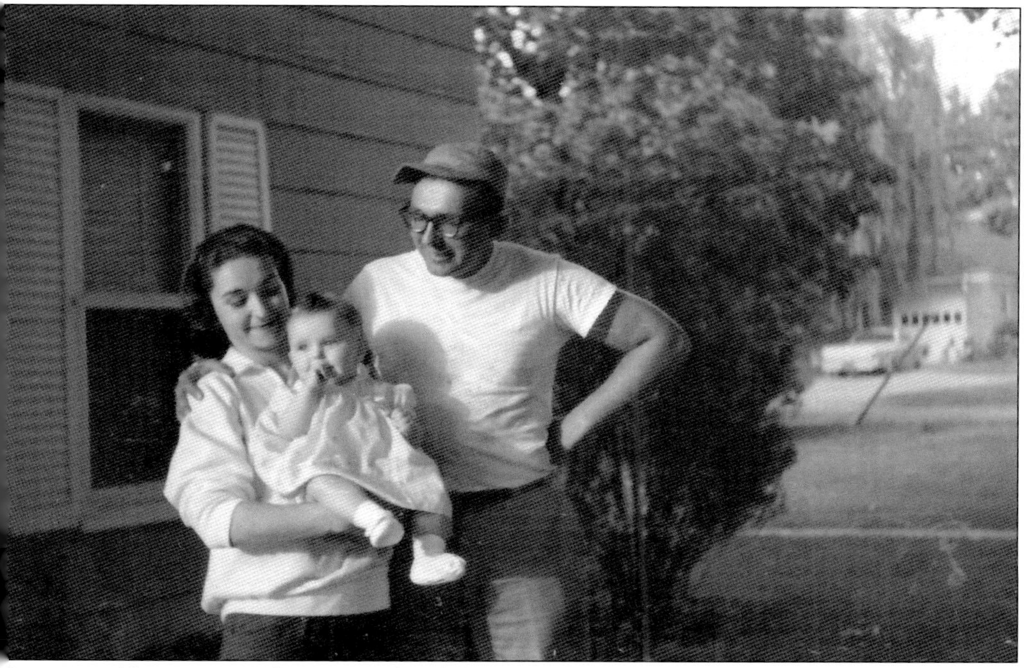

One-year-old Nancy Capek is pictured with her parents, Pat and Richard Capek, in 1964. Pat was suspicious that Nancy was deaf for a while. After numerous unsuccessful trips to the local doctors, Pat took Nancy to Detroit to see an audiologist, who finally diagnosed Nancy as deaf at four years old. Nancy was then placed in an oral-deaf program. Later on, Nancy and her deaf husband produced two deaf children and communicated in ASL. (Courtesy of Nancy Capek McCall.)

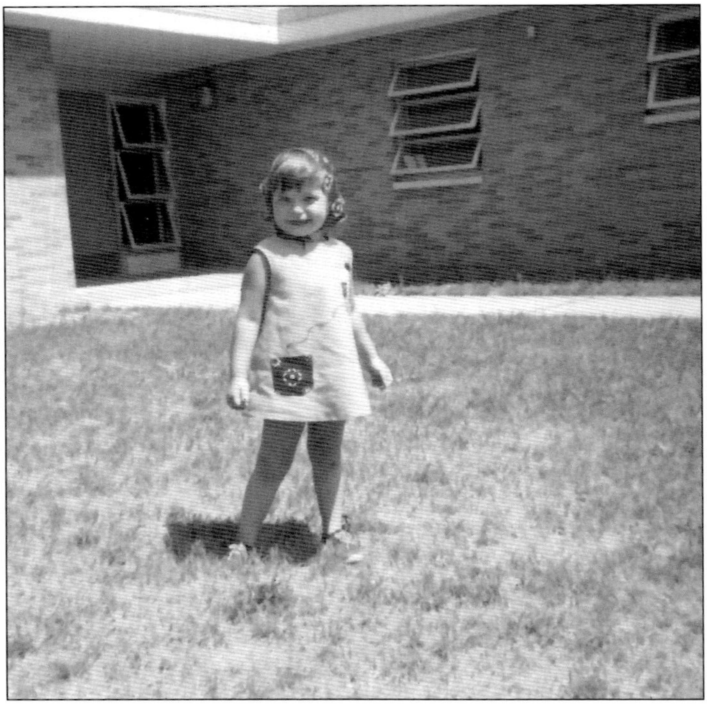

Nancy Capek is modeling an outfit sewn by her own mother, Pat Capek, in front of her grandparents' home in Whitehall, Michigan. The back of the photograph, dated July 1966, reads, "Pat made the outfit—notice how she standing like a model, yet." (Courtesy of Nancy Capek McCall.)

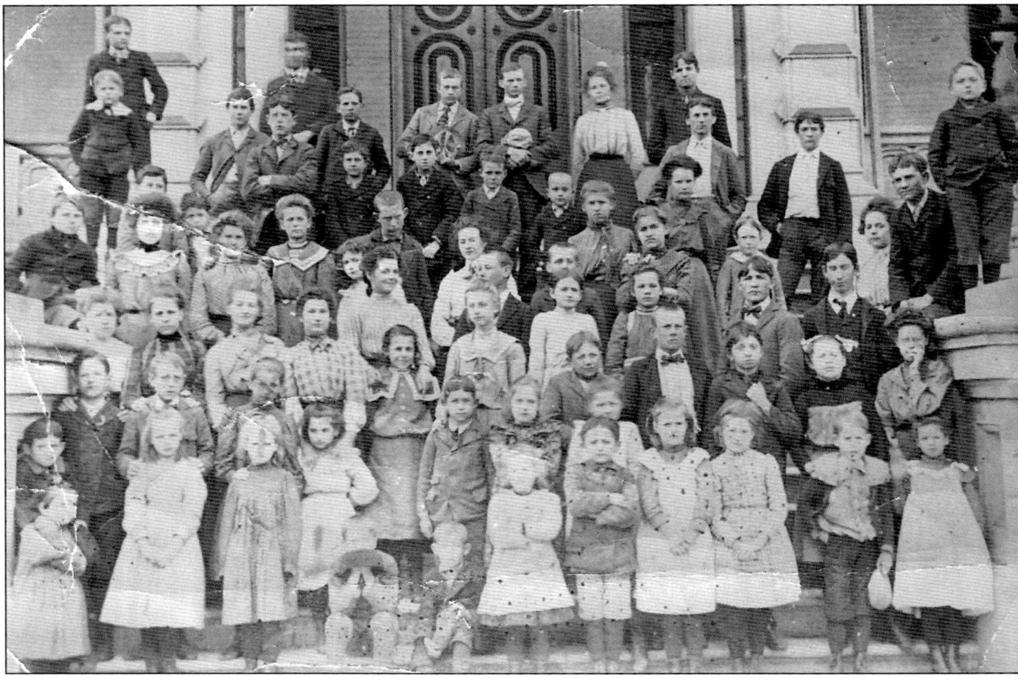

All of the deaf siblings at MSD stand on the front steps of Fay Hall in the early 20th century. There were many deaf siblings due to the fact that vaccinations had not yet been developed for illnesses from rubella to whopping cough that affected the hearing. (Courtesy of Anson and Kathy McCall Mitchell.)

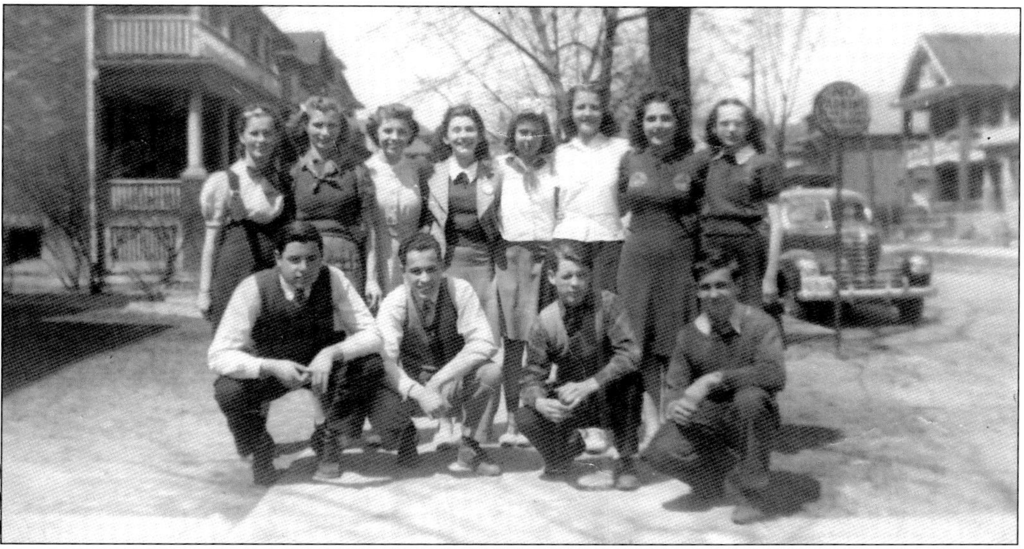

This group socialized after school at DDSD on April 29, 1940. They are Charles Mully (first row, far left), Arlyn Meyerson (first row, second from right), Annie Roscoe (second row, fourth from right), Betty Lancaster Weingold (second row, third from right), Frances Maniace Tomalin (second row, second from right), and Loretta Bruszewski Kuplicki (second row, far right). The others are, in unknown order, Jean Michael, Elaine Weiss, Charlotte Minkin, Violet Zaborawski, Bernice Szymanski, Robert Murphy, and Malcolm Hughes. (Courtesy of Carol and Paul Kuplicki Sr.)

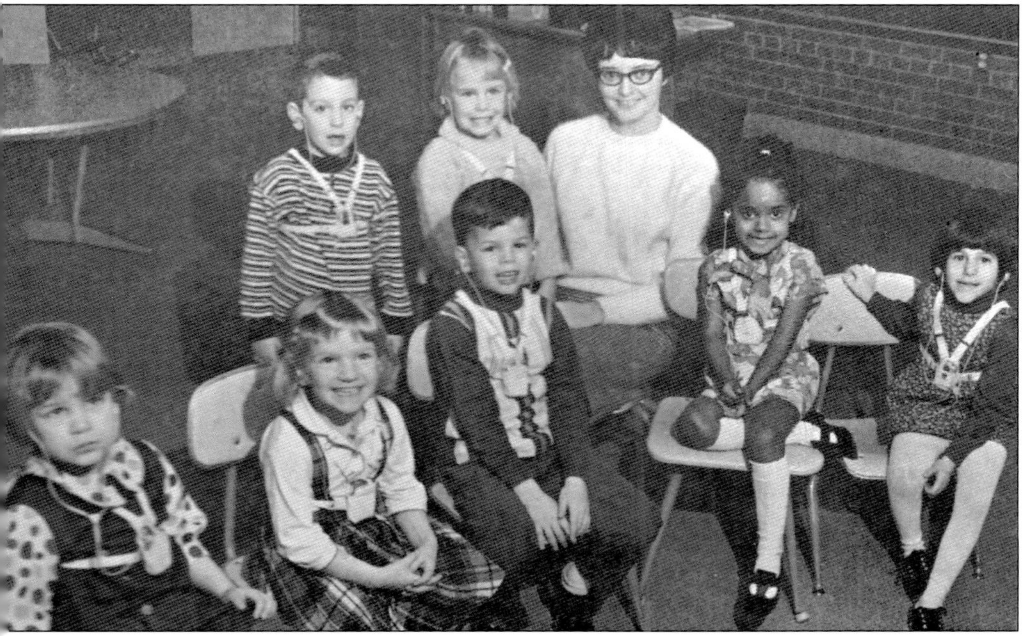

This photograph was taken during the 1967–1968 Shawnee Park Oral-Deaf School year. From left to right are (first row) Linda Klamer, Debbie Wendt, Scott Smith, Belinda Peay, and Sandy Karrip; (second row) Vernon Witte, Katie Kellar, and Carol Shook. It is interesting to note that an oral-deaf architect, Roger Allen, designed the original Shawnee Park School building. (Courtesy of Nancy Capek McCall.)

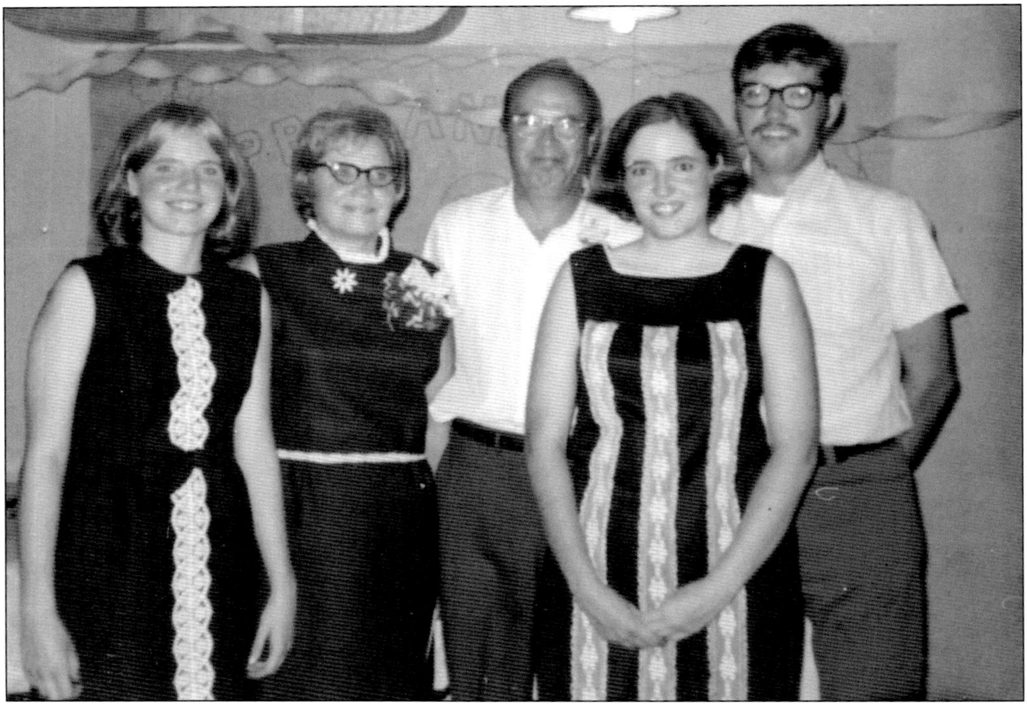

The photograph above, taken on August 8, 1970, shows, from left to right, Patricia, Virginia "Orene," Joseph, Diana, and Henry Strandell on the occasion of Joseph and Virginia's 25th anniversary. The photograph below was taken in April 1956 with the full deaf Strandell family, from left to right, Henry, Joe (holding little Patricia), Diana, and Virginia "Orene." Orene came from Tennessee, where her mother decided to learn sign language. The course her mother took turned out to be British Sign Language (BSL)! Orene grew up communicating in two languages between school and her own family. Patricia recalled her mother signing very fast in BSL with her mother's family. (Courtesy of Christopher and Patricia Strandell Schultz.)

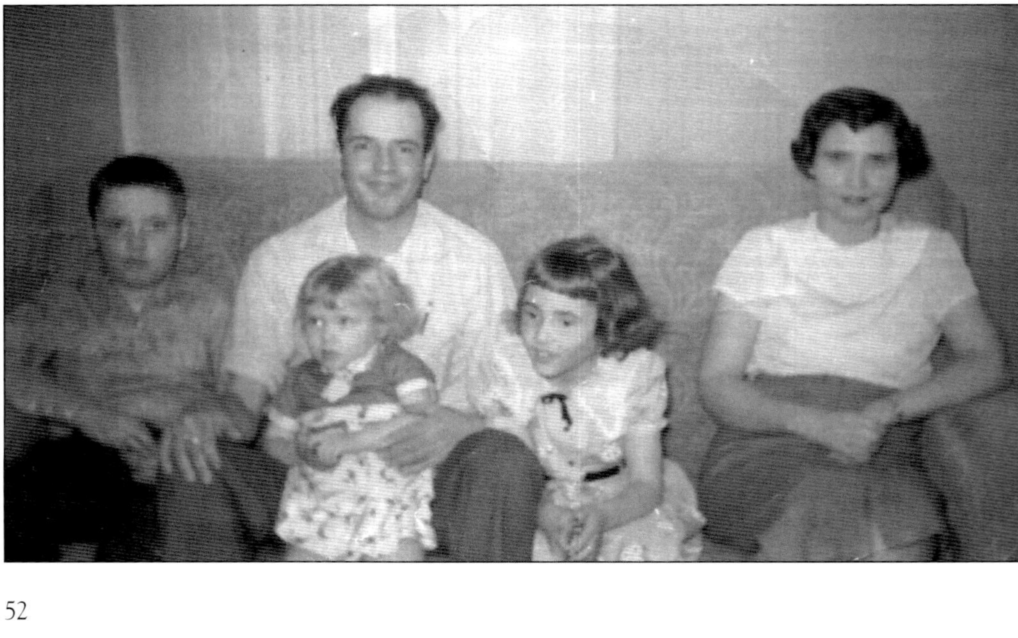

A teacher in the kindergarten class at MSD demonstrates a bow in this 1945 photograph and has a student act or sign the word. The student made a bow. MSD was the only school in Michigan in the early days that fully used sign language. The rest of the schools in the state used the oral method in their programs for the deaf. (Courtesy of Robert and Diane Strandell Snider.)

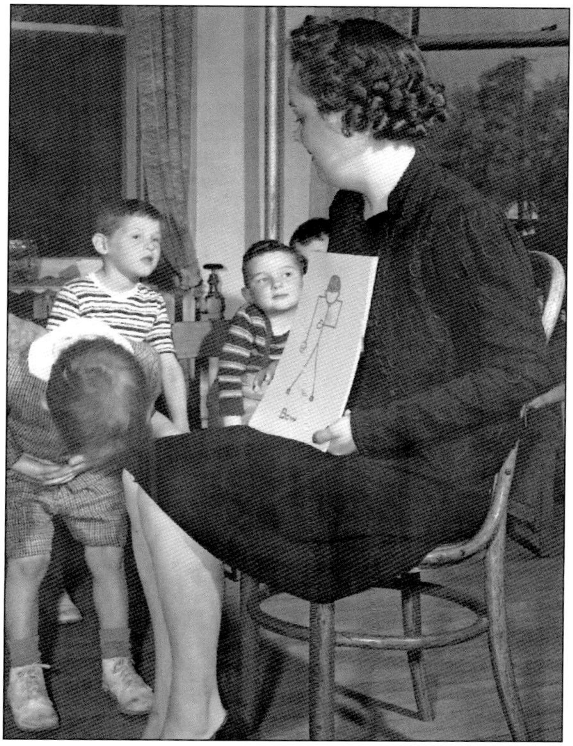

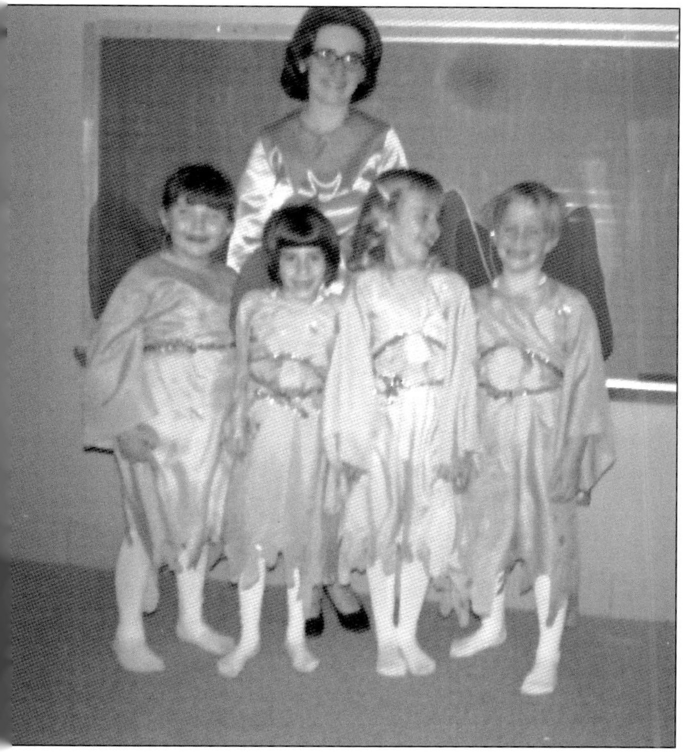

In December 1969, all the girls are dressed up in pink outfits for the Christmas pageant. From left to right are Nancy Capek, Sandra Karrip, Jill Van Sleighright, and Katherine Kellar; Marie Courtemanche is standing behind them. Shawnee School had a Christmas pageant directed by Courtemanche. Capek recalled that that school year, the teacher invited the entire class to her wedding, when Marie Courtemanche became Marie Hadiaris. (Courtesy of Jill Van Sleighright Veldkamp.)

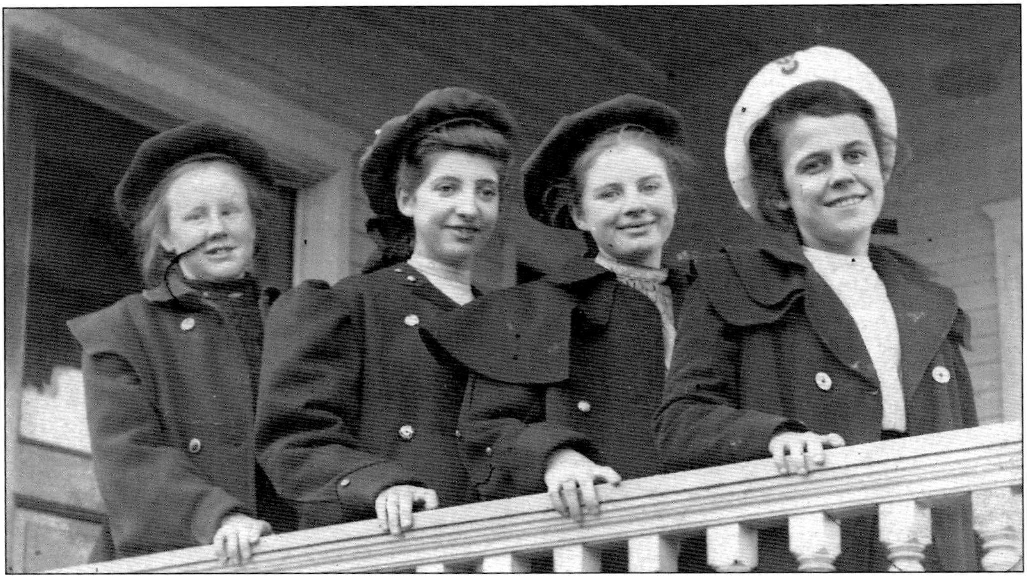

It's a family affair for these MSD students. From left to right are Mattie Sundquist, Georgianna Dumais Wahowiak, Annie Demick, and Amelia Blodgett. Georgianna and Annie are with the McCall deaf family. Annie used to work for Superintendent Francis D. Clarke in the superintendent's cottage. Clarke came from New York and helped MSD expand with new buildings. He served as superintendent for 21 years before he passed away in 1913. (Courtesy of Anson and Kathy McCall Mitchell.)

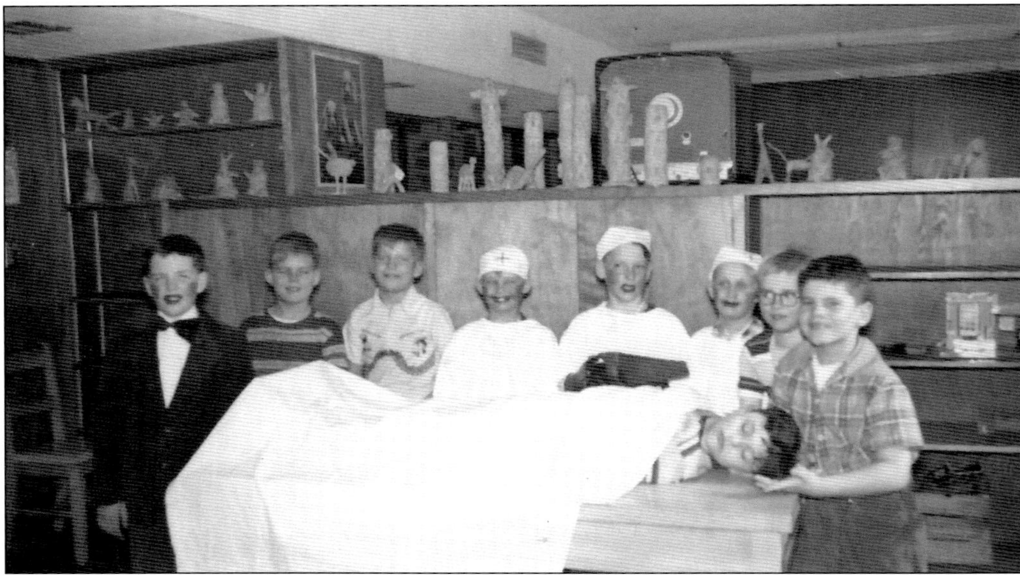

Around the 1950s, this group of elementary students played hospital in Stevenson Hall dormitory at MSD. The most noticeable thing is the papier-mâché made by the students placed on the shelves to show off their work. Shown from left to right are unidentified, Buddy Whaley Campbell, Bobby Chaffin Beck, David Takacs, Paul Lemper, Steven Gemmill, Kenneth Terwing, and Robert Morrison. Lying on the table in front is Istvan "Steve" Kovacs. Most of the boys were around seven years old. (Courtesy of Istvan "Steve" Kovacs.)

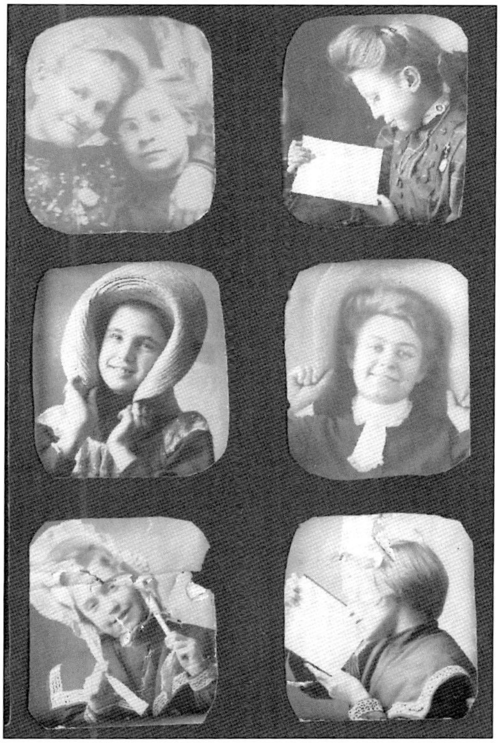

Both of these photographs show MSD classmates dressed up in props and clowning for the camera. The variety of expressions and emotions is fascinating. Some photographs are poor quality but still capture excitement. (Both, courtesy of Anson and Kathy McCall Mitchell.)

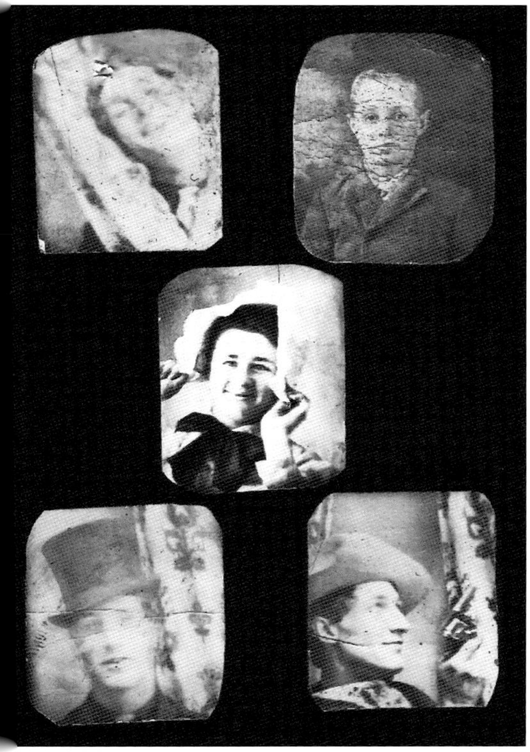

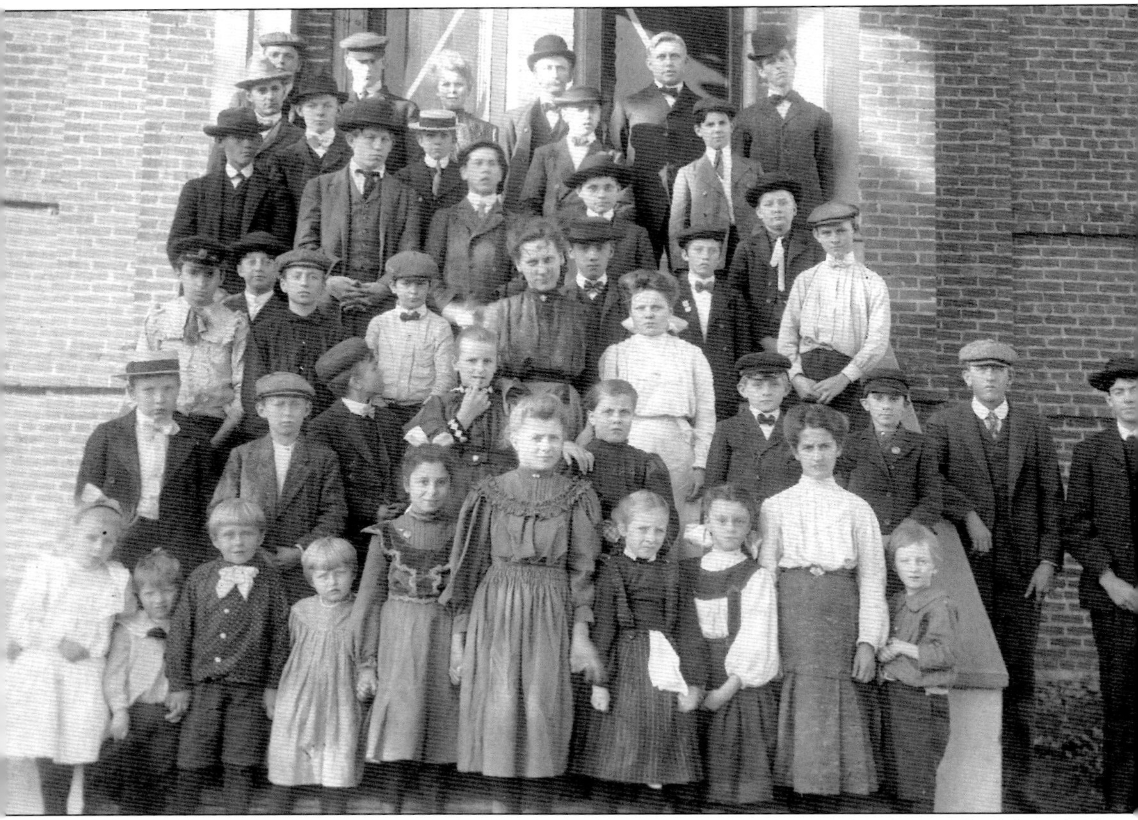

Pictured in 1903, the students from LSD stand on the stairway of the former building before the modern complex of buildings was constructed. The students learned both orally and in sign language. The woman at center in the first row was a deaf houseparent. Rev. William Gielow served as director for 31 years, from 1902 to 1933, when he resigned to become a full-time missionary to the deaf. (Courtesy of Judy and Larry Vardon.)

Five

Organizations

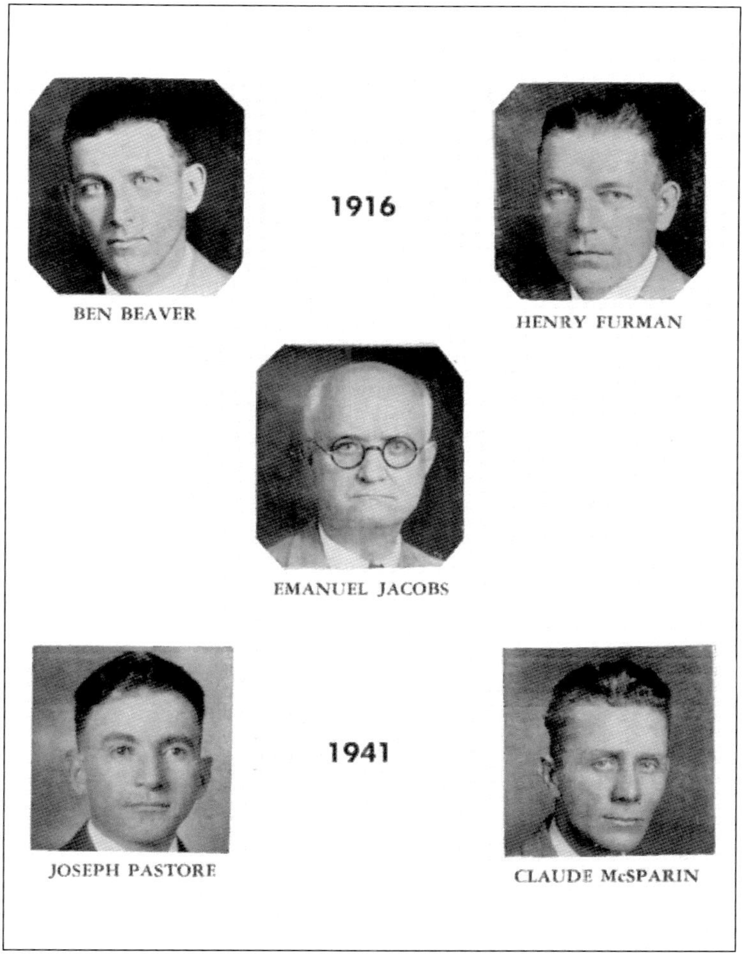

These were the five original DAD members from 1916 to 1941. DAD was officially founded in 1916. From left to right are (top row) Benjamin Beaver and Henry Furman; (center) Emanuel Jacobs, the founding president; (bottom row) Joseph Pastore and Claude McSparin. They were honored in the Silver Jubilee Program for the 25th-anniversary banquet. (Courtesy of DAD.)

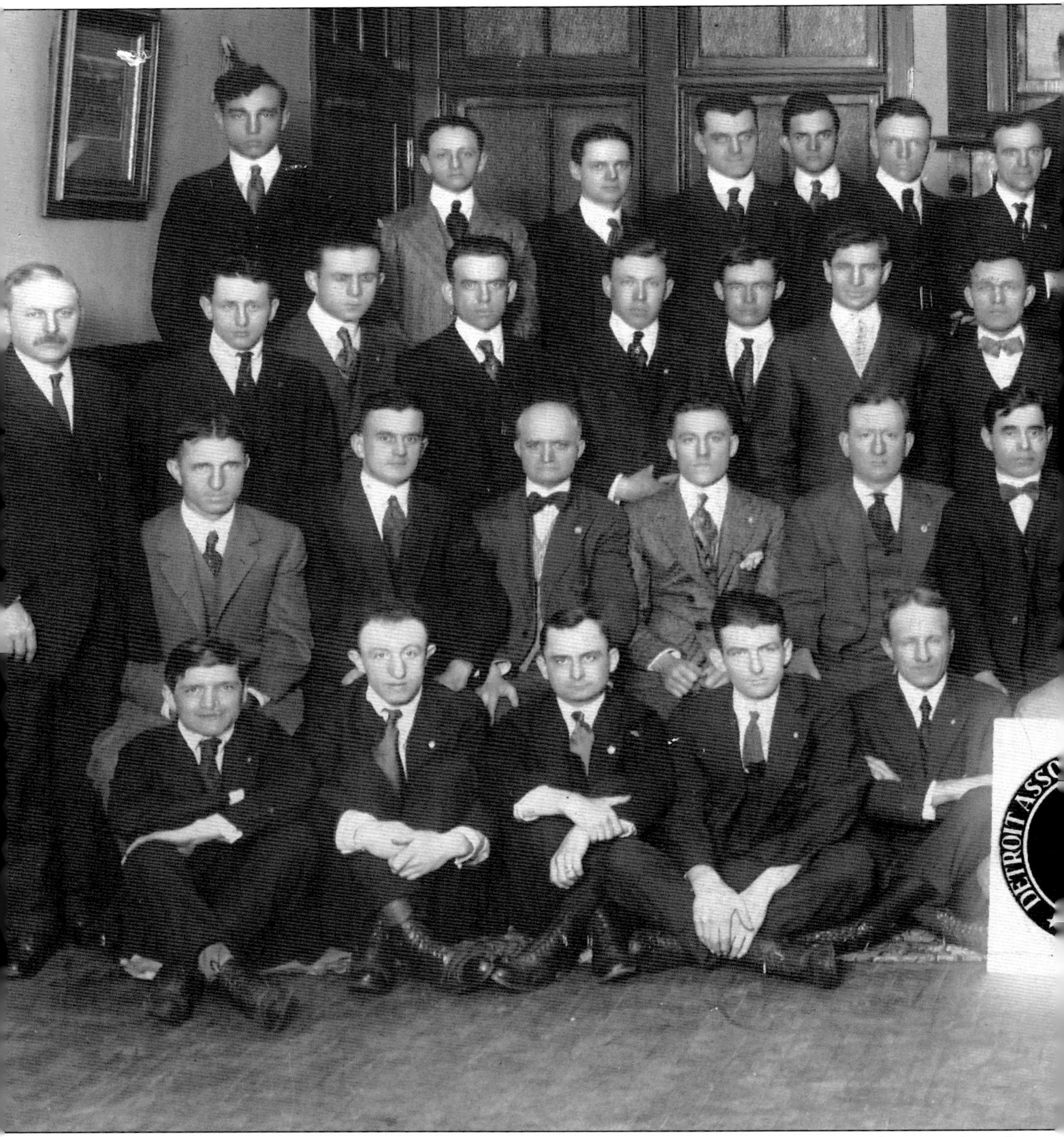

This may be the first photograph of DAD members; the organization started in 1916 and was incorporated in 1918. Emanuel Jacobs was the first president. The original group of men had set up as an athletic organization. Later on, DAD became a social, athletic, and political organization.

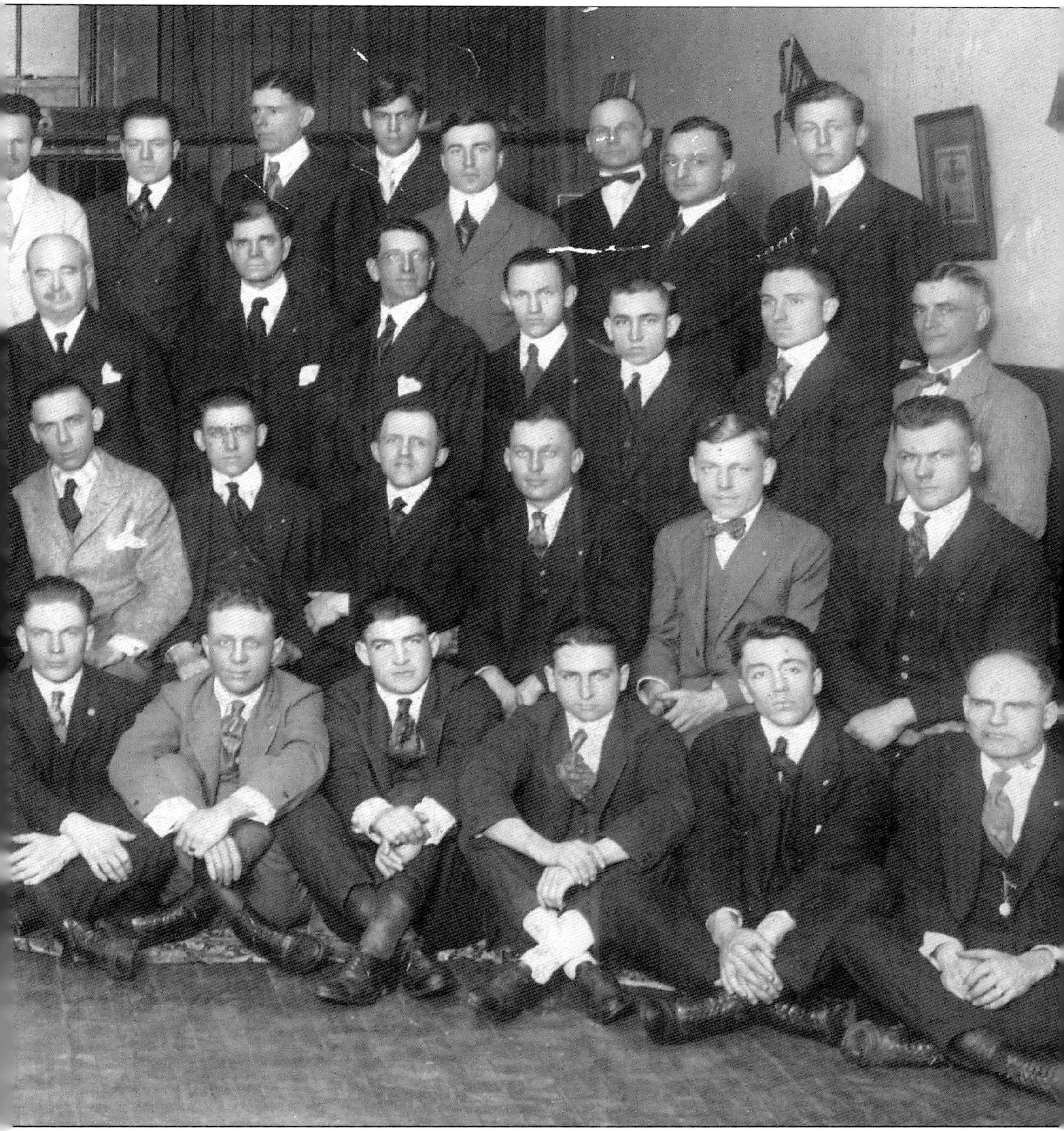

In 1934, the organization was reincorporated. DAD had a long run of excellent officers who kept it going. October 2016 will be the 100th anniversary of the organization. (Courtesy of DAD.)

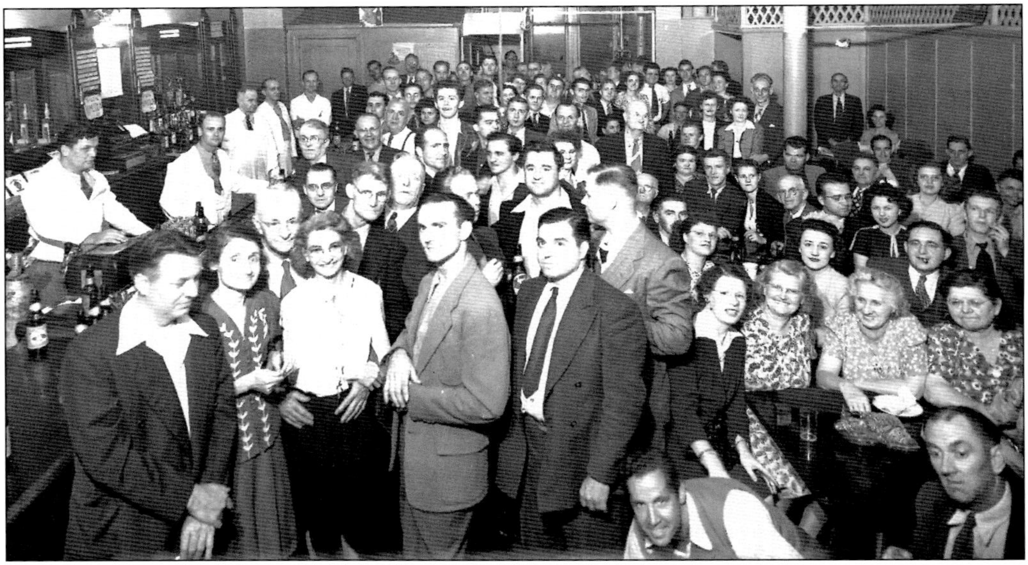

A large group of DAD members is pictured at the East Jefferson Street location in the 1950s. All of them, including Sam Gompers (standing at left next to the pole), enjoyed socializing and having drinks to unwind after work or during the day. The bar was open seven days a week in those days. It was a comfort zone where many enjoyed talking and catching up on the news. (Courtesy of DAD.)

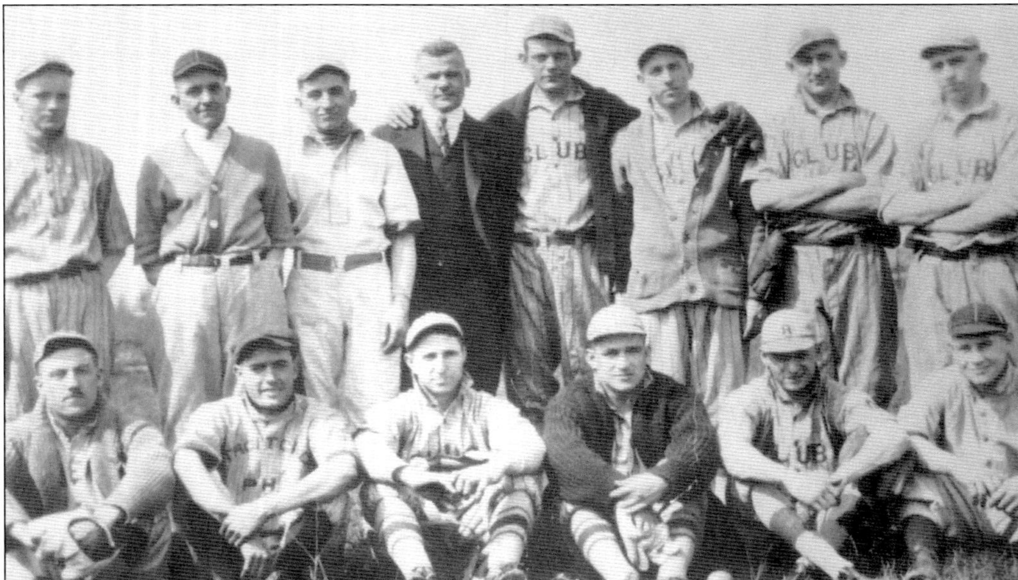

This proud team, shown in 1917, was first called the Rosedalers before they changed their name to DAD. From left to right are (first row) Ralph Beaver, Louis Sherwood, Charles Rosenbaum, Frank Friday Sr., Fennard Herring, and George Gellatly; (second row) J. Chapman, Haley Day, Joseph Pastore, Philip Bednarek, Marcus Osmonson, Benjamin J. Beaver, Edward Bourlier, and Theodore Liedberg. (Courtesy of DAD.)

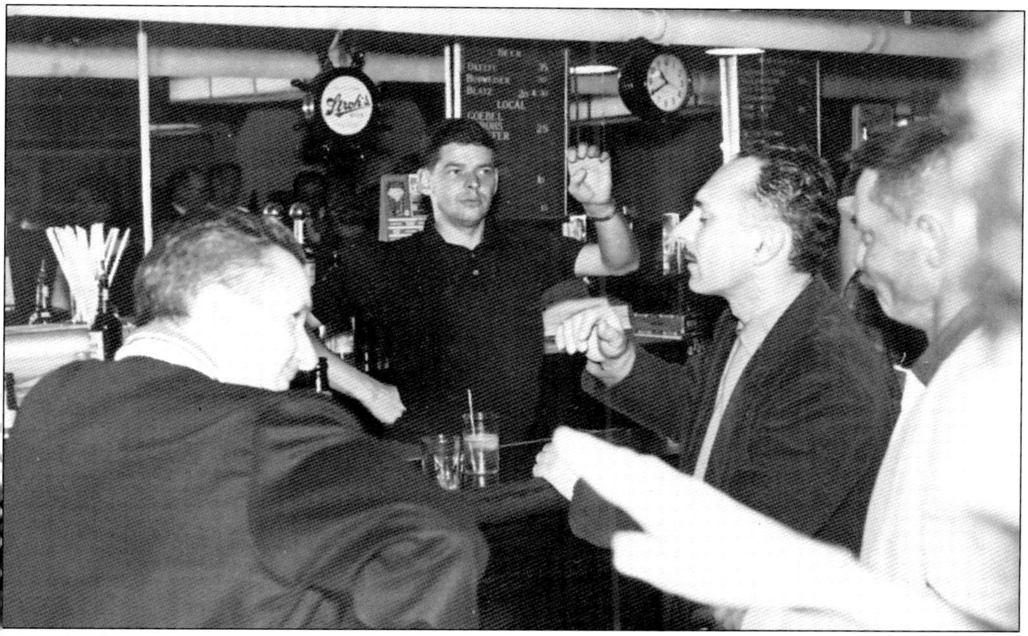

DAD had another location with a bar at Third Street. From left to right are unidentified, Fred Hall, David Soultanio, and unidentified. Notice the boards listing beers and prices: O'Keefe, 35¢; Budweiser, 30¢; Blatz, 20¢ and 30¢; and Goebel and Stroh's, 25¢. The other board lists various whiskeys at 50¢. (Courtesy of DAD.)

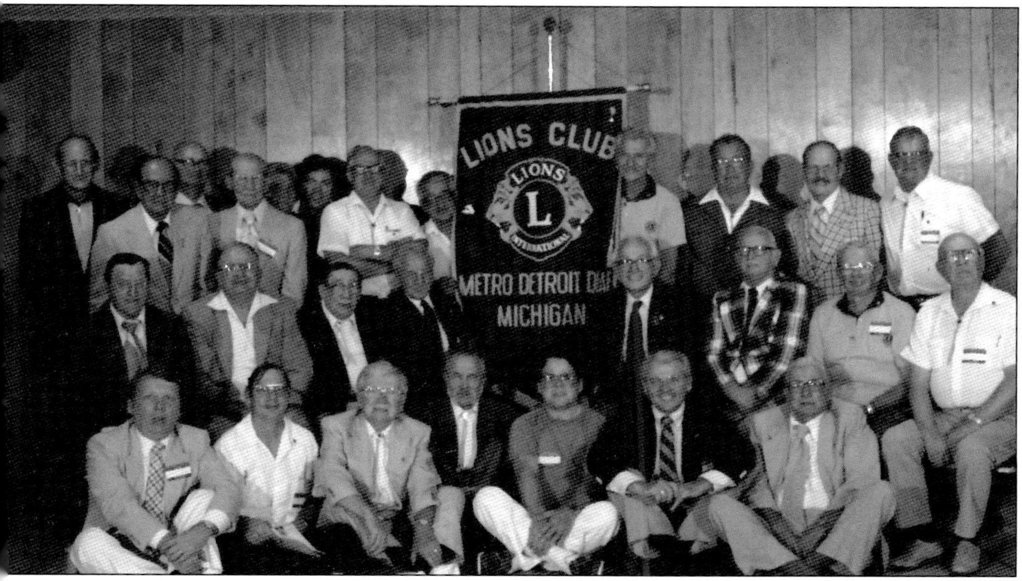

The Detroit Metro Lions Deaf Club included, from left to right, (first row) Harmon Beekman, Charles Miller, Homer Beekman, Delbert Carter, Dale Makar, Larry Grant, and Ernest Maitre; (second row) John Kaniuk, Ray Babuska, Clifford Groves, Blodie Virkstis, Robert Hopkins, Fred McCall, unidentified, and Everett Stevick; (third row) Arthur Englen, David Curso, unidentified, Benjamin Beaver, unidentified, Anson Mitchell, Frank Kozar, Dominic Zito Sr., Daniel Vondrak, Tony Strang, unidentified, and Walter Denecuk. (Courtesy of Anson and Kathy McCall Mitchell.)

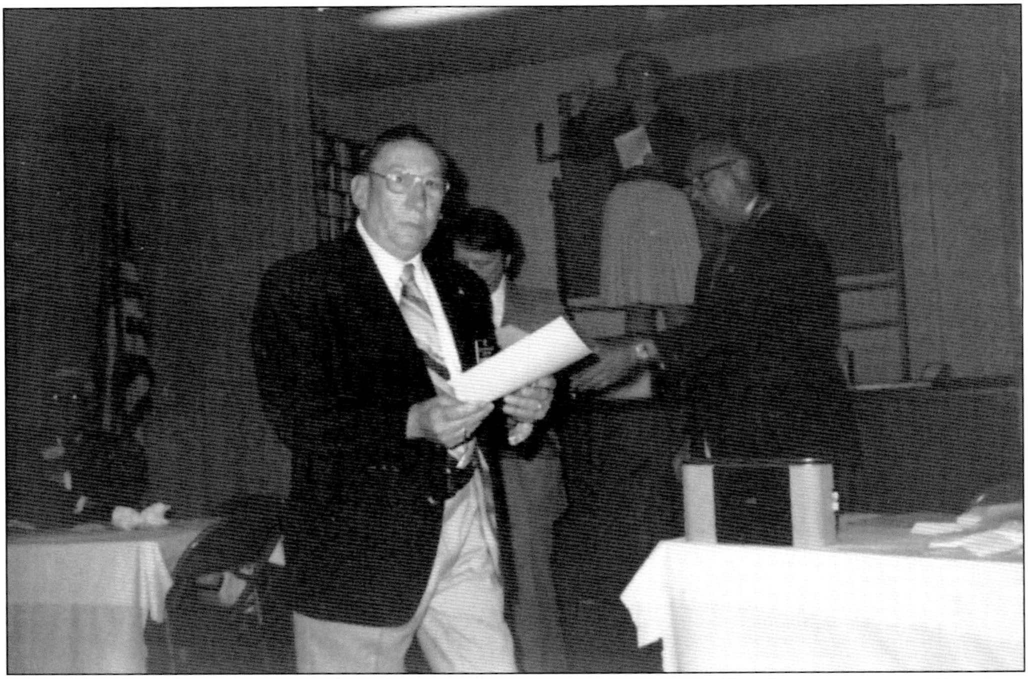

Founder Clifford Groves was quoted in the December 1980 *Lions of Michigan* as saying that "the language of Lionism of helping to make the life better for others is truly universal. . . . Lionism presently reports 19 deaf clubs among its membership. The first in Michigan, the Detroit Metro Club . . . a heartwarming example of the handicapped reaching out to help others who are even more handicapped." The club rented the DAD Hall at Third Street. (Courtesy of Anson and Kathy McCall Mitchell.)

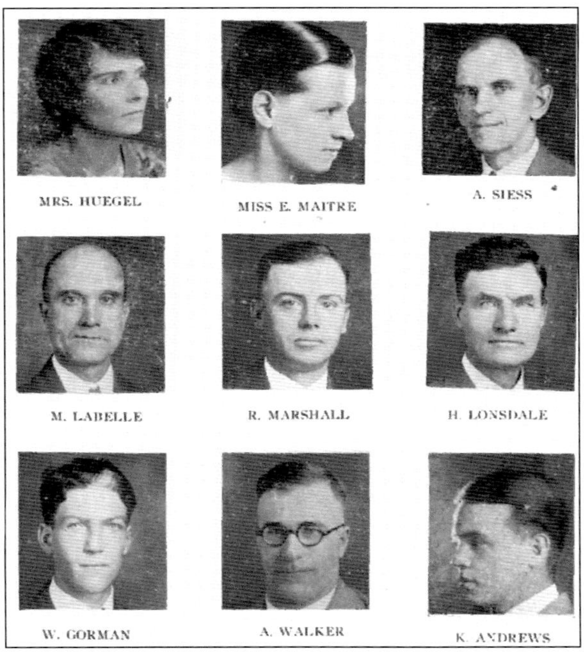

Shown are some of the deaf Canadians who were members of DAD. From left to right are (bottom row) W. Gorman, A. Walker, and K. Andrews; (middle row) M. Labelle, R. Marshall, and H. Lonsdale; (top row) Dorfna Huegel, Evelyn Maitre, and A. Siess. According to the August 1935 *Disc and Docket* newsletter, subtitled "Our Canadian Cousins," "the Canadian group deserves a goodly share of credit for the success of the club. Some have been members almost since the beginning, and some of the newer ones are among the best workers." (Courtesy of DAD.)

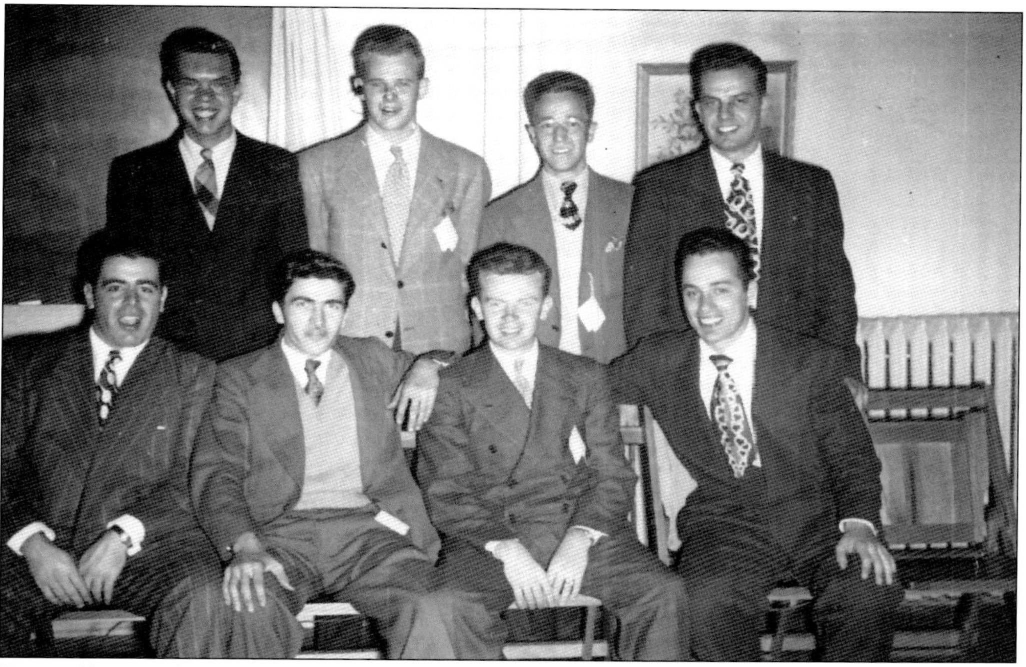

Pictured here in the first row are, from left to right, Charles Mully, Constance "Connie" Marchione, Gordon Bachman, and Arlyn Meyerson. This photograph was taken at Grand Rapids for the bowling league in October 1946. Connie was well known as a news writer at that time. (Courtesy of Arlyn and Hester Meyerson.)

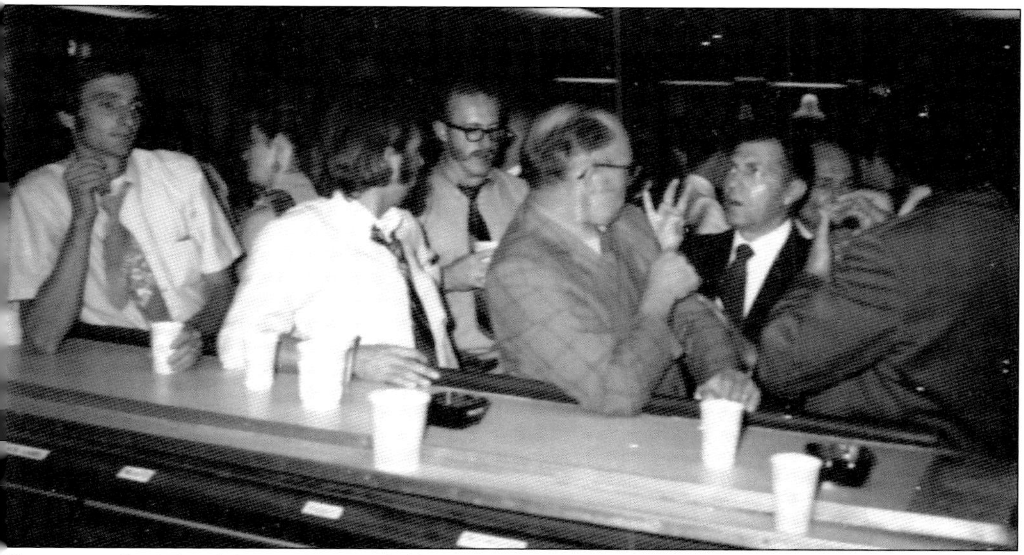

Shown at the Third Street DAD clubhouse are, from left to right, Dennis "Rick" Kaufman, unidentified, Harry Lewis, Merrill Frelich, Bernard Trayner, and unidentified. Kaufman was a frequent visitor and a FAD member. DAD and FAD are friendly sports rivals, but members make visits to each other's clubs for events and activities. DAD's Third Street clubhouse was a very popular spot but was sold. Today, the former clubhouse stands nicely next to the casino and nearby stadiums. (Courtesy of Charles and Diana Cutshaw McKittrick.)

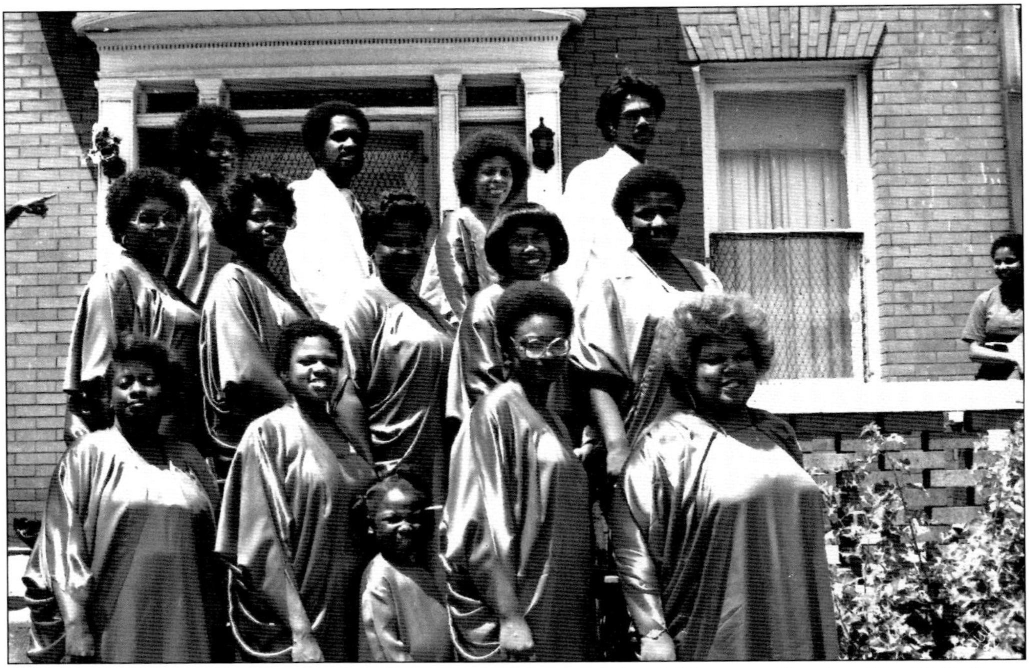

Ella Kambrick founded the Unity of Hands Community Deaf Choir on October 20, 1978. From left to right are (first row) Mary Longmuier, Shari Smith, Yimiko ? (little girl), Sarah Edwards, and Vera Johnson; (second row) Vicki Clark, Yvonne Smith, Pat Fowler, Deborah Logan, and Tanya Vanessa Dunigan; (third row) Rosa Emery, April ?, and Glenn Stewart. This photograph was taken on October 21, 1981, at the Ford Auditorium at Jefferson Street and Woodward Avenue in Detroit. (Courtesy of Glenn and Susan Stewart.)

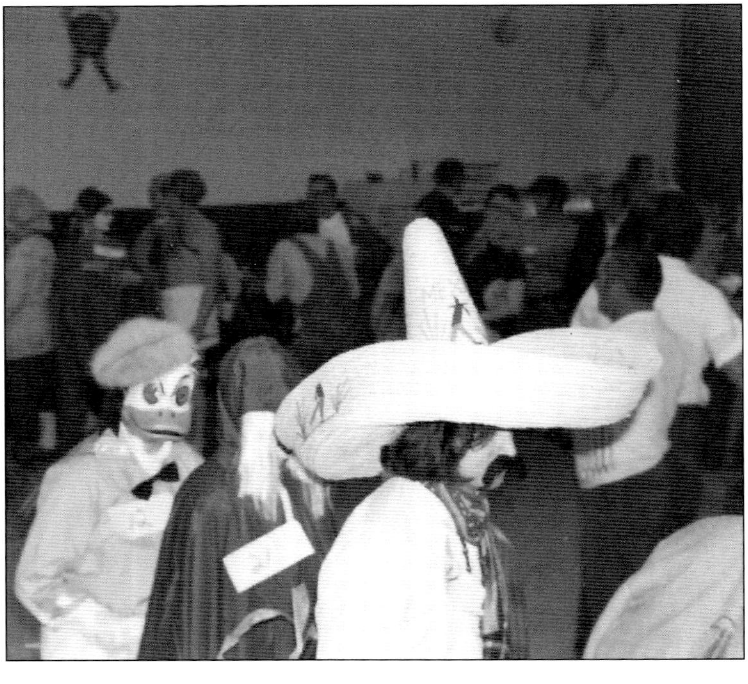

This 1970 Halloween party held at DAD included someone in a Donald Duck costume. The party had prizes and games for the kids and adults, including prizes for costumes. Dudley Cutshaw as usual gave good surprises. (Courtesy of Charles and Diana Cutshaw McKittrick.)

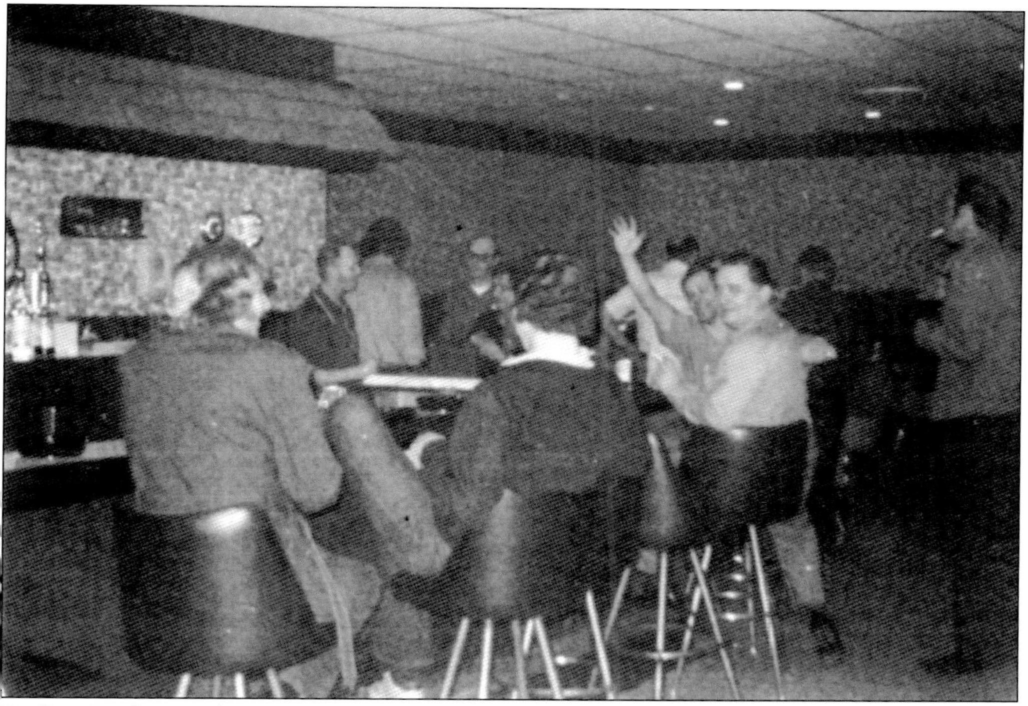

Dudley Cutshaw is shown visiting the FAD clubhouse bar in the late 1960s. He was a frequent guest at FAD and was once invited to give a keynote speech at FAD's anniversary. He was always friendly with FAD members. They visited the DAD clubhouse, too. From Flint to Detroit is approximately a one hour drive. (Courtesy of Charles and Diana Cutshaw McKittrick.)

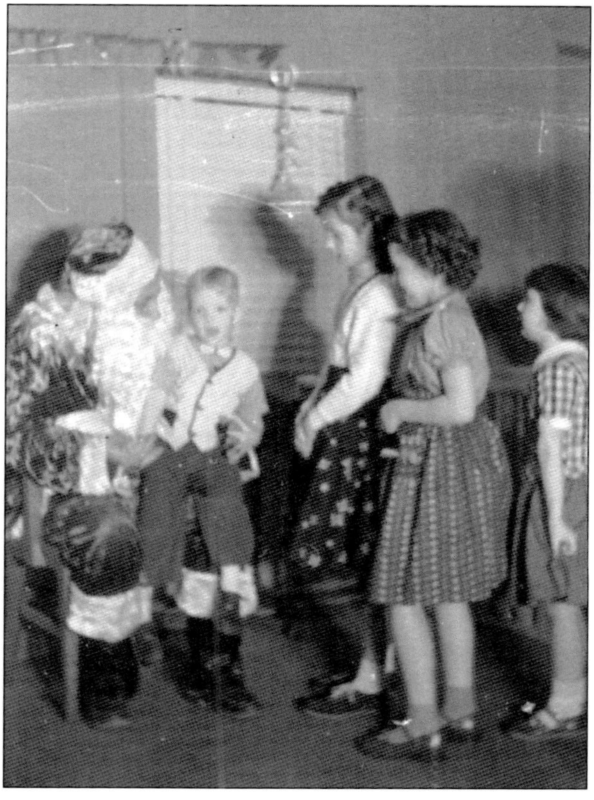

Dudley Cutshaw's daughter remembers attending this Christmas party for the children hosted by DAD along with all of her cousins. Diana was around eight years old and stands in the middle of this c. 1957 photograph. (Courtesy of Charles and Diana Cutshaw McKittrick.)

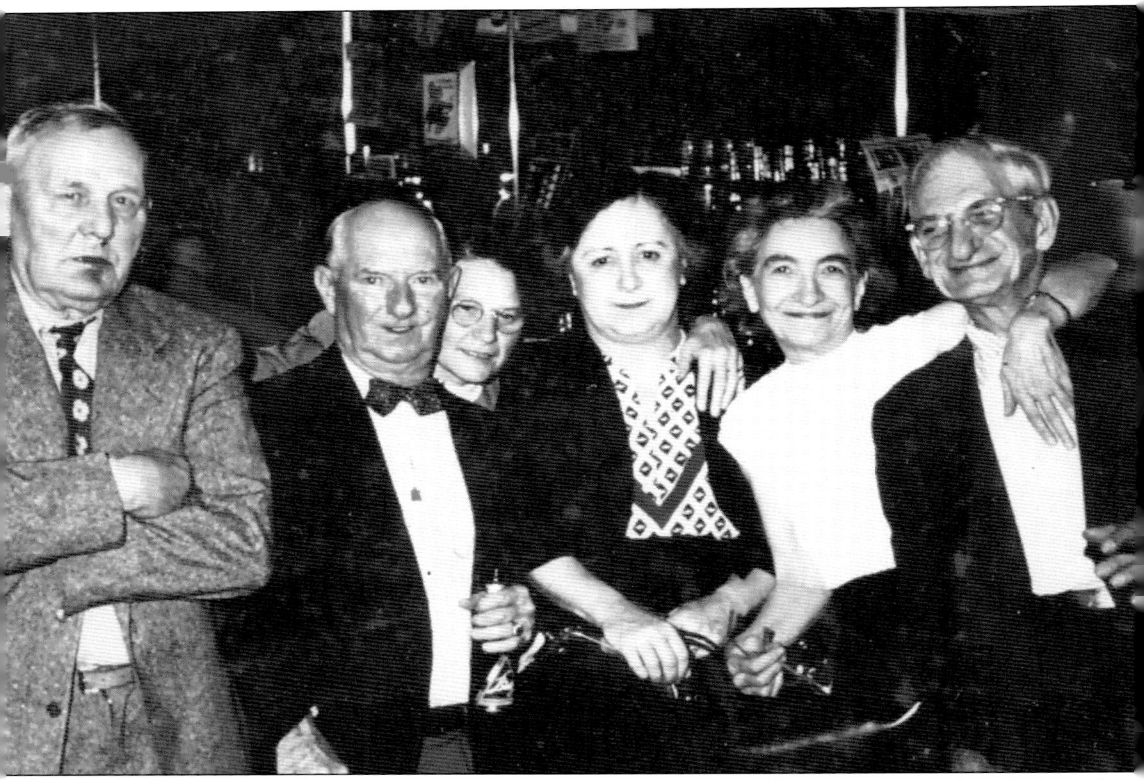

These people pictured at one of the early clubhouses are possibly N. Yeager, unidentified, Madge La Tondress, Miss E. Maitre, Mary Provst, and G. May. La Tondress and Provst were active in the DAD Ladies Auxiliary. Provst also was a family friend of the Wahowiaks and McCalls. (Courtesy of Charles and Diana Cutshaw McKittrick.)

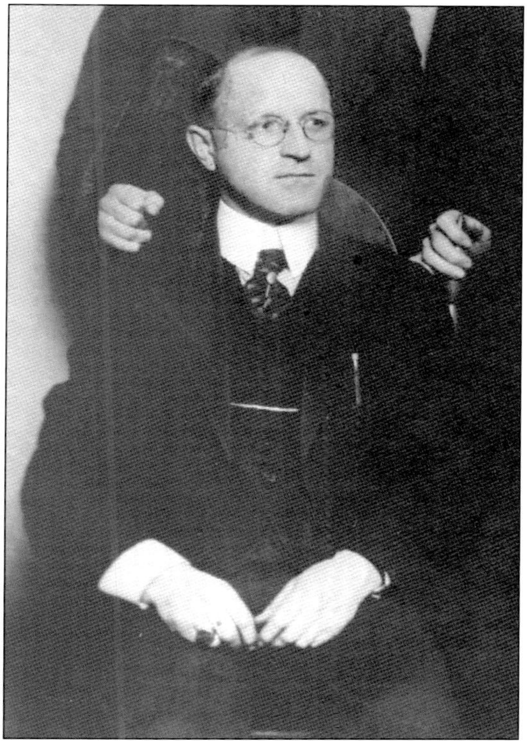

George Ashley (right) arrived in Flint from New York to find that there was no club for the deaf. He and other deaf men first gathered in Old Mac's Cigar Store on the east side of Saginaw Street to discuss the details. At E.M. Bristol's home at 623 East Third Street (below), Ashley, Bristol, and a group of deaf men agreed to establish the Flint Association of the Deaf on February 19, 1919. The first temporary officers were Ashley as president, Bristol as secretary-treasurer, and L.F. Williams, Andrew Gilbert, and P.L. Schreiber on the board of trustees. The first hall was found at 424 Buckham Alley with a lease for five years starting on May 10, 1919. (Both, courtesy of FAD.)

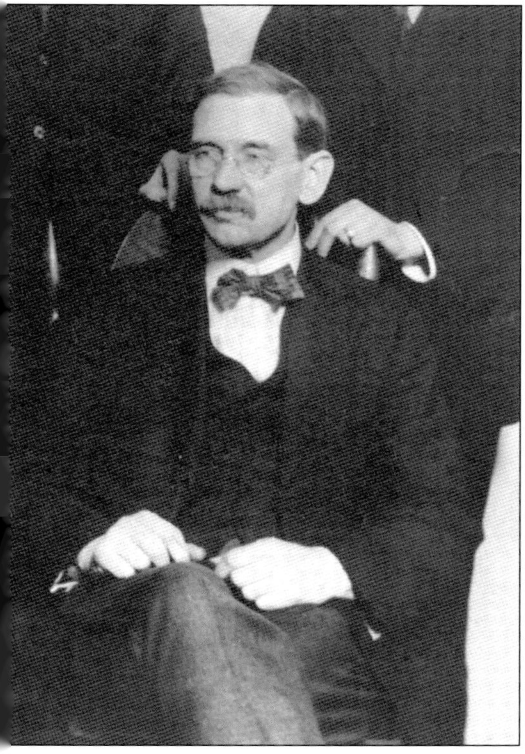

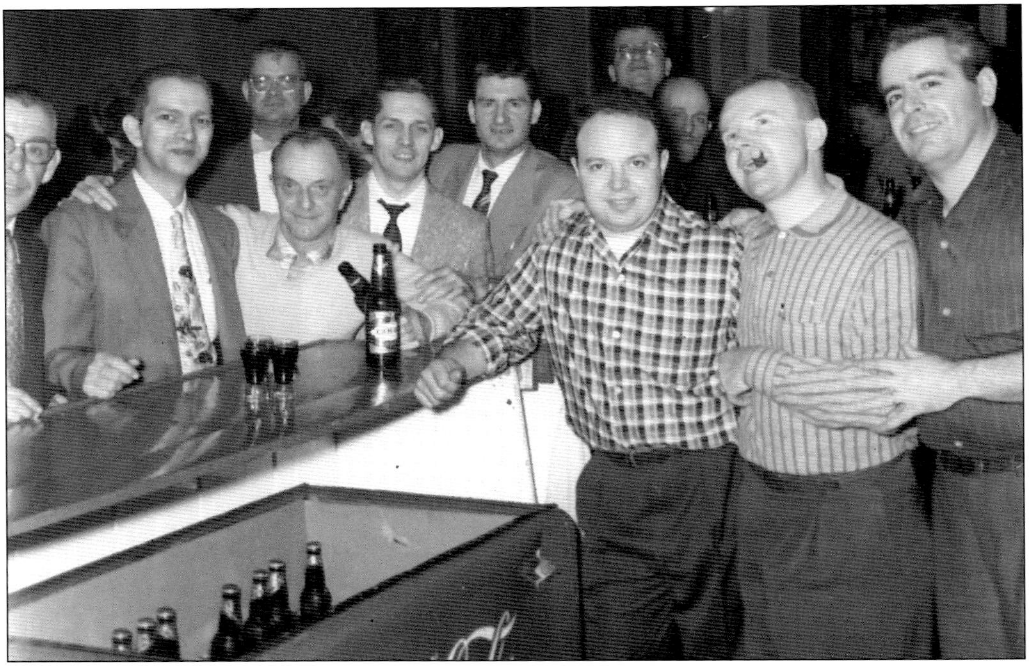

The Motor City Association of the Deaf rented a hall with a bar on Park Avenue. Shown in this c. 1952 photograph are, from left to right, Jim Ellerhorst, Roger Jacques (with an unidentified man behind him), Tom Crowley, William Kein, Albert Monacelli, Gordon Bachman, and Charles Mully. During that time, Arlyn Meyerson, a long time MCAD member, was a hobby photographer and developed the negatives on his own for many events like this one. (Courtesy of Arlyn and Hester Meyerson.)

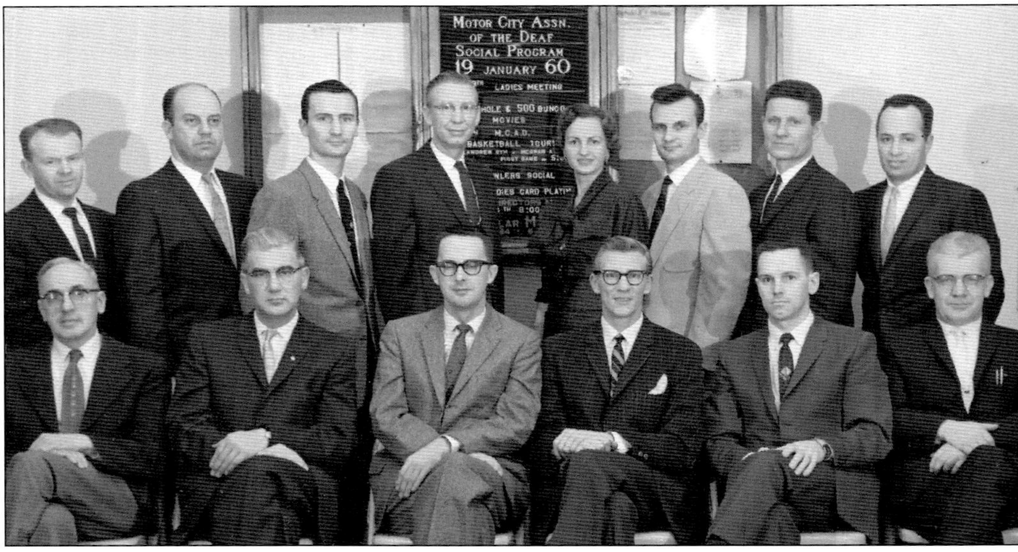

Shown here are the MCAD officers in January 1960. From left to right are (seated) Odell Ballman, Theodore Deska, Walter A. Hanes, Max Johnson, William Roscoe, and Kenneth Mantz; (standing) Gordon Bachman, William Miller, Val DiFalco, Edwin Drolet, Helen DiFalco, Phil DiFalco, Stanley Jendritz, and Arlyn Meyerson. (Courtesy of Arlyn and Hester Meyerson.)

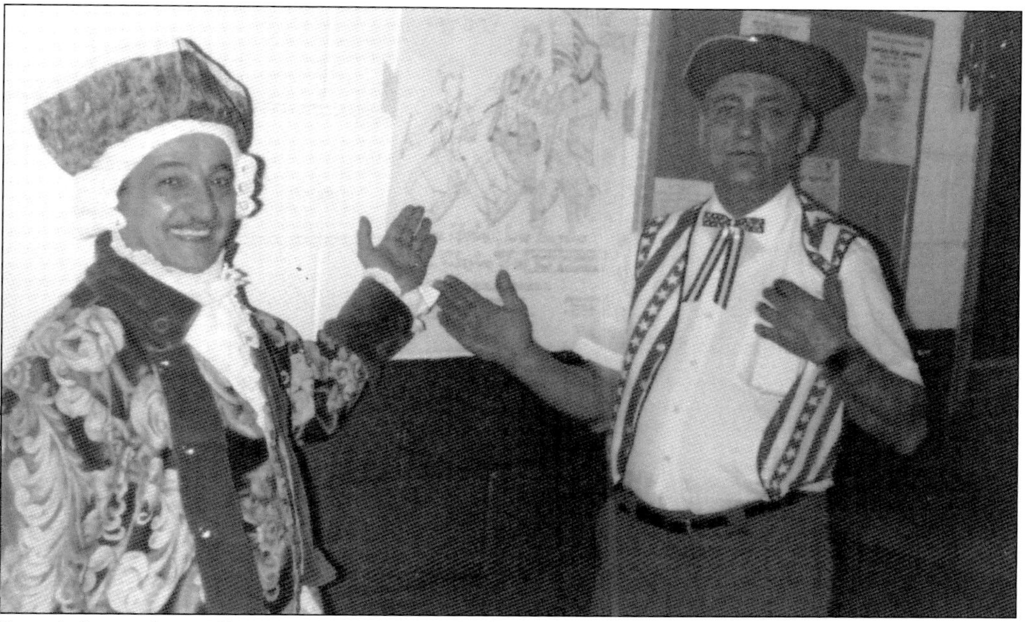

From left to right are Dominic R. Zito Sr. and Alexander Radanovich. The photograph was printed in April 1976, although it was possibly taken in July 1975, as these DAD members are dressed to celebrate the Fourth of July. Alexander Radanovich passed away on December 28, 2014. (Courtesy of Dominic and Dorothy Etkie Zito.)

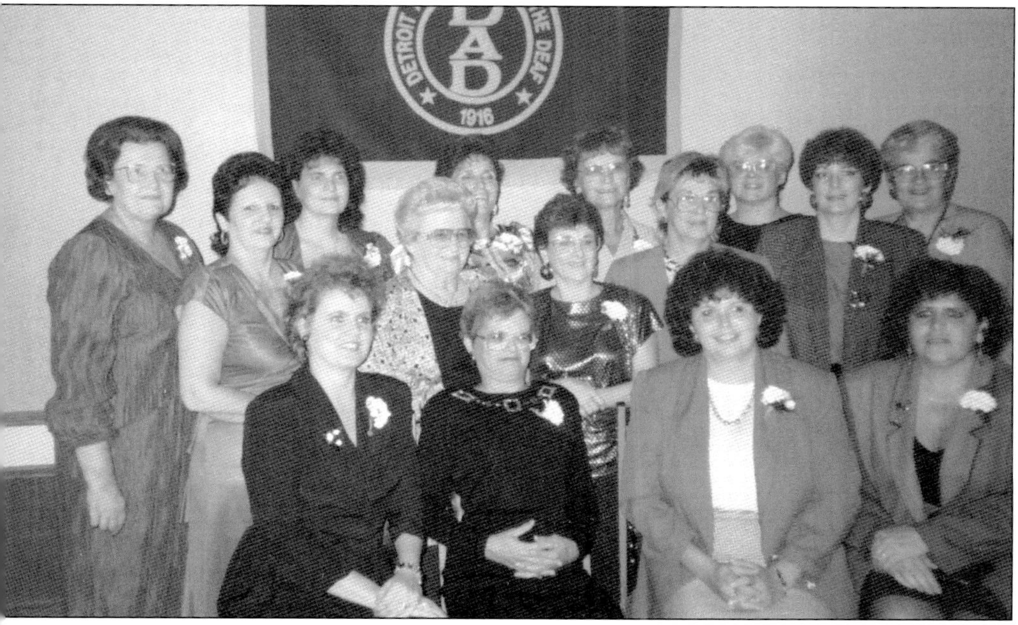

The DAD Ladies Auxiliary is shown at the 75th anniversary in October 1991. From left to right are (first row) Patricia Schultz, Anita Gable, Nancy McCall, and Mary Kay Crawford; (second row) Donna M. Klarr, Phillis Keuping, Judy Cachia, Maureen Arrowsmith, and Dalee Strandell; (third row) Delphine Soultanian, Jean Scott, Mary Evans, Irene Kettinger, Beverly Lemker, and Angie Oliasz. (Courtesy of John and Donna Delikta Klarr.)

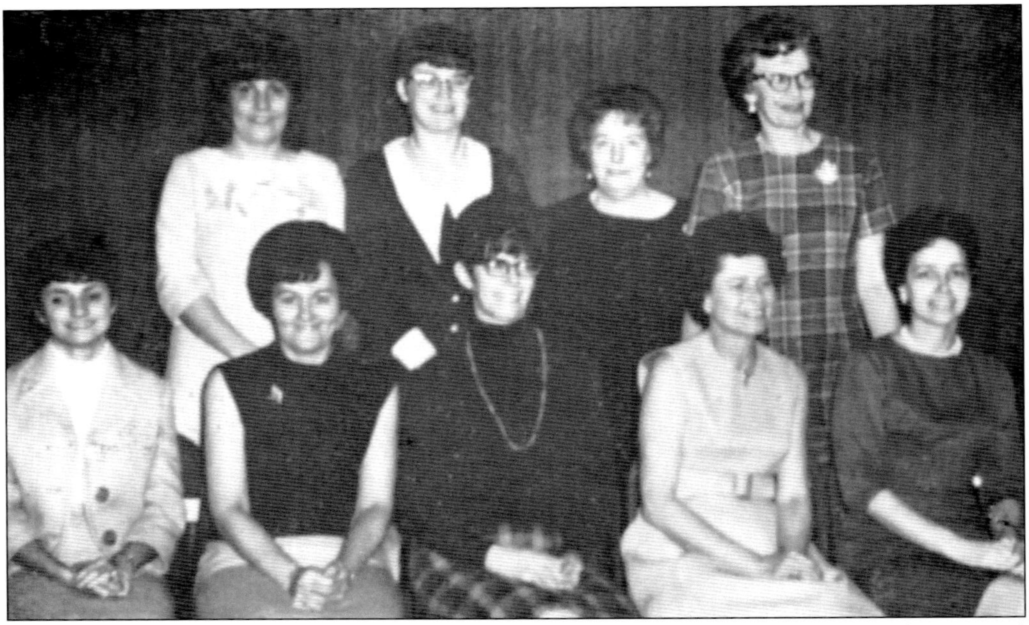

Flint's ladies auxiliary is a separate organization from FAD and is believed to be the only separated deaf ladies auxiliary organization in the nation. Shown in 1969 are, from left to right, (seated) Ruth Richards, secretary; Alice Phillips, second vice president; Ella Rich, president; Aleta Dennison, first vice president; and Yvonne Brow, treasurer; (standing) Dora Jean Corrin, Sheila Wollard, Eleanor Strang, and Josephine Arnold, all on the board of governors. (Courtesy of Flint Deaf Ladies Auxiliary.)

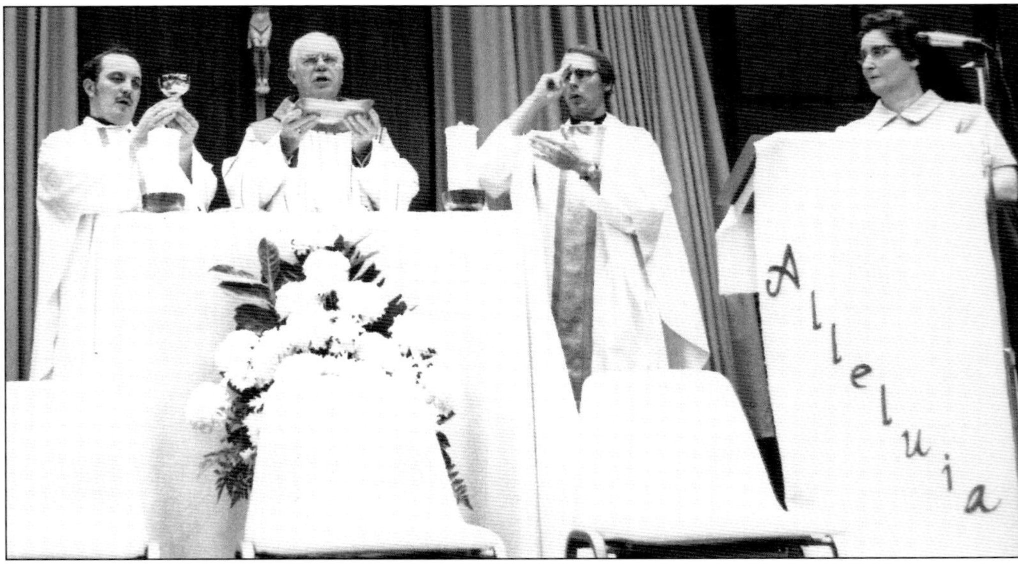

In 1974, the new St. John's Deaf Center's opening ceremony included a mass. From left to right are Rev. Edmund Borycz, director of pastoral ministry; Cardinal John Dearden, archbishop of Detroit; Rev. Gary Bueche, director of the deaf apostolate; and Sr. Dolores Beere, codirector of the deaf apostolate. The center was located on Fisher Avenue in Warren. Since 2015, the center has been on Chesterfield Avenue in Eastpointe. (Courtesy of SJDC.)

Six

SPORTS

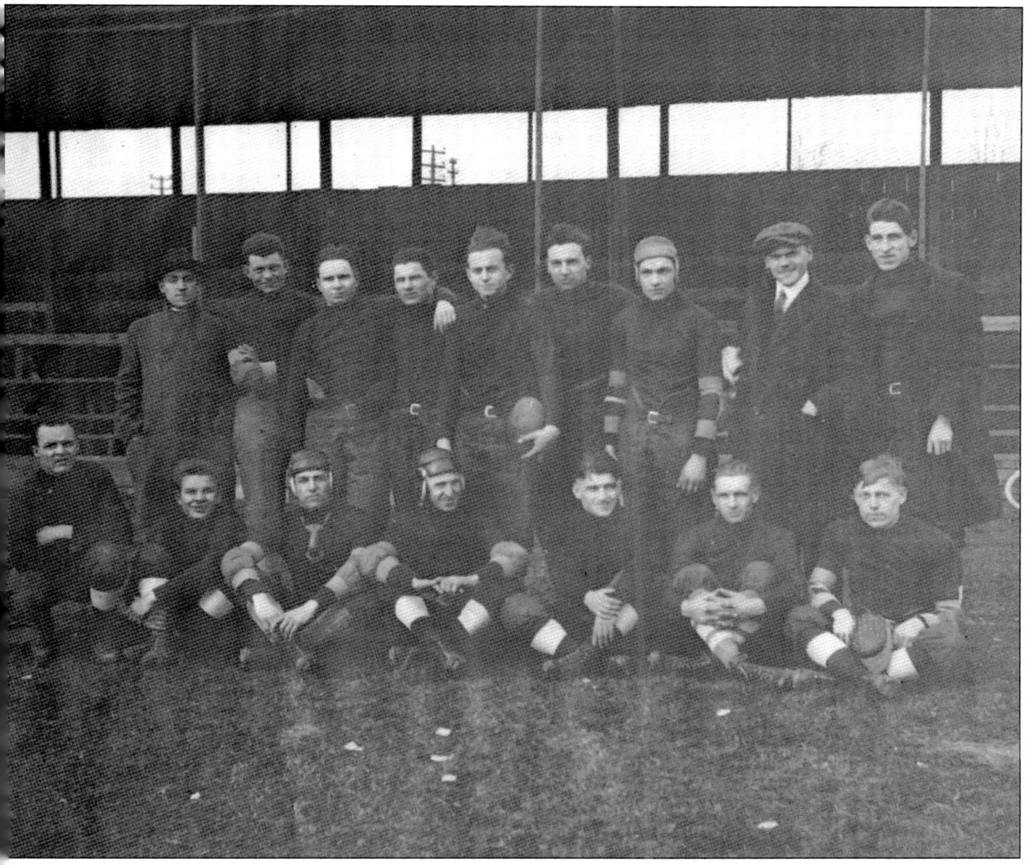

This photograph of the 1916 football team might be the most sentimental in DAD history. The team was made up of members who helped form the DAD organization. The club was originally intended to be an athletic club. Before DAD began, the club was called the Rosedalers, because it started on Rosedale Court in Benjamin and Ralph Beaver's home. The man third from left in the first row is believed to be Benjamin Beaver. (Courtesy of DAD.)

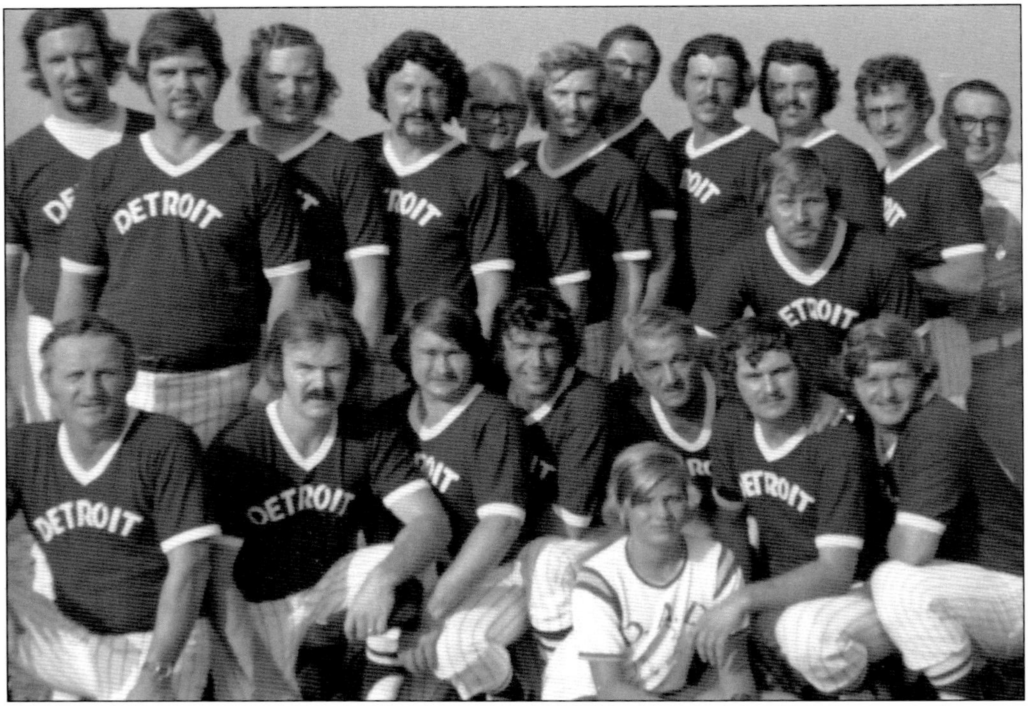

The 1973 Central Athletics Association of the Deaf (CAAD) championship team was, from left to right, (first row) Steve Popp, Donald Morris, Gary Kirby, Anson Mitchell, coach Dominic Zito Sr., Christopher Schultz, and Ronald Rood; (second row) David Takacs, Earl Parks, John Bogden, Antal "Tony" Kovacs, Eddie Riley, Jerome Beaver, Edward Mangold Jr., Ronald Smith, Gregory Harrison (in front of Ronald), Istvan "Steve" Kovacs, Dominic Zito Jr., and Bill Stasczaczk. Seated in front is Alan McCall. Rood was selected as the most valuable player, and Popp was the best manager. (Courtesy of DAD.)

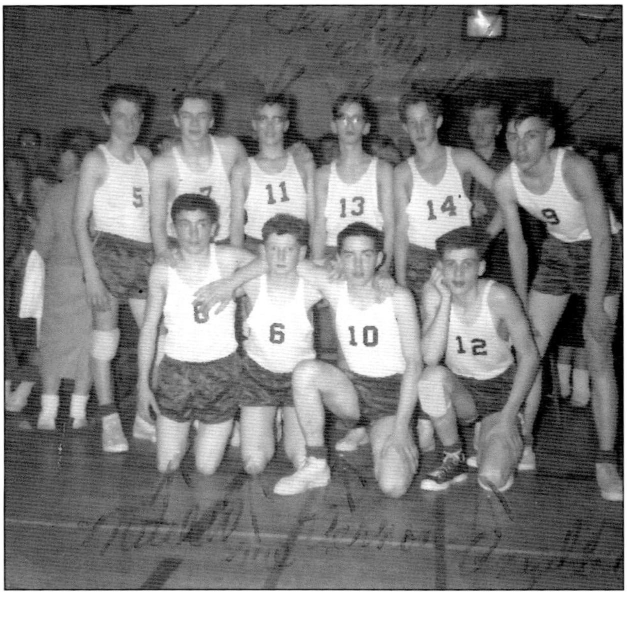

At MSD, the high school freshman boy's basketball team posed for a March 1959 picture with their names written on the front. From left to right are (first row) Anson Mitchell, Dominic E. Zito Jr., Gerald Vernon, and W. Angelbeck; (second row) ? Bailey, Dennis Schemenauer, Stephen Gemmill, Rodney Phillips, Glindel Young, and Frank Fickies. (Courtesy of Dominic and Dorothy Zito.)

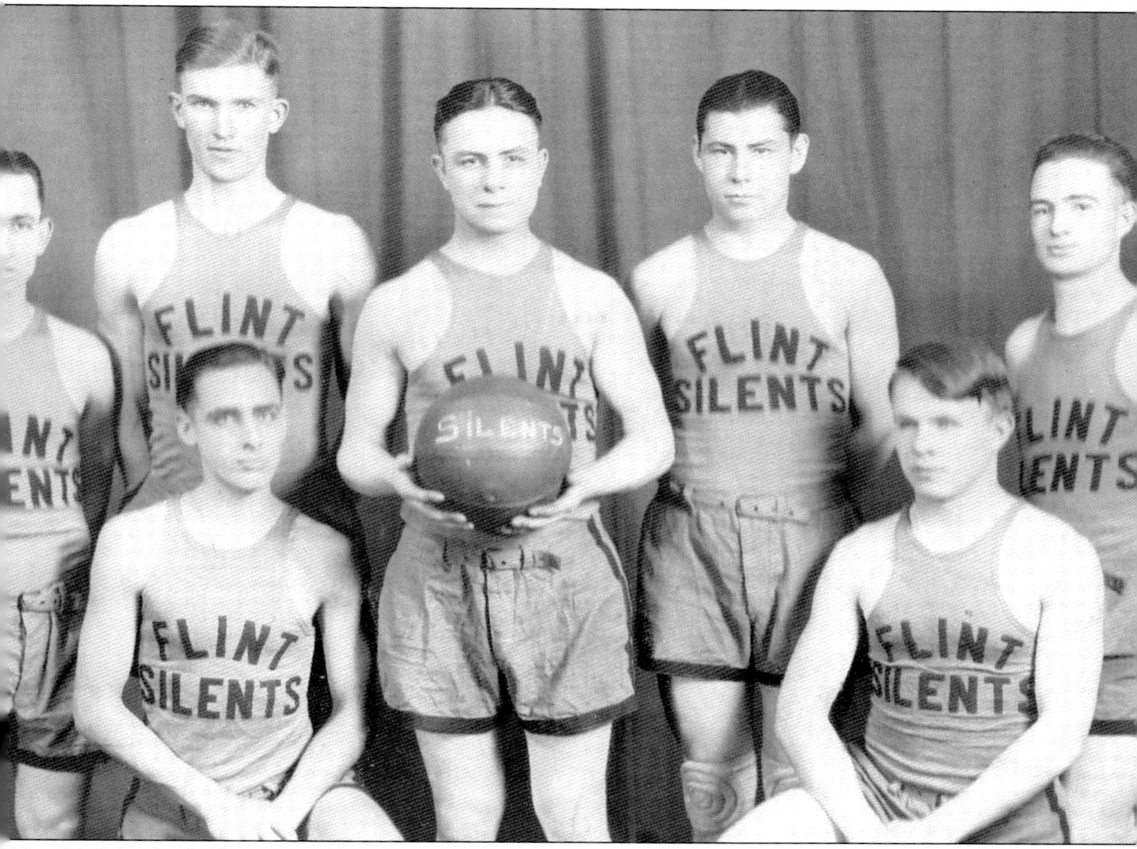

The FAD basketball team, called the Flint Silents, joined the Industrial Mutual Association Factory League for the 1926–1927 season. From left to right are (first row) Clifford Sims and Elmer Beuerle; (second row) LaVerne Misener, Octavesicotte, Albert Locker, Ernest Leach, and William MacDonald. FAD also played softball and bowled against other leagues or deaf clubs. (Courtesy of FAD.)

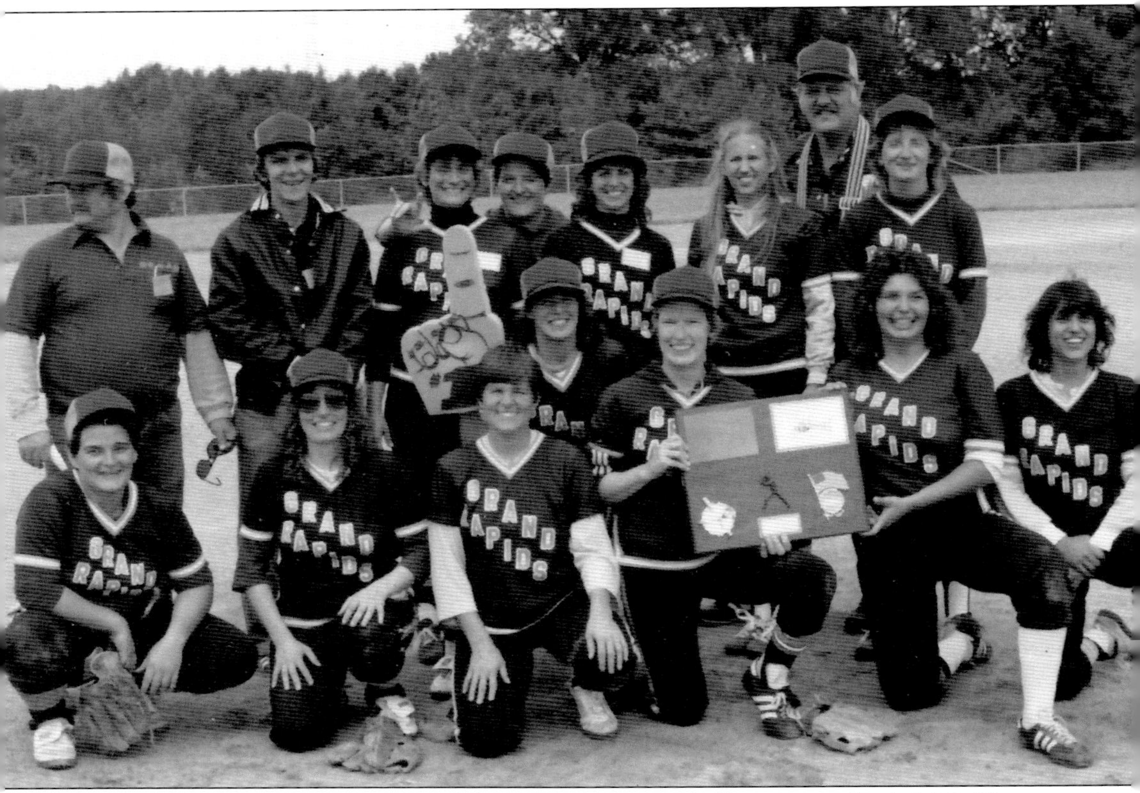

The Grand Rapids Association of the Deaf women's softball team won the AAAD Championship in 1984. From left to right are (first row) Tina Hicks, Linda Ross, Rosemary Martin, Tammy Chestnut, Julie Dlugoss, Nancy Capek, and Dina Kerbuski; (second row) coach Gary Kirby, Marty Jansen, Chris Beach, Tita Lewis, Kathy Spicer, Maureen Dixon, Dale Phillips, and Karen Karpinski. Gary Kirby was a great activist on the west side of Michigan for the Kalamazoo Deaf Club. (Courtesy of Nancy Capek McCall.)

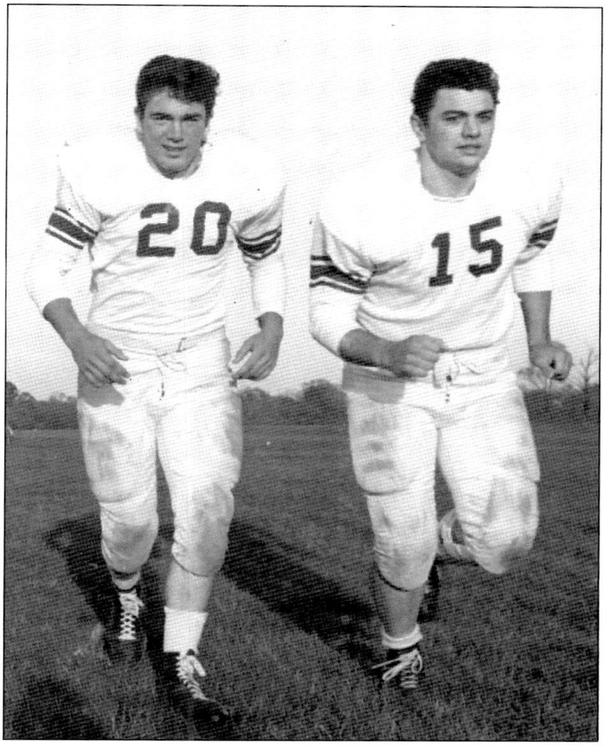

At right are defensive star Anson Mitchell (left) and fullback Istvan "Steve" Kovacs; below are halfback Abram Powell (left) and quarterback Dominic Zito Jr. According to the October 25, 1962, *Detroit News* article "MSD, Lake Fenton Take Unbeaten Records Into Friday Nonleaguer," "MSD's most versatile backfield in history includes power runner Steve Kovacs with a 5.2 average on 585 yards in 112 rushes, speedy Abram Powell with a 6.7 average on 261 strides in 39 rushes and Anson Mitchell, who filled in for Zito as a quarterback. Zito was recovering from a left hand injury. Mitchell was gaining 304 yards, S. Kovacs, 201 and Powell, 133." Deaf coach Earl Roberts managed the team. (Both, courtesy of Dorothy and Dominic Zito Jr.)

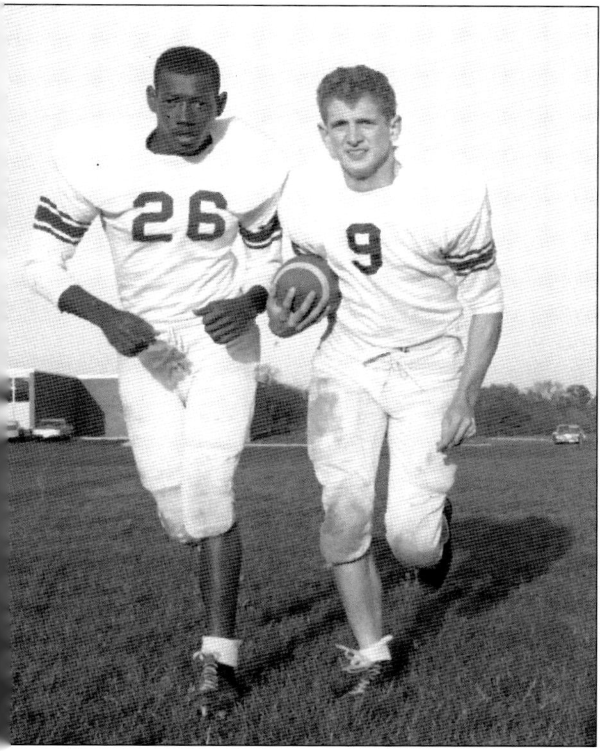

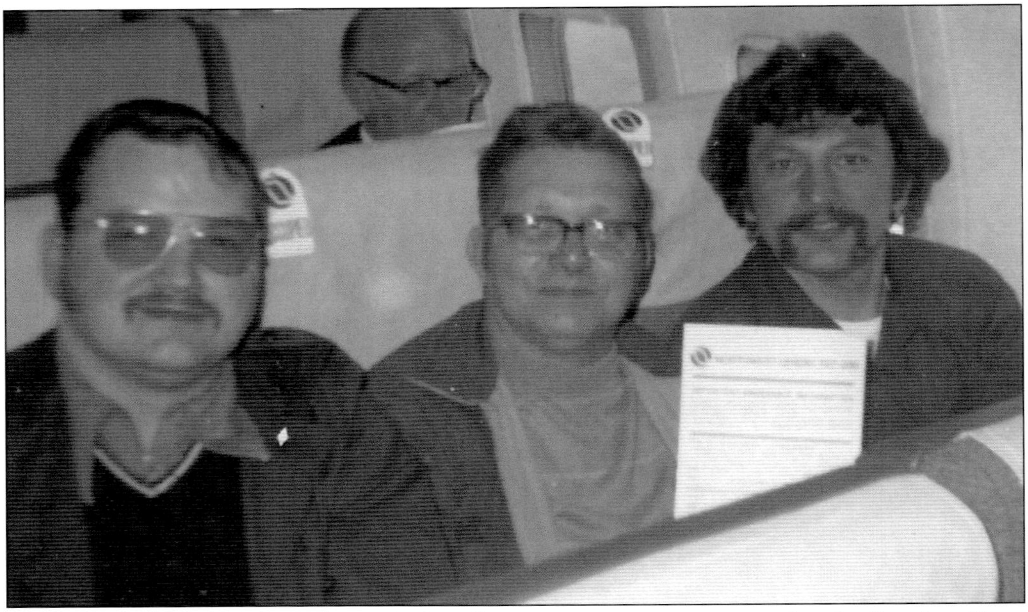

The bowlers flew overseas to play at the Deaflympics, competing against other deaf bowlers. From left to right are unidentified, Harvey Ellerhorst, and Antal "Tony" Kovacs. Both Ellerhorst and Kovacs were avid bowlers besides playing basketball and softball. Some stated that bowling was a great way to keep busy and an excuse to get out of the house for exercise. (Courtesy of Antal Kovacs and Lisa Heck.)

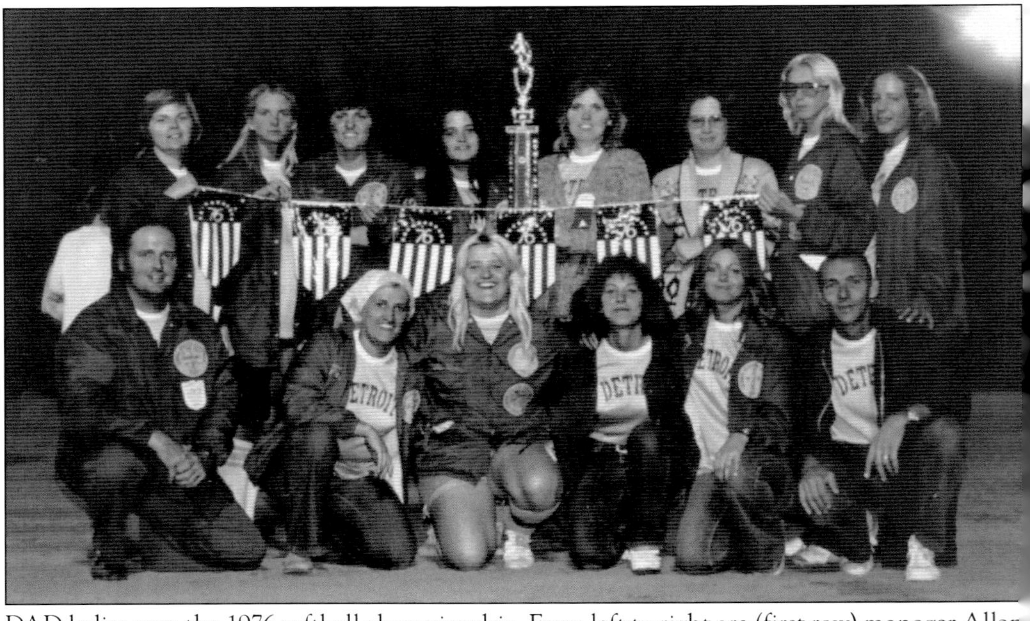

DAD ladies won the 1976 softball championship. From left to right are (first row) manager Allan Russeman, Donna Klarr, Tita Lewis, Mary Guastella, Dorothy Etkie Zito, and coach Henry Swinney; (second row) Joann Gablo, Sue Etkie, Carol Johnson, Tina Hicks-Takacs, Patty Schultz (pregnant with her second deaf child), Fredia Morrison, Loretta Etkie-Decker, and Joann Klarr. (Courtesy of DAD.)

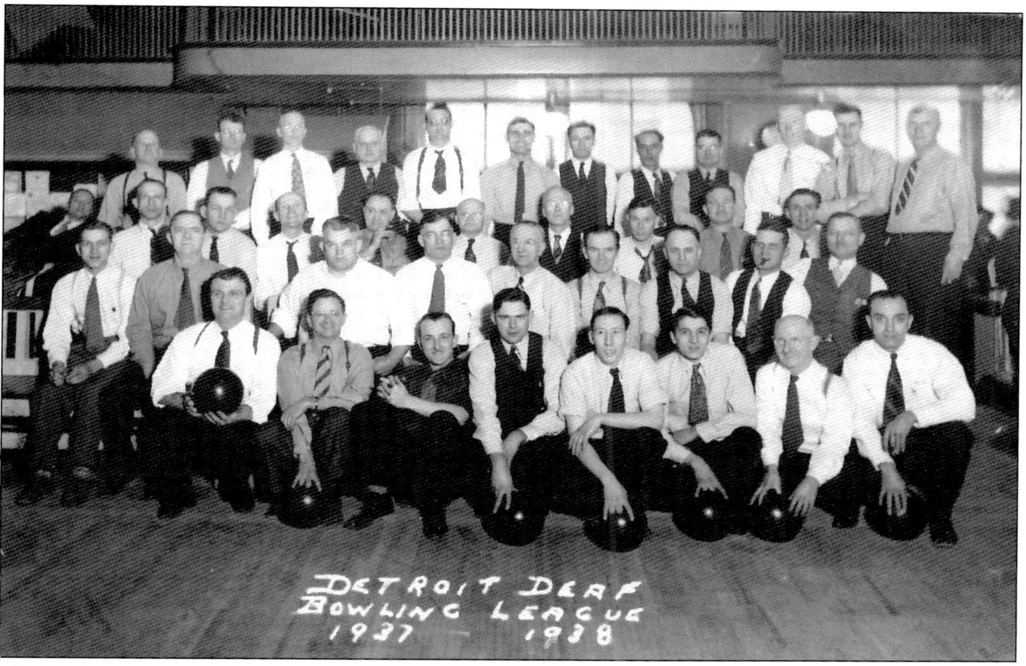

Shown here is the DAD bowling league that played in 1937–1938. DAD still has a big love for bowling. Most teams bowled against others in the Great Lakes region. Some bowlers are recognized members who were longtime activists to keep DAD going. (Courtesy of DAD.)

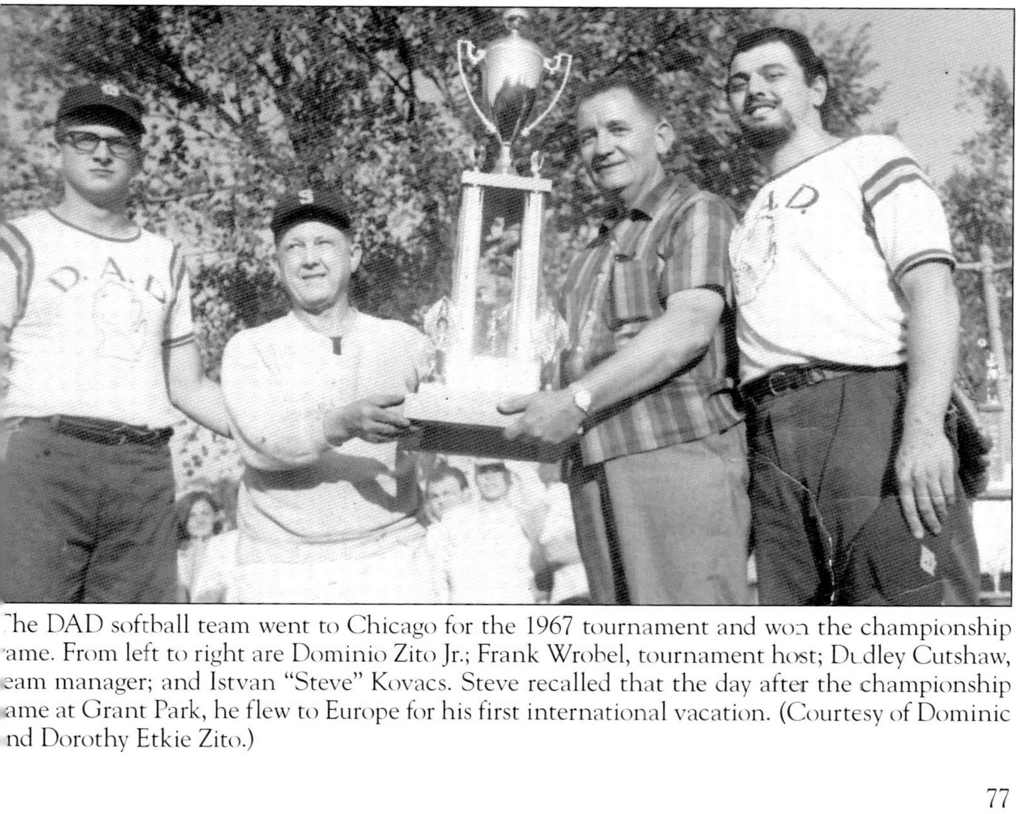

The DAD softball team went to Chicago for the 1967 tournament and won the championship game. From left to right are Dominio Zito Jr.; Frank Wrobel, tournament host; Dudley Cutshaw, team manager; and Istvan "Steve" Kovacs. Steve recalled that the day after the championship game at Grant Park, he flew to Europe for his first international vacation. (Courtesy of Dominic and Dorothy Etkie Zito.)

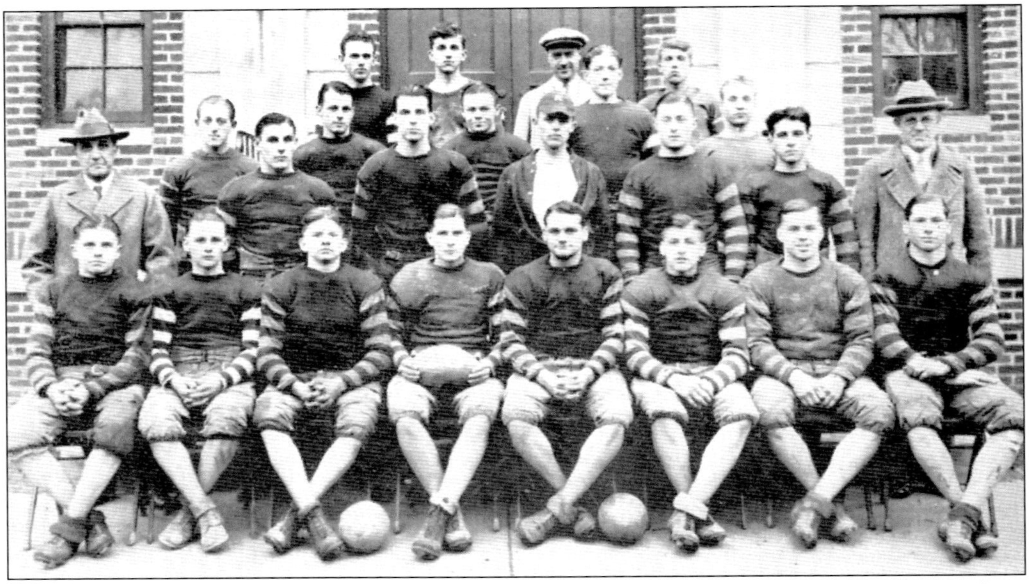

The MSD football team shown in this image from the October 1929 issue of *Silent Worker* was, from left to right, (first row) J. McKenzie, Adams, C. McKenzie, Captain Laura, C. Shaffer, Weinkauf, Vickstrom, and Zimmer; (second row) Superintendent Gilbert, Kerns, Waters, Coach Wright, Davies, and Lackind; (third row) Kannick, Wood, J. Wood, Jastrezemski, Gorman, and Virkstis; (fourth row) Osewald, Suejda, Newsome, and Conklin. (Courtesy of DAD.)

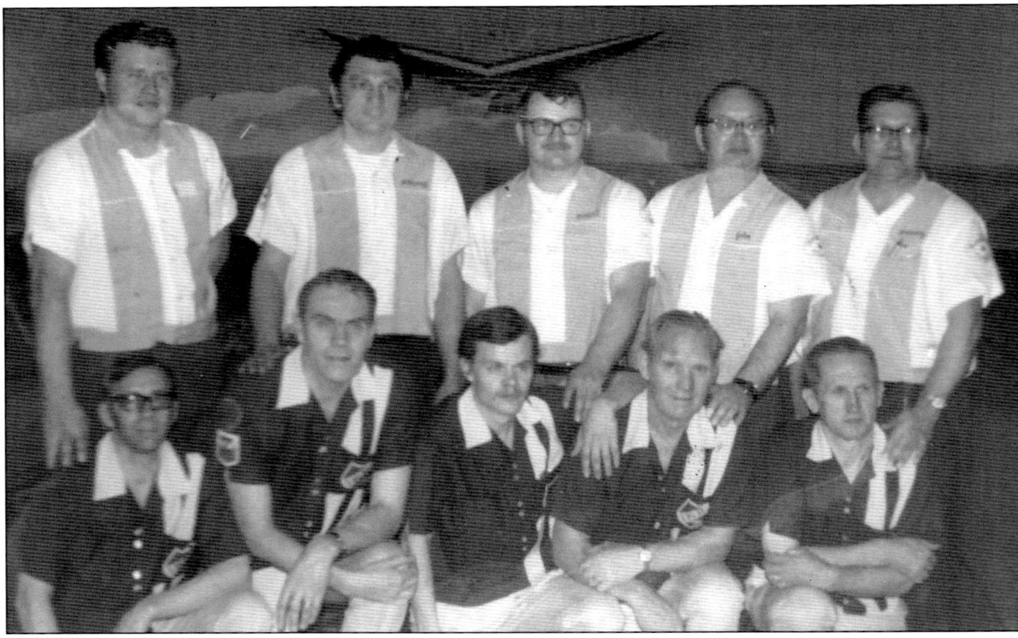

The DAD bowling league played against the deaf Swedish bowling league for fun. The Swedish team came to Detroit in 1971. The first row is unidentified. The second row is, from left to right, Alexander Marchuk, Antal "Tony" Kovacs, Hobert Smith, John Judich, and Harvey Ellerhorst. (Courtesy of Harvey and Camille Ellerhorst.)

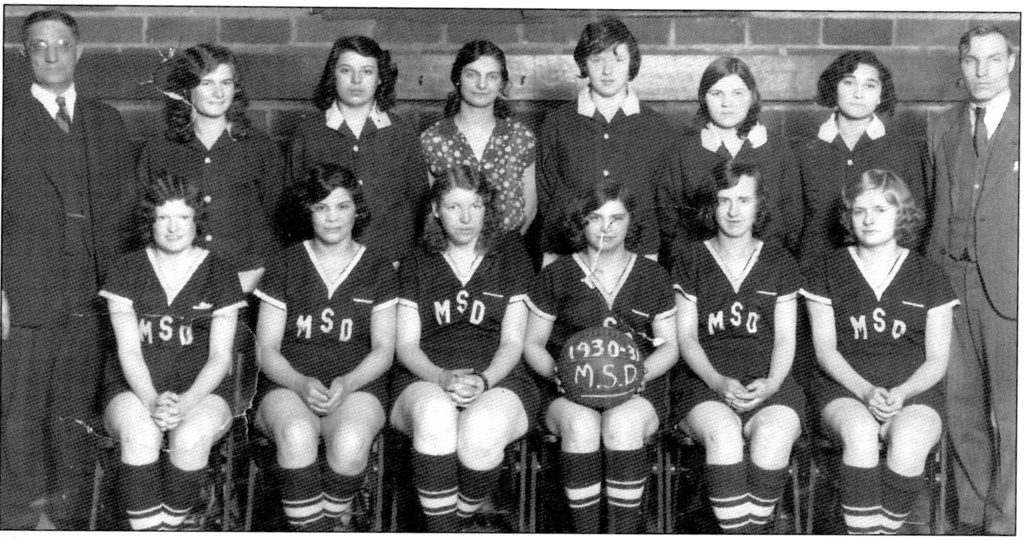

Shown is the 1930–1931 MSD high school girls' basketball team. The difficult-to-read writing on the back of the photograph lists players but not their order. Pictured are Paula Davies, Mary Smith, Mary Beck, Laura Davis, Bessie Campbell, Jessie Wheeler, Gina Gainframaggio, Edith Landi, Antionetta Di Falzio, June McCarty, Geraldine Trayner, and Margaret Vickstrom. The coaches are unidentified. (Courtesy of Stanley and Elidia Grabowski.)

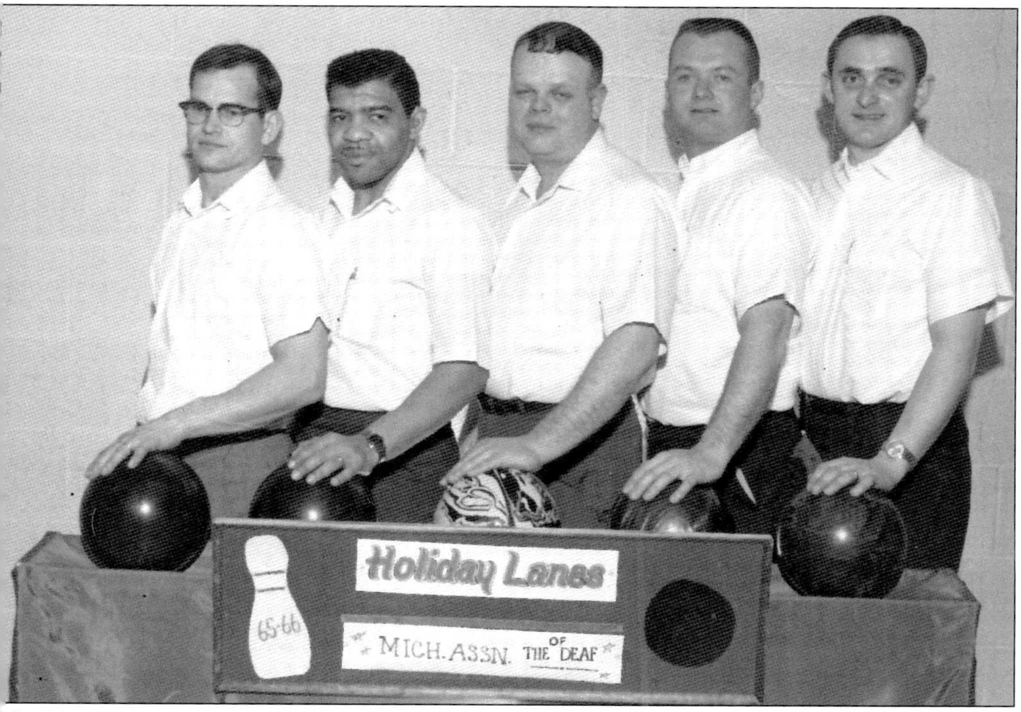

The Michigan Association of the Deaf (MAD) later changed its name to Michigan Deaf Association (MDA). This unique photograph shows its bowling team. Ernest Hairston (second from left) recalled that he joined to keep himself busy away from working hard in Lansing, Michigan. He later coauthored *Black and Deaf in America* with Linwood Smith in 1982. (Courtesy of Ernest Hairston.)

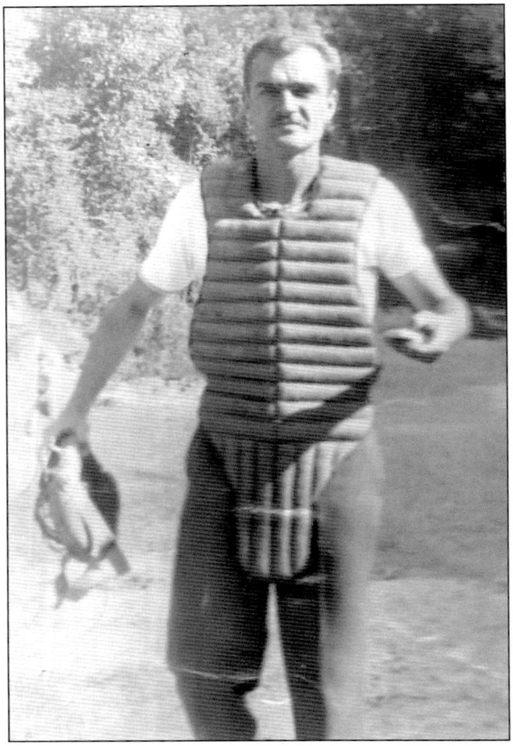

Ray Wahowiak was a deaf umpire for a hearing team in the Upper Peninsula. He umpired for many teams in the local area when he took over the shoe repair shop his deaf father owned in Gladstone, Michigan. He played softball with DAD sometimes and attended FAD for activities as well, along with his family. (Courtesy of Anson and Kathy McCall Mitchell.)

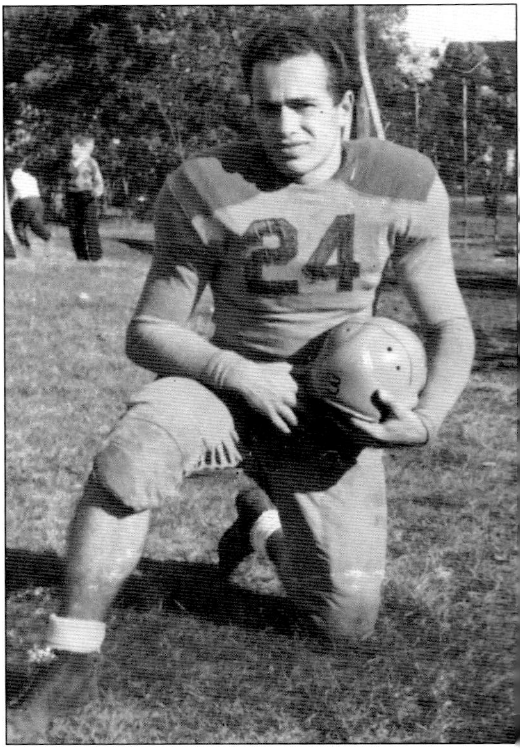

Arlyn Meyerson was the only deaf student at Wilbur Wright High School without an interpreter. He collected nine letters in sports. Arlyn remembered that he played three years straight in football and never won a single game from 1941 to 1944, but he had a wonderful experience playing and interacting with the high school students with his hearing brother. (Courtesy of Arlyn and Hester Meyerson.)

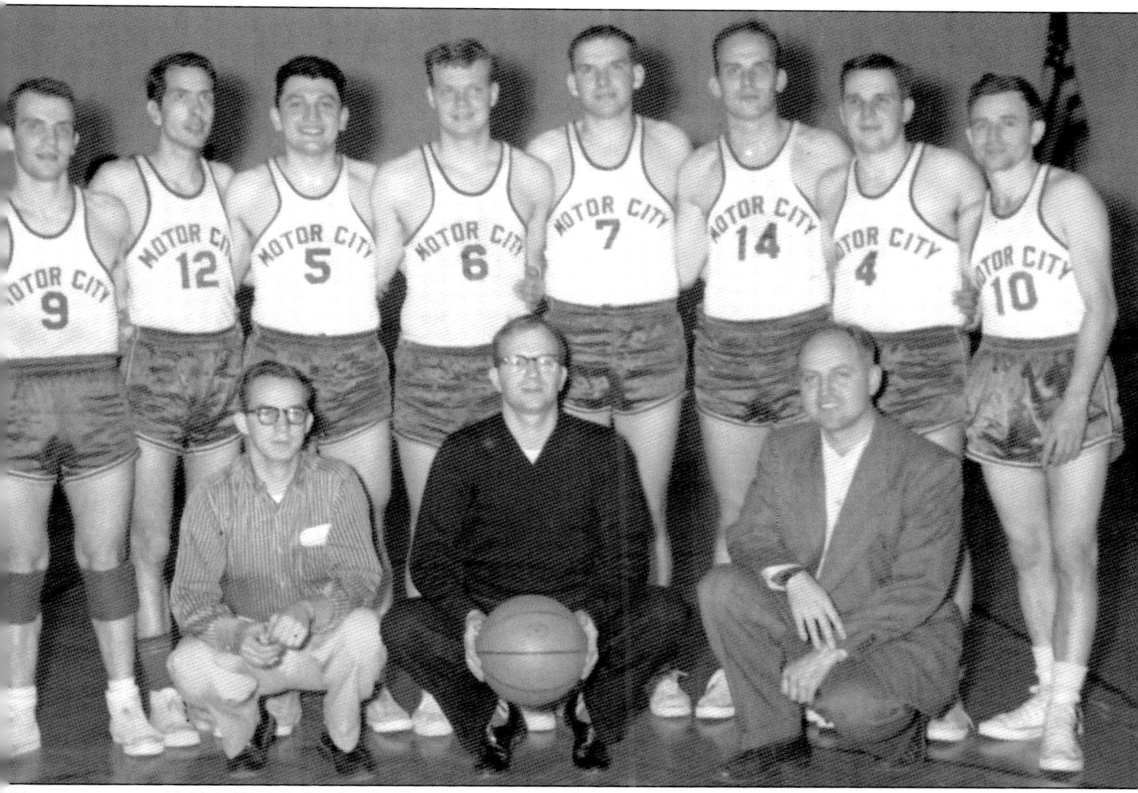

Shown is a c. 1961 MCAD basketball team. From left to right are (seated) L. Anderson, coach Charles Allen, and unidentified; (standing) unidentified, Martin Pierce, Antal "Tony" Kovacs, Nelson Finks, unidentified, Carl Groth, Bill Knight, and unidentified. Martin and Bill would be gone a year later in a tragic car accident that killed four out of the six MCAD members en route to Pittsburgh's invitational basketball tournament. (Courtesy of Arlyn and Hester Meyerson.)

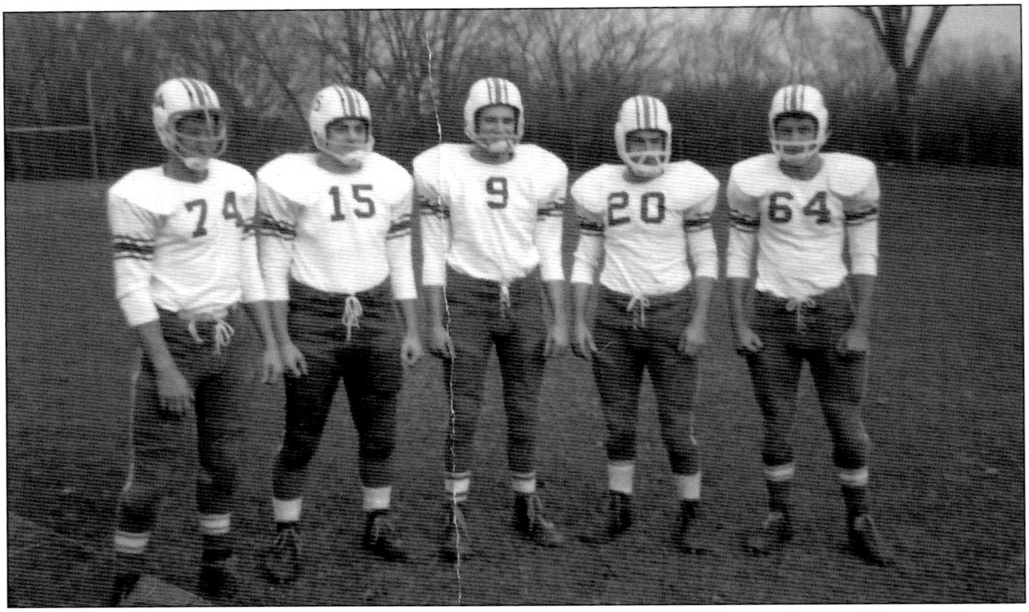

In this October 19, 1962, photograph are, from left to right, Glindel Young, Istvan "Steve" Kovacs, Dominic E. Zito Jr., Anson Mitchell, and Ronald Scripter during practice on the MSD football field. Sports reporter Vince Sickora noted in the October 12, 1962, *Detroit News* that the speed, power, alertness, and spark of each player kept MSD going. (Courtesy of Dominic and Dorothy Etkie Zito.)

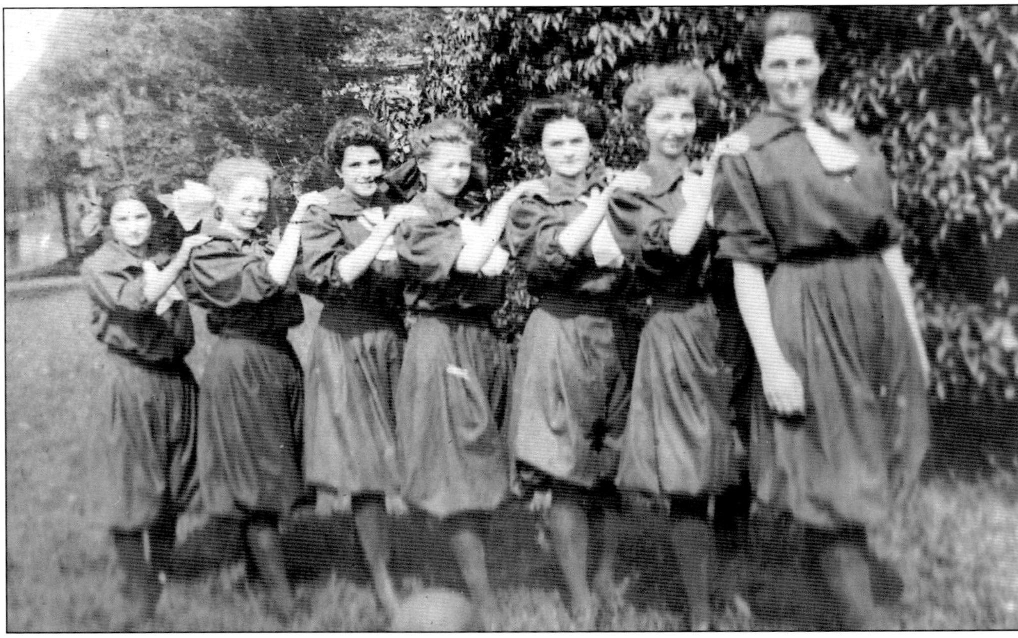

This is a c. 1910 MSD girls' basketball team dressed in what was considered appropriate sports clothes for women, with pulled-up stockings and ribbons in their hair. The sporting activities during that period also included fencing. Beside the athletic activities, the girls cooked and took turns serving in the dining room at MSD. (Courtesy of Anson and Kathy McCall Mitchell.)

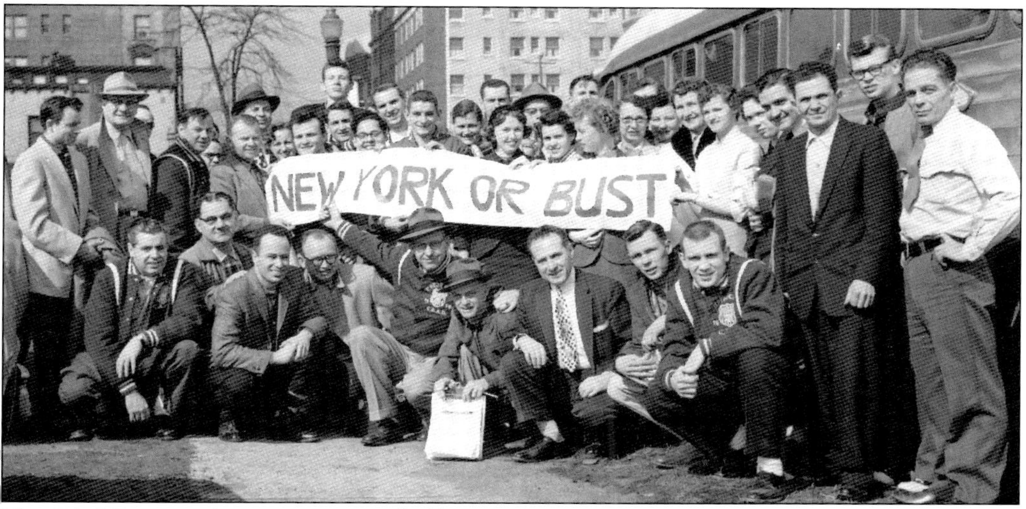

The CAAD regional tournament was held in Rockford, Illinois, in 1957. Before they traveled from Detroit, the MCAD basketball team decided to put up a "New York or Bust" sign, hoping to win and head to New York for the AAAD national tournament. The team lost and did not go. Arlyn Meyerson is kneeling third from left in the first row. (Courtesy of Arlyn and Hester Meyerson.)

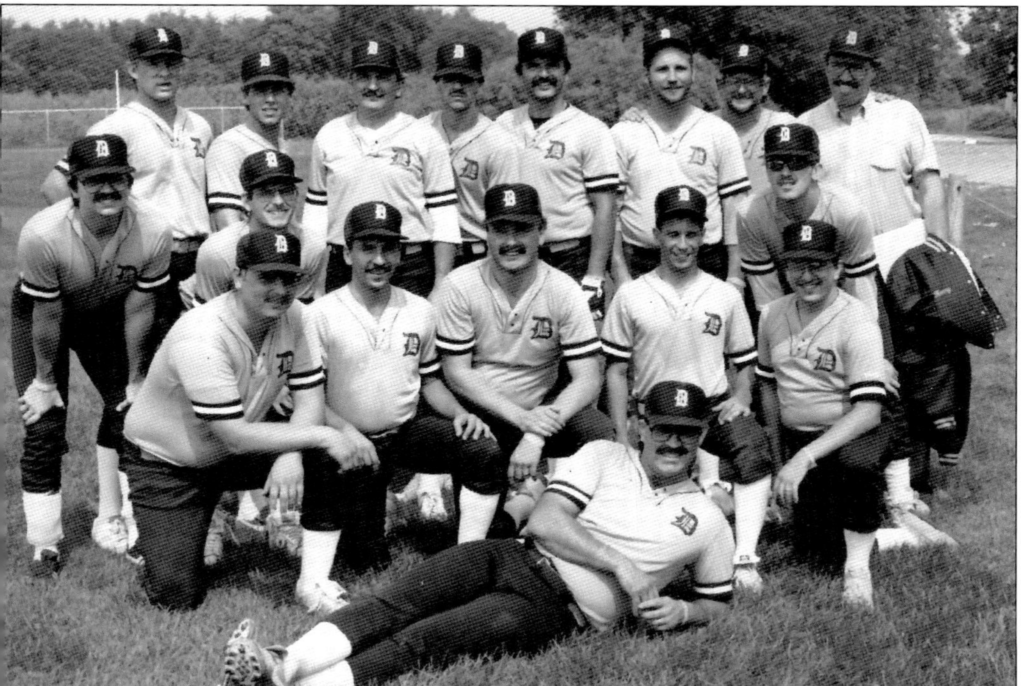

This DAD "A" men's softball team played in 1987 and won second place at the CAAD and ninth place at the AAAD. From left to right are (first row) Bobby Madden; (second row) Alan McCall, Paul Trayner, Jerry Beaver, Jerry Trayner, and Larry Trayner; (third row) Craig Schlorff, Dana Harmon, and Richard Beaver; (fourth row) Darrell Hovinen, Steve Mitchell, Antal "Tony" Kovacs, Danny Beaver, Willie Van Dyck–Dobos, David Zanavich, Dominic Zito Jr., and Henry Strandell. (Courtesy of Nancy Capek McCall.)

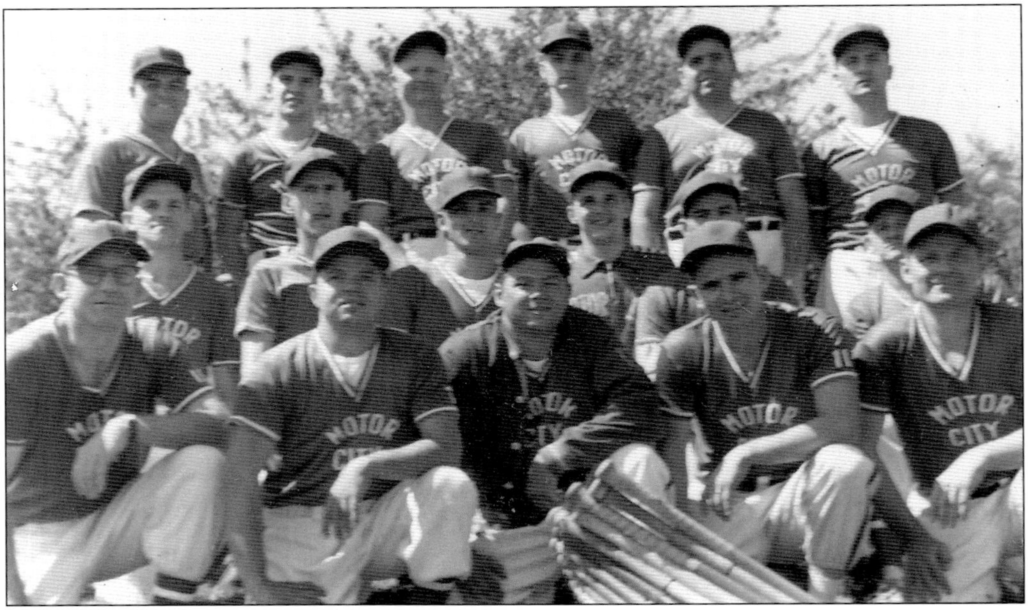

The MCAD team in this September 1947 photograph was participating in the CAAD softball tournament. In no particular order are Emil DeMeyere, Harry Petrowske, Frank Lytle, Charles Mully, Bill Graff, Stanley Jentriz, Walter ?, Albert Montacelli, Marcel Viene, Bill Roscoe, Arlyn Meyerson, Alexander Marchuk, and Henry Lipinski. (Courtesy of Arlyn and Hester Meyerson.)

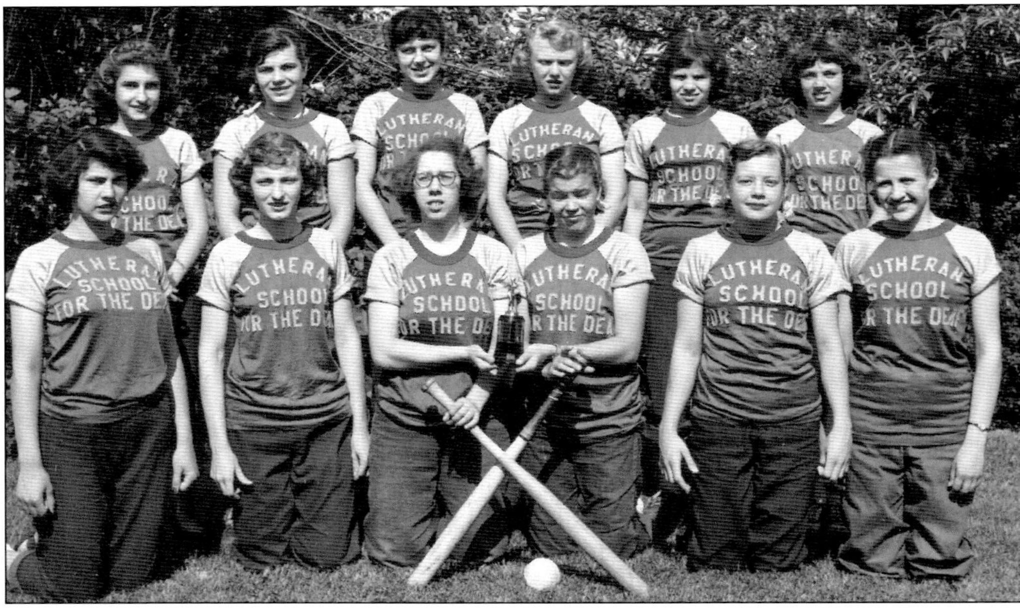

LSD girls played against hearing Lutheran school teams. This photograph shows the 1951 girls' softball team. They were proud to display their trophy after they won the championship for the South and East Detroit Lutheran Girls League. From left to right are (first row) Marilou Laford, Margaret Hopf, Joyce Rossow, Gay Haigler, Grace Meilander, and Marlene Schluz; (second row) Monica Gable, unidentified, Roberta Clawson, Geraldine Smith, Eilleen Snyder, and unidentified. (Courtesy of Judy and Larry Vardon.)

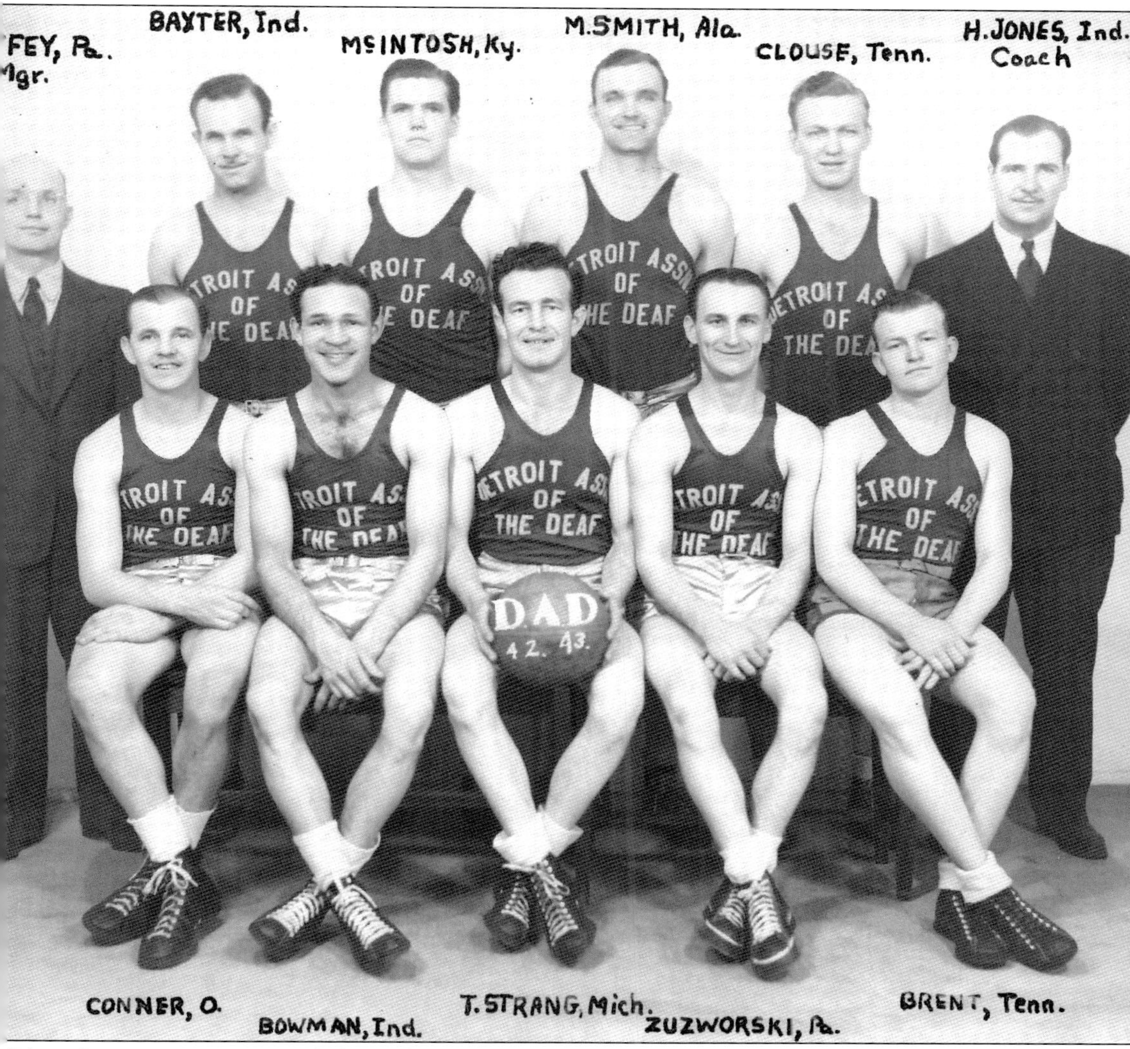

Often the sports teams invited players from other states to join teams to play in every tournament. Some were called "free agents." This photograph shows a DAD basketball team with players mostly identified by last name and home state. From left to right are (first row) O. Conner; Bowman, Indiana; T. Strang, Michigan; Zuzworski, Pennsylvania; and Brent, Tennessee; (second row) Coffey, Pennsylvania, manager; Baxter, Indiana; McIntosh, Kentucky; M. Smith, Alabama; Clouse, Tennessee; and H. Jones, Indiana, coach. (Courtesy of DAD.)

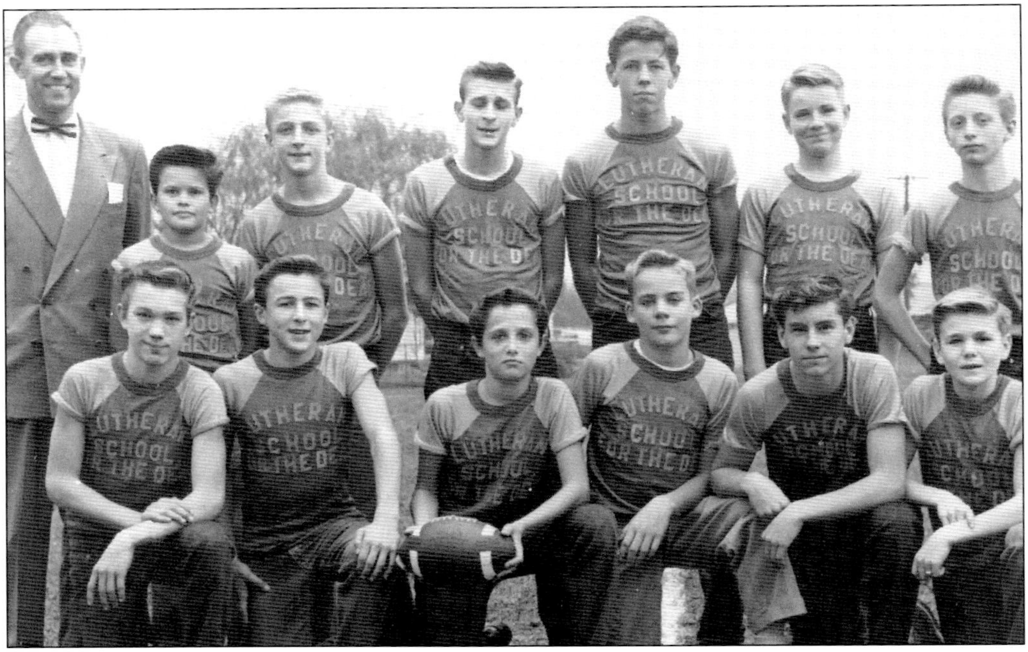

The LSD boys team were the touch football champions for 1956 in the East Side League. From left to right are (first row) James Katzel, Gary Larson, Hugh Blankenship (quarterback), James Allen, Caswell Hassel, and Donald Morris; (second row) coach R. Tegeder, Alan Nelson, Reed Lee, Gary Blumerick, Roger Lindstrom, James Johnson, and Curtis Coveyou. (Courtesy of Judy and Larry Vardon.)

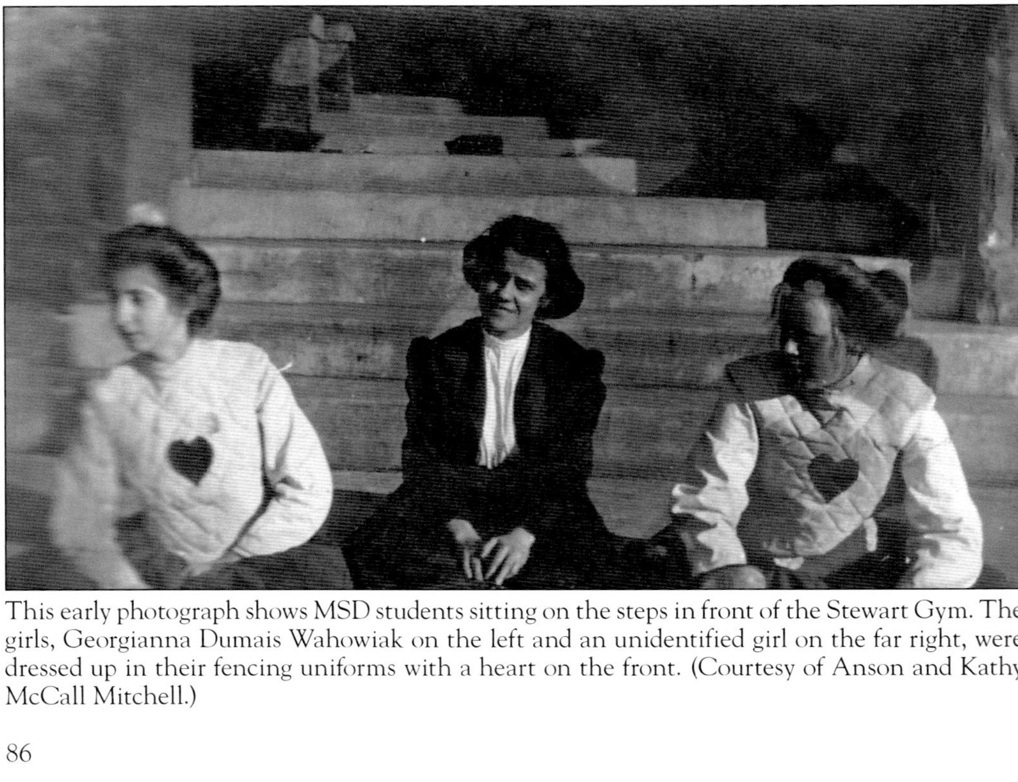

This early photograph shows MSD students sitting on the steps in front of the Stewart Gym. The girls, Georgianna Dumais Wahowiak on the left and an unidentified girl on the far right, were dressed up in their fencing uniforms with a heart on the front. (Courtesy of Anson and Kathy McCall Mitchell.)

Seven

EVENTS AND GATHERINGS

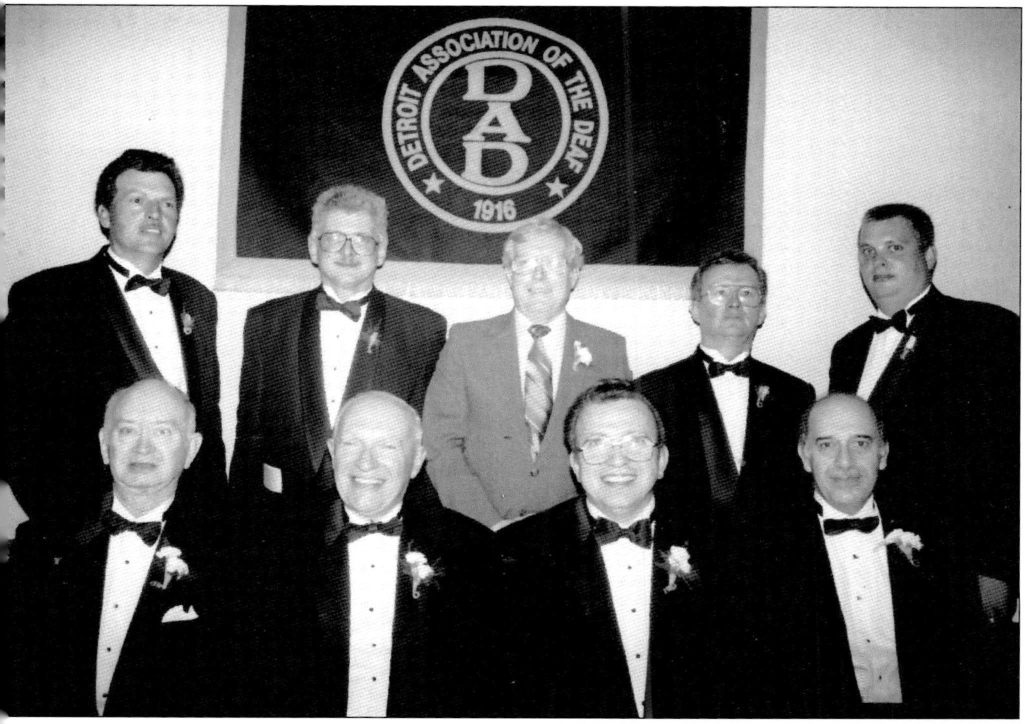

These DAD club officers are dressed up in their tuxedos for an unknown event. From left to right are (first row) John Judnich, Jim Lombardi, Anthony Genna, and George Bozaan; (second row) Ron Smith, Dominic Zito Jr., John Klarr, Robert Lemker, and Alan McCall. (Courtesy of Dominic and Dorothy Etkie Zito.)

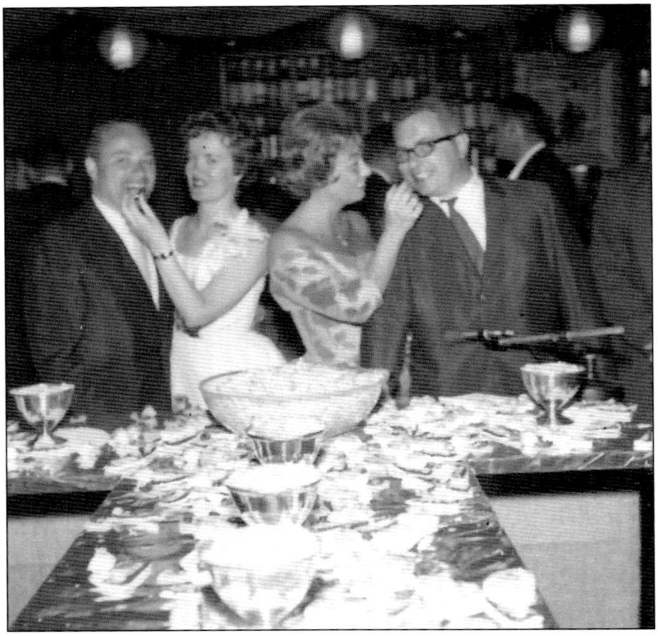

Arlyn Meyerson and Hester Wayner (left) got married on June 25, 1961, in a double wedding with Arlyn's brother, Jerry Meyerson (right). It was a second marriage for both Arlyn and Hester. The Meyerson brothers opened the Scotch 'n' Sirloin restaurant the day after Labor Day 1960 in the center surrounded by James Couzen Highway, Greenfield Avenue, and Eight Mile Road. (Courtesy of Arlyn and Hester Meyerson.)

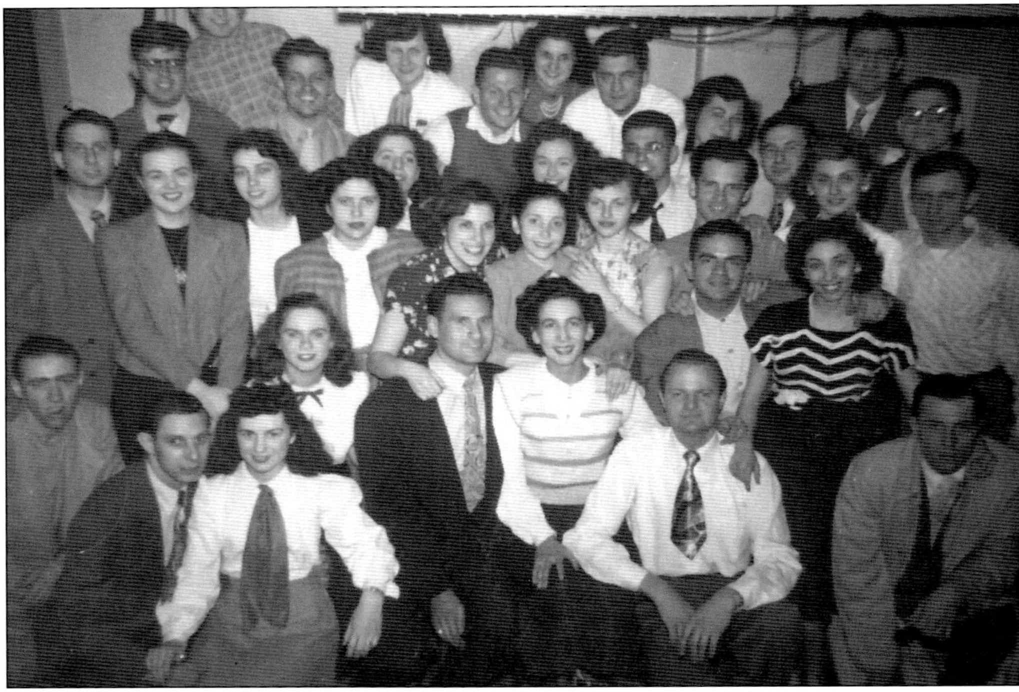

The MCAD basketball team traveled to Philadelphia for the AAAD tournament in April 1948. After the tournament was over, the team traveled to New York City and joined with the Naismith Silent Athletics Club members. Arlyn Meyerson boasted he was a cupid. He introduced Gene Zeni, his teammate, to Julie Zuzzi at the tournament, where she was visiting friends. Gene (second from left) and Julie (third from left) are shown holding hands. They got married a year later. (Courtesy of Arlyn and Hester Meyerson.)

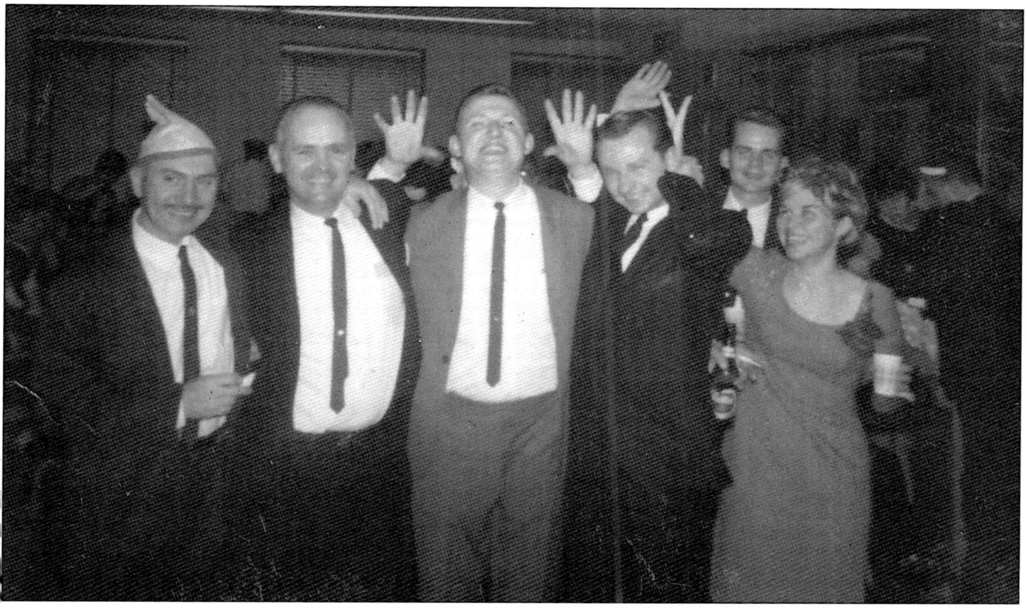

This c. 1950s photograph shows a themed party hosted by DAD. From left to right are David Soultanian, Eddie Riley, Steve Spurgis, Gerald Grifford, James Allen, and an unidentified woman. DAD would often host social events to keep the club going. The club is approaching its 100th anniversary in October 2016 as one of the oldest and longest-running deaf clubs in the United States. (Courtesy of DAD.)

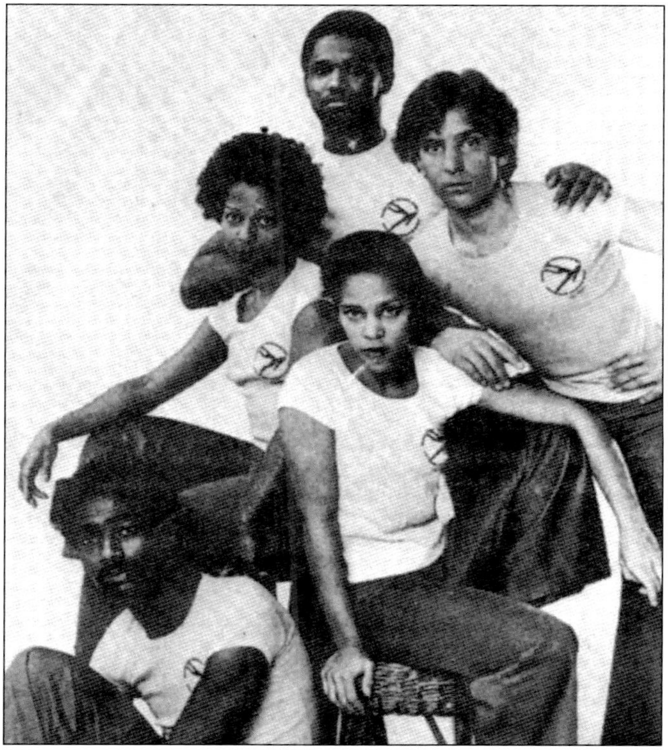

This photograph is from a 1983 issue of *Black Arts Magazine*. Penny Godboldo, a choreographer, founded the Writhm Dance Company in 1976. Glenn Stewart, the only deaf member in the company, did classical, modern, jazz, and ethnic dance. The company toured throughout Michigan. From left to right are (first row) Glenn Stewart; (second row) Penny Godboldo and Sylvia ?; (third row) two unidentified. Glenn loved to dance and sing in the chorus. (Courtesy of *Black Arts Magazine*.)

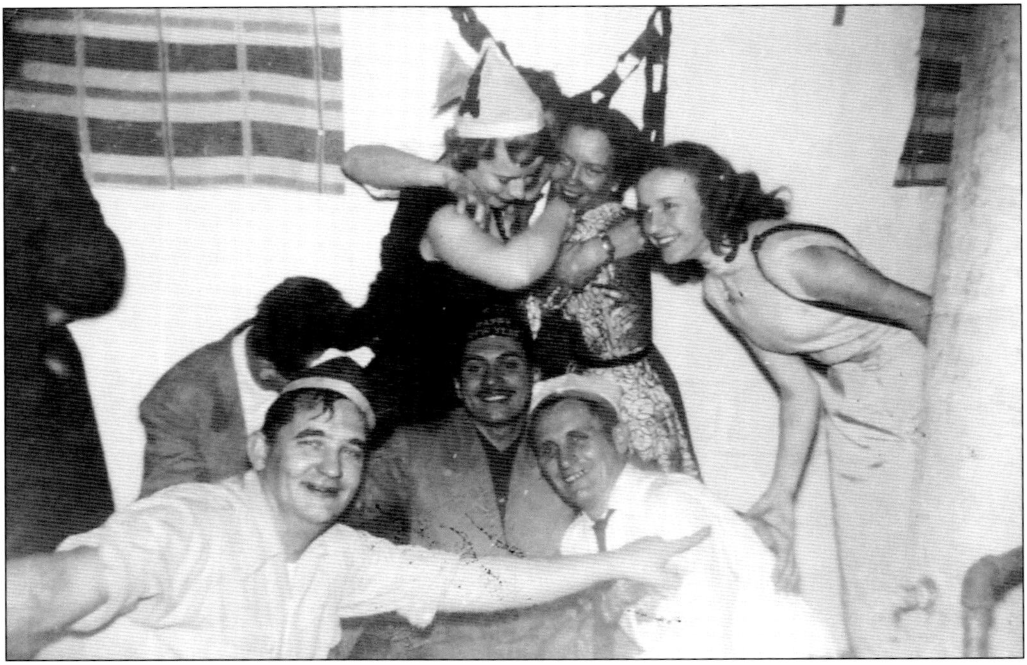

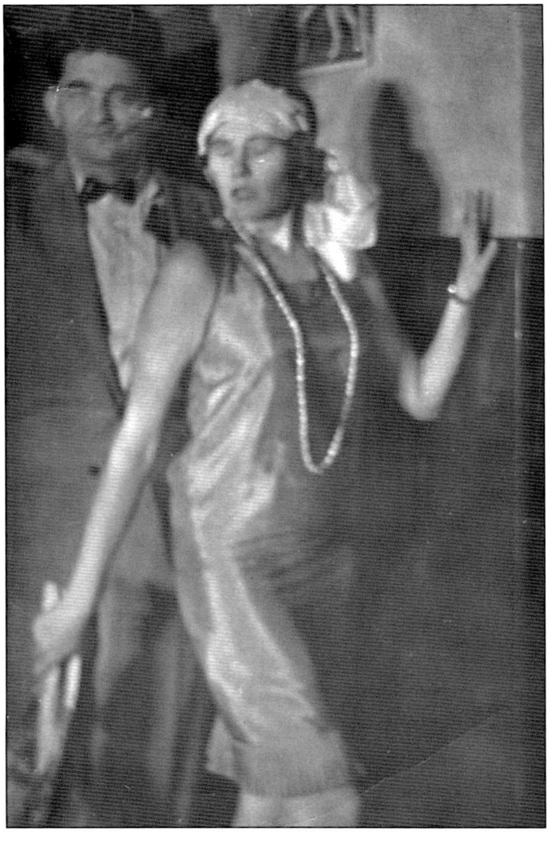

At this DAD New Year's celebration, Susan Beer is at the top left. In the first row are, from left to right, Dudley Cutshaw, David Soultanian, and Steven Popp. (Courtesy of DAD.)

Dudley Cutshaw celebrates at a DAD Roaring Twenties party with Dorothy Taylor around 1960. DAD promised better trends to entertain members and nonmembers that year. DAD offered a drama club with fabulous plays like *Paris Escapades* and *Babes Are Cute*. (Courtesy of DAD.)

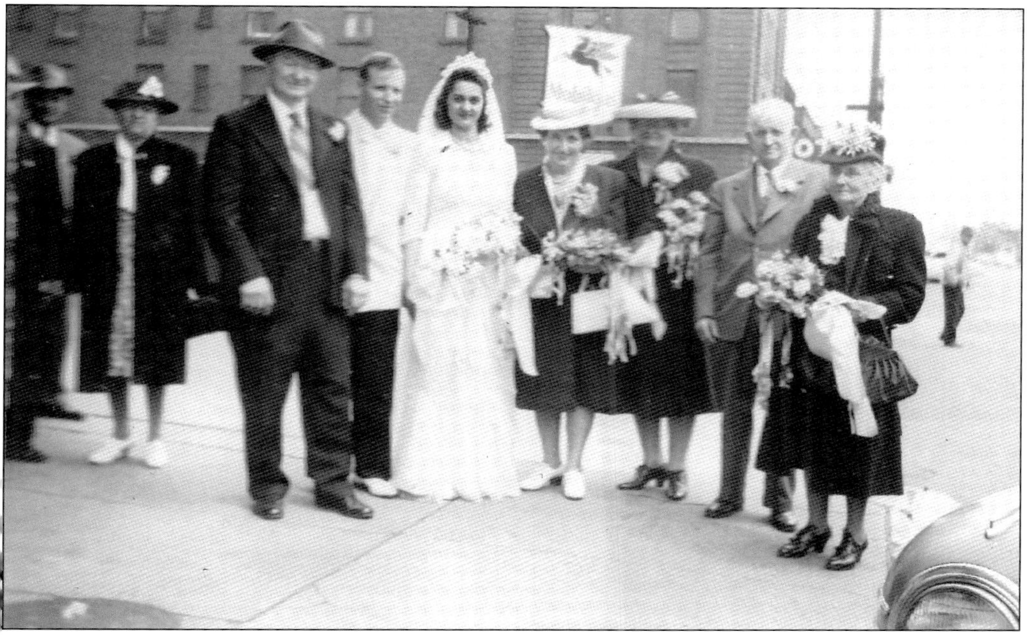

This wedding took place between the Wahowiak and McCall clans on May 26, 1945, at All Saints Catholic Church in Gladstone, Michigan. From left to right are John Wahowiak, Frederick McCall, Melvina Wahowiak McCall, Georgianna Dumais Wahowiak, Mary Demick McCall, Eugene McCall, and Ida McCall Englebrecht. According to an issue of the *Escanaba* newspaper from May 1945, the couple celebrated a pre-wedding breakfast and then a post-wedding dinner and reception with 25 guests at the Sherman Hotel in Escanaba, Michigan. (Courtesy of Anson and Kathy Mitchell.)

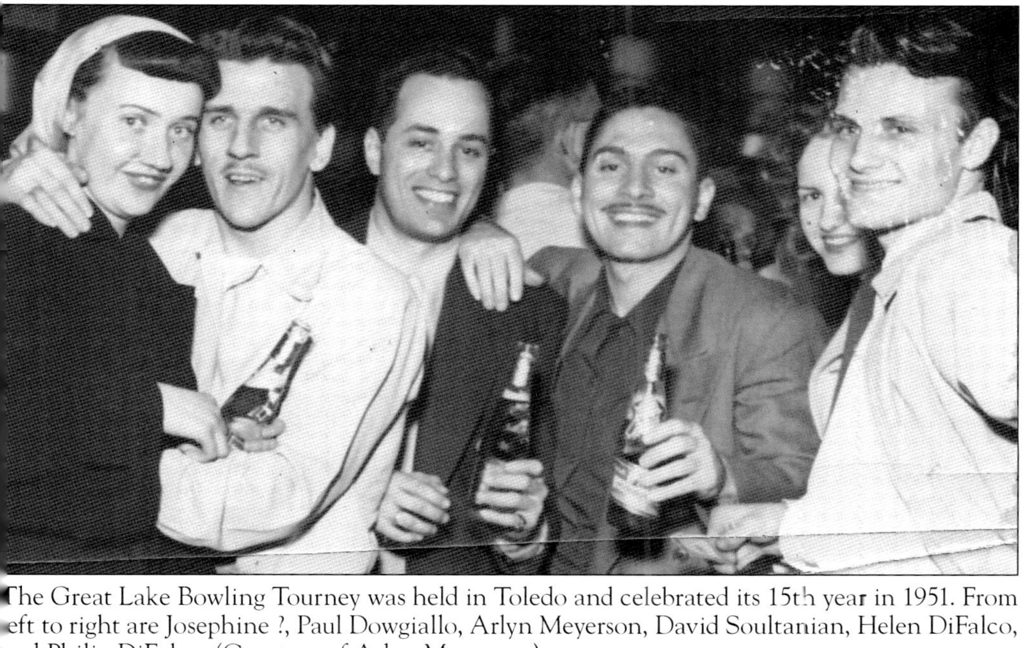

The Great Lake Bowling Tourney was held in Toledo and celebrated its 15th year in 1951. From left to right are Josephine ?, Paul Dowgiallo, Arlyn Meyerson, David Soultanian, Helen DiFalco, and Philip DiFalco. (Courtesy of Arlyn Meyerson.)

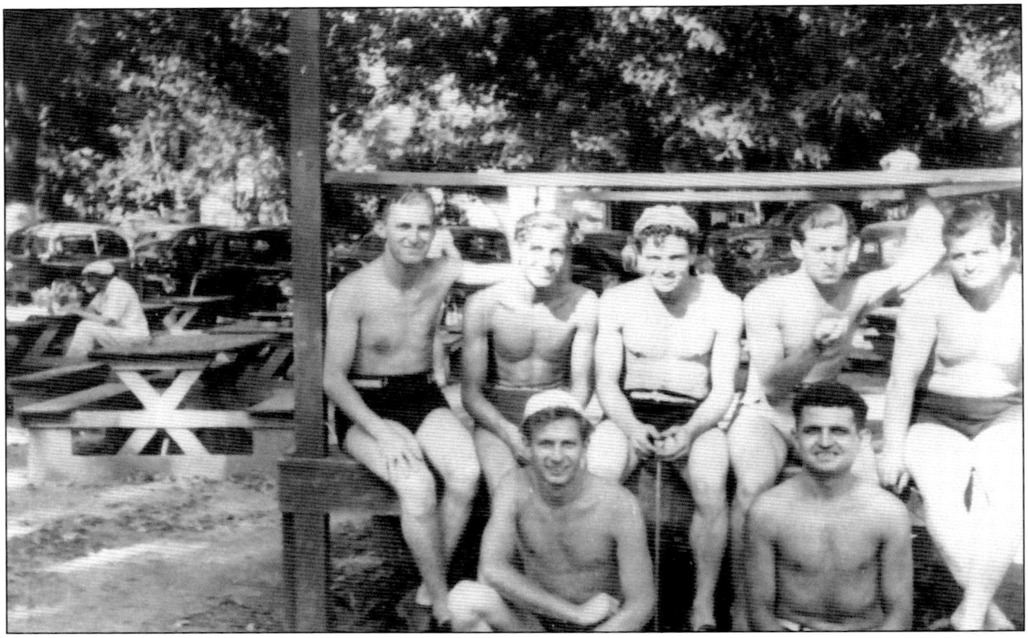

During the summer of 1943, Walled Lake was the popular hangout for this group of deaf men from New York who worked defense jobs in Detroit during World War II. Shown below, they rode in a nice 1938 Pontiac convertible. Arlyn Meyerson is sitting third from left in the back. Ever since he met the New York gang in his father's restaurant, he hung out with them and communicated in sign language. Some were members of DAD and MCAD as well. (Both, courtesy of Arlyn and Hester Meyerson.)

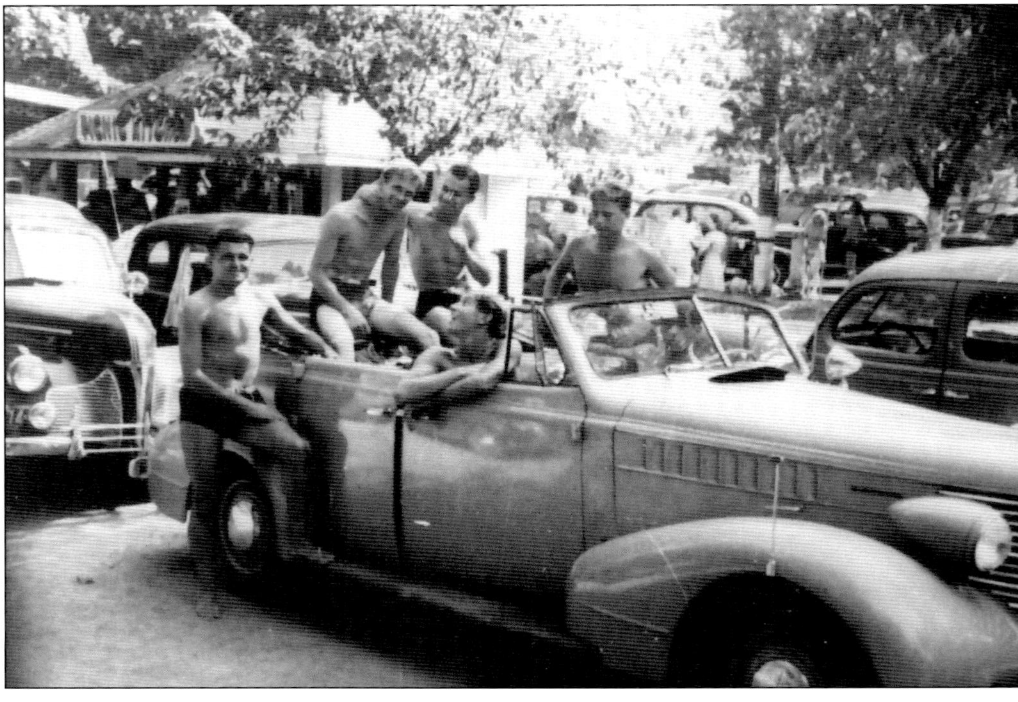

A group of deaf people swam and socialized at the Whitemore Lake every Sunday during warm weather in the late 1950s. They all look so cheerful dressed in summer clothes and bathing suits, ready for a fun day. Diana Cutshaw McKittrick recalled attending with her father, Dudley Cutshaw, and their family. There was no technology to communicate, and they all relied on getting together regularly to hang out. (Courtesy of Charles and Diana Cutshaw McKittrick.)

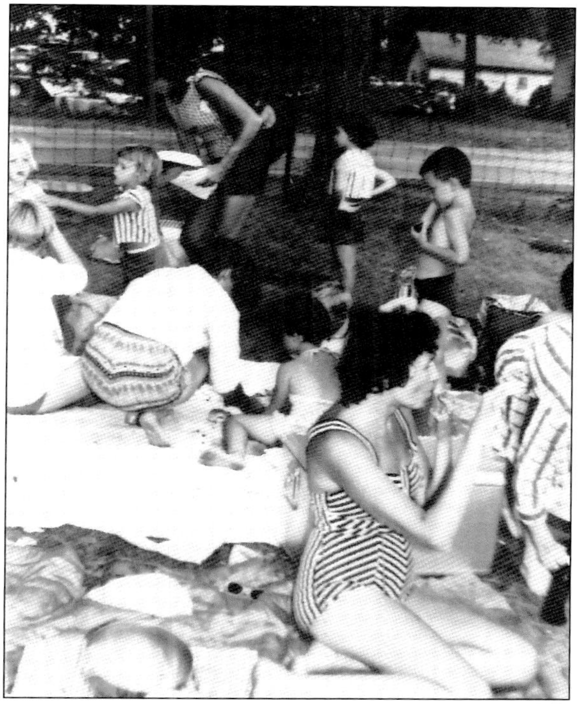

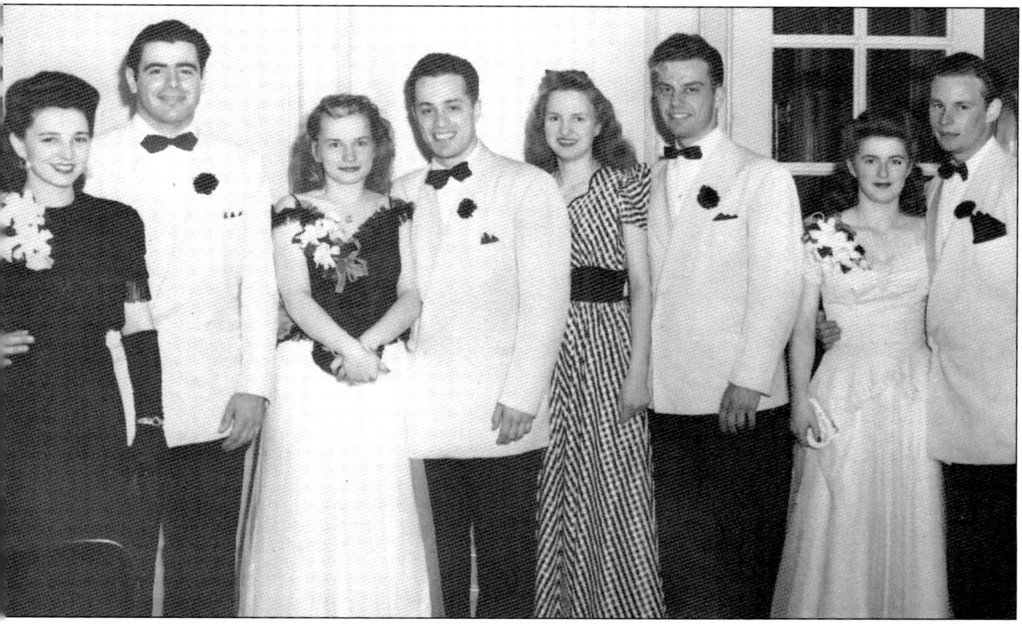

Arlyn Meyerson attended Wilbur Wright High School as the only deaf student. His brother was always around at high school to keep him company. Prom was approaching, so he decided to invite his former DDSD classmates and their dates to join him at the Dearborn Inn in June 1945. Shown from left to right are Connie ?, Charles Mully, Susan Beer, Arlyn Meyerson, Helen Gellenbeck, William "Bill" Miller, unidentified, and Jerry Raskin, Arlyn's best friend. (Courtesy of Arlyn and Hester Meyerson.)

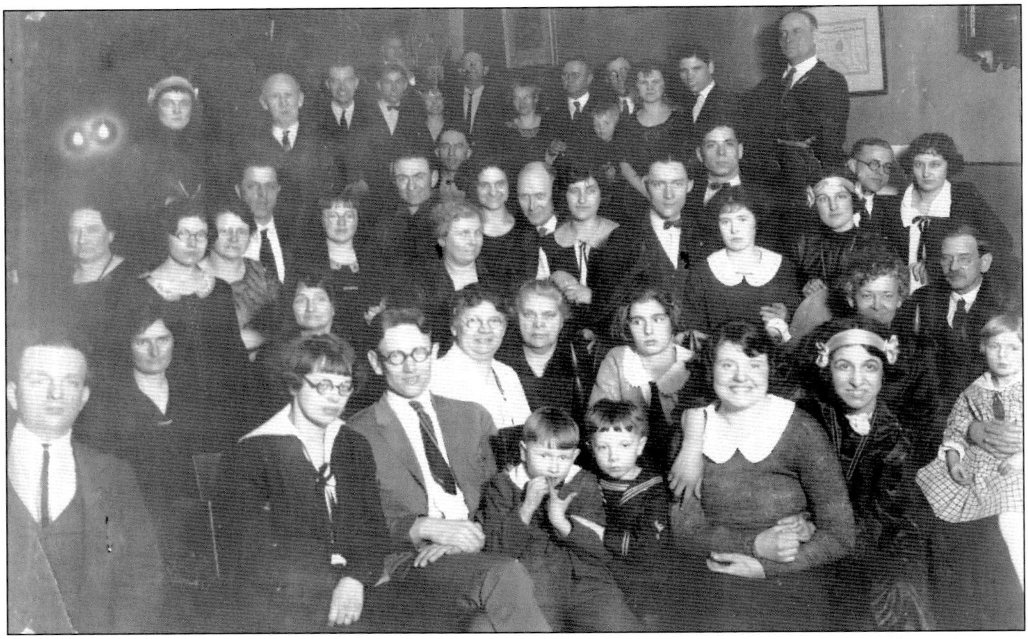

In 1924, FAD had a Christmas party at the clubhouse at 100 1/2 Saginaw Street in Flint. Among the revelers are Vernnet Johns, John Rumbold, William Gibney, L. Bakkala, Oren Dechamplain, John Wiakowiak, Wilfred Vicks, George Trine, Harry Neely, Fred A. Laurason, William Heck and his daughter Thelma, Ed Cauthier, V. Fredoris, and Mrs. Fouthier. (Courtesy of FAD.)

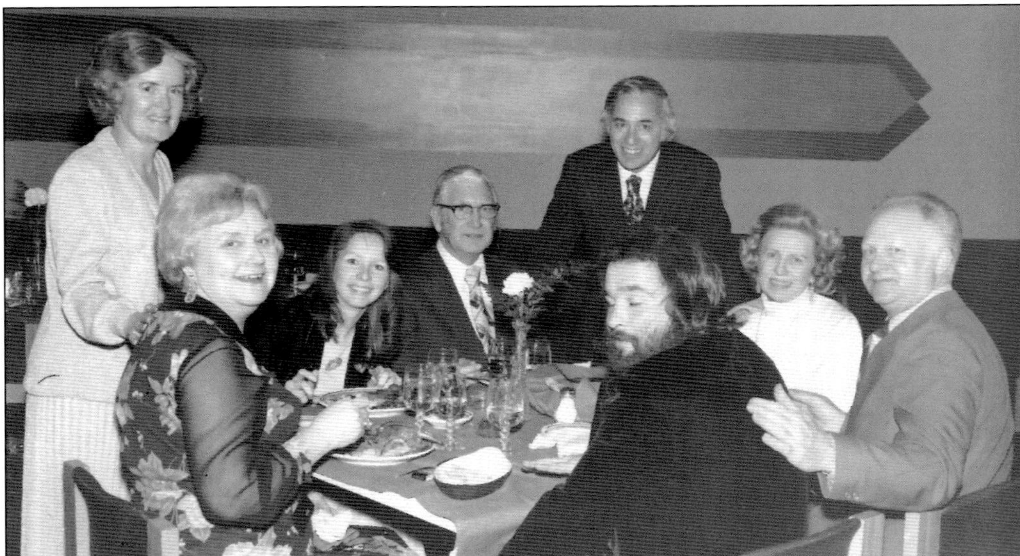

In 1975, after Arlyn and Jerry, the Meyerson brothers, closed their previous restaurant, Scotch 'n' Sirloin, they opened a new restaurant, Trio at Franklin, with 400 seats. Some MCAD members came to give support at the opening night. From left to right are Hester Meyerson (standing), Evelyn DeMeyere, unidentified, Ted Deska, Arlyn Meyerson (standing), unidentified, Helen Deska, and Emil DeMeyere. (Courtesy of Arlyn and Hester Meyerson.)

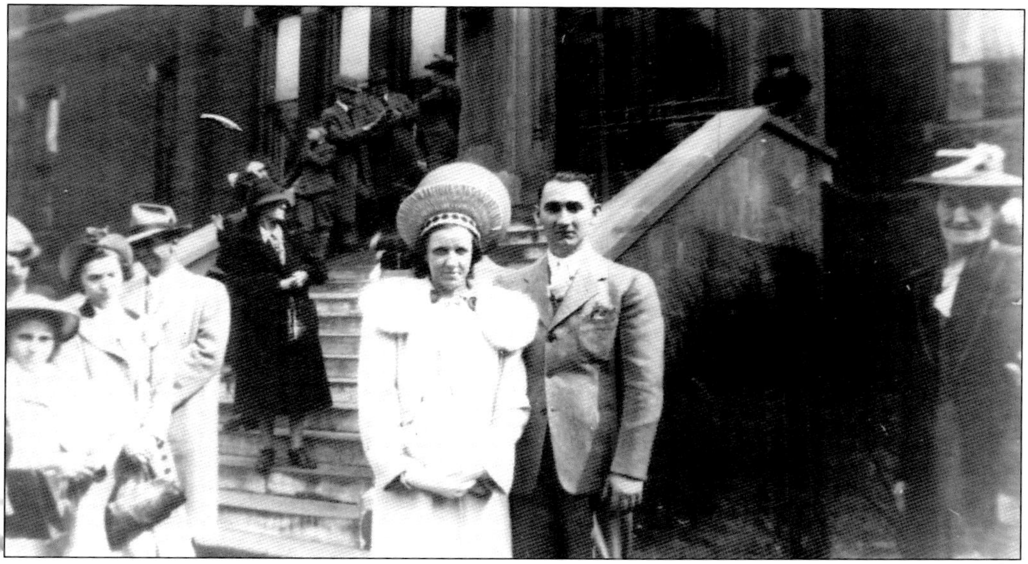

This photograph was taken in November 1942. Standing at center are Adele and John Perlisky dressed for a Detroit Association of Catholic Deaf service in a rented room at St. Mary's Hospital. (Courtesy of SJDC.)

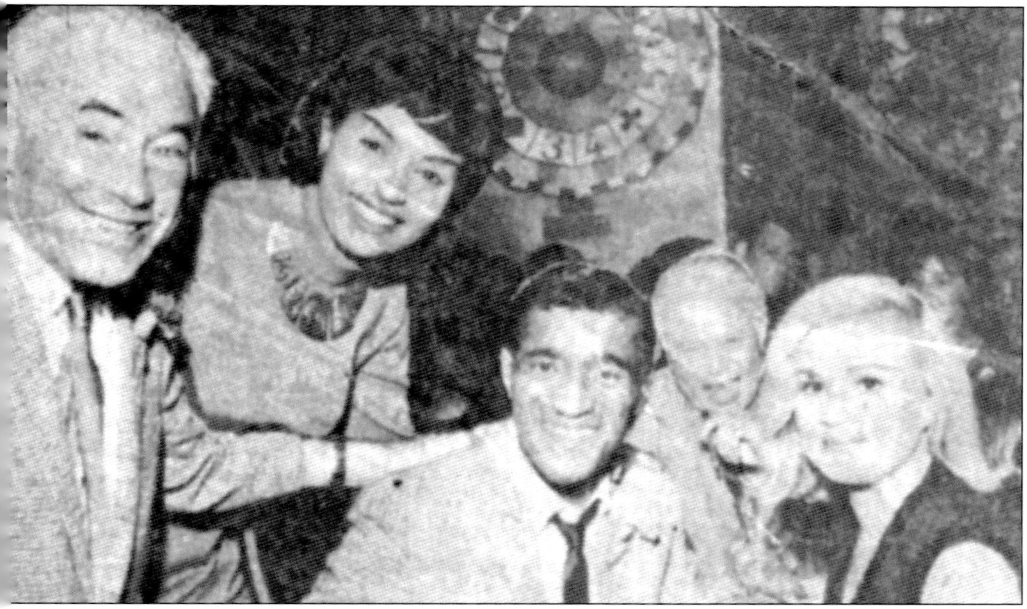

Actor Sammy Davis Jr. was performing at the popular Northland Playhouse and ate at the popular Scotch 'n' Sirloin restaurant nearby, owned by Arlyn and Jerry Meyerson. In this picture from the theatrical news section in the *Detroit News* between 1961 and 1962 are, from left to right, Buddy Meyerson, Arlyn's father; Jo Thompson, vocalist; Davis, star of the show; and his co-stars Billy Daniels and Paula Wayne. During that time, the restaurant had 145 seats and 50 employees. (Courtesy of the *Detroit News*.)

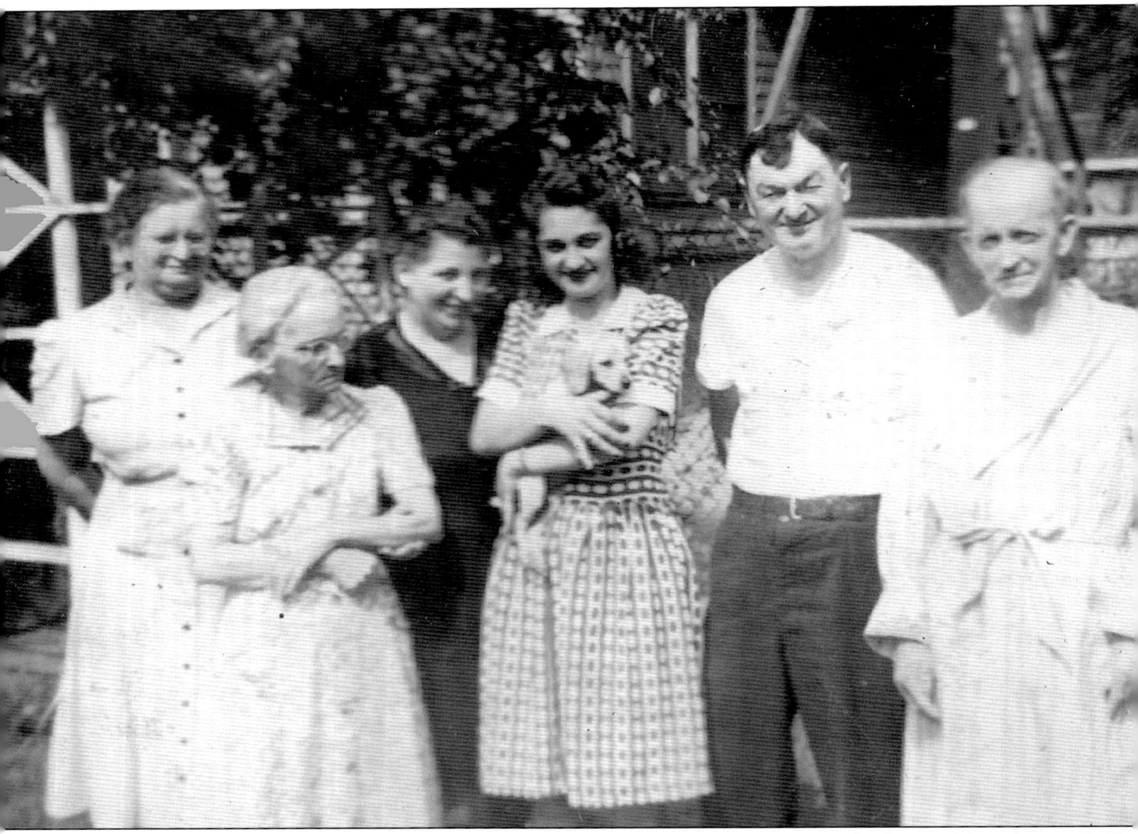

This c. 1945 photograph shows, from left to right, Mary Demick McCall, Ida Englebrecht McCall, Georgianna Dumais Wahowiak, Melvina Wahowiak McCall, John Wahowiak, and Eugene McCall. Eugene was the founder of National Fraternal Society of the Deaf Detroit Chapter No. 2. (Courtesy of Anson and Kathy McCall Mitchell.)

Frederick "Fred" McCall (left) and Dominic Zito Sr. (right) were the cochairmen of the DAD Bazaar in the early 1970s. Fred married Melvina Wahowiak and resided in Dearborn for a long time. He was active with DAD, Detroit Metro Lions Deaf Club, and Tri County Deaf Seniors. After 1992, Fred and his wife, Melvina, had 10 hearing and deaf grandchildren from their four deaf children. (Courtesy of Dominic and Dorothy Etkie Zito.)

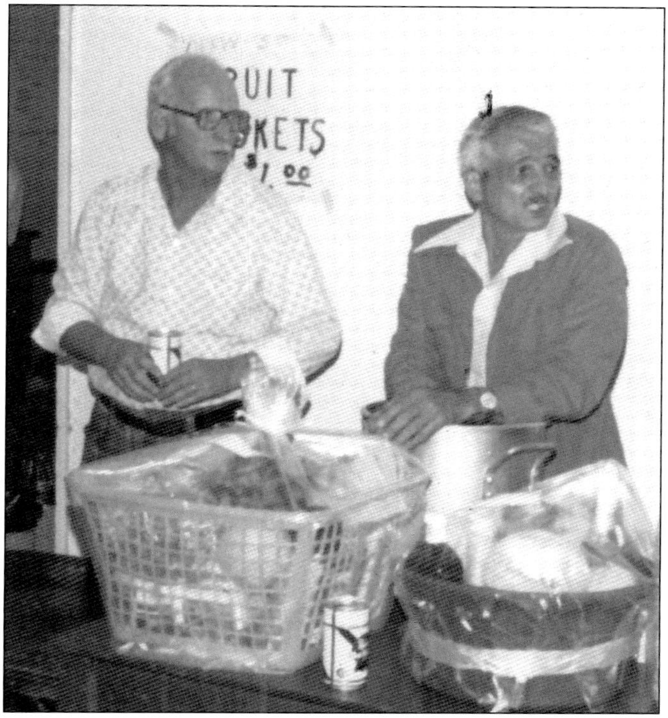

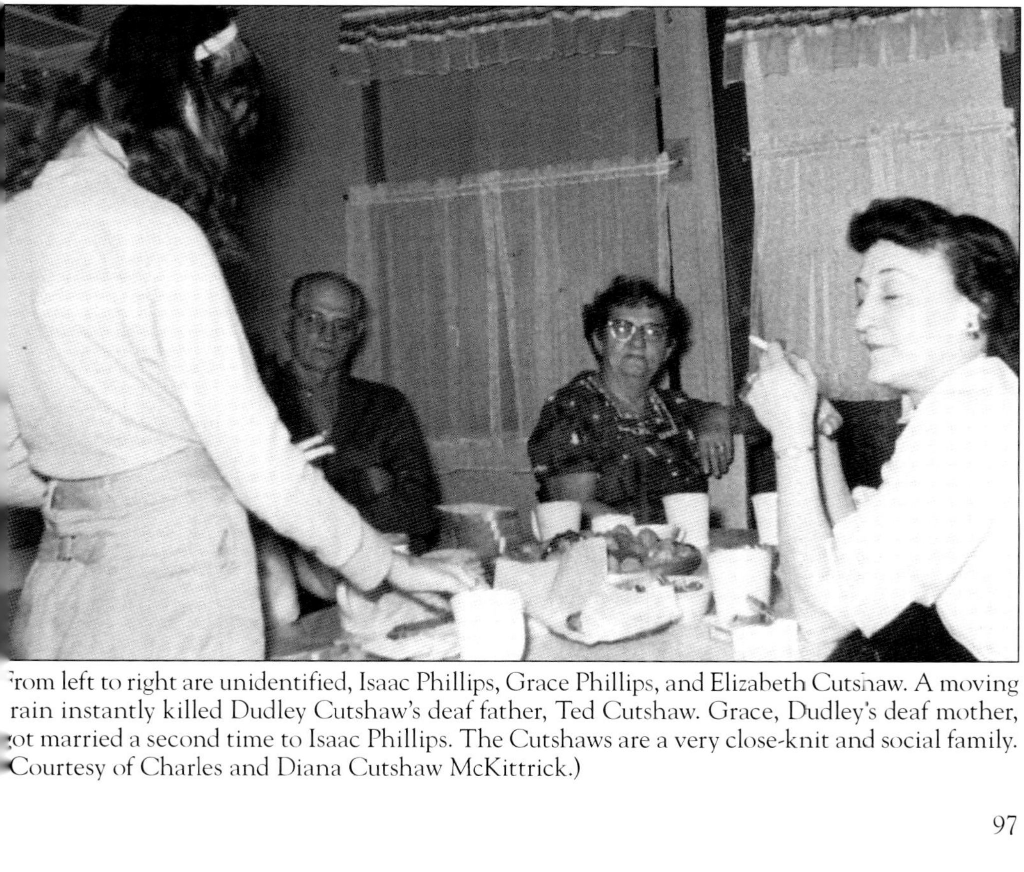

From left to right are unidentified, Isaac Phillips, Grace Phillips, and Elizabeth Cutshaw. A moving train instantly killed Dudley Cutshaw's deaf father, Ted Cutshaw. Grace, Dudley's deaf mother, got married a second time to Isaac Phillips. The Cutshaws are a very close-knit and social family. (Courtesy of Charles and Diana Cutshaw McKittrick.)

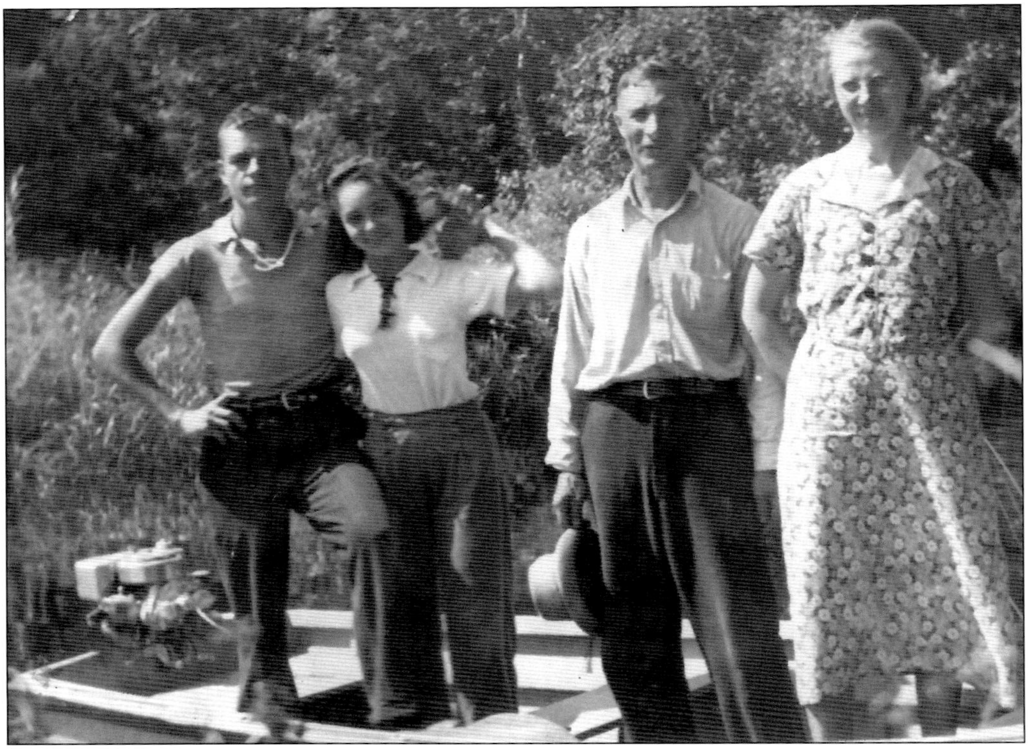

In Gladstone, on the Upper Peninsula, the Wahowiak family enjoyed one of their favorite activities on break from the shoe repair shop and away from MSD. Shown are, from left to right, Ray Wahowiak, Melvina Wahowiak McCall, and Louis and Alma Dumais. Ray sometimes volunteered as an umpire for the hearing softball teams in the area. (Courtesy of Anson and Kathy McCall Mitchell.)

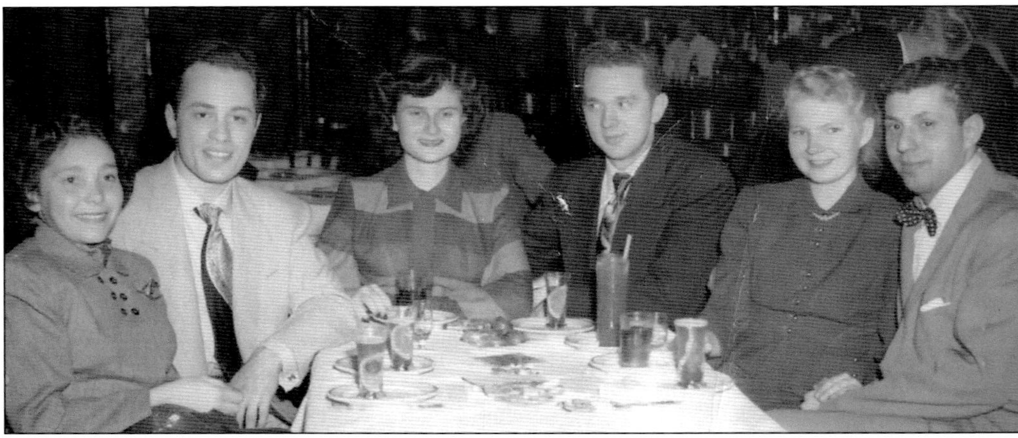

Arlyn Meyerson traveled to New York City with his DDSD buddy Paul Naeyert and Sammy Lewis. They took their deaf dates to Leon and Eddie's nightclub in April 1950. Shown from left to right are Alice Peck, Arlyn, Gloria Faerman, Paul, Ruth Pease, and Sammy. Paul later got married and settled in Flint, working as a linotype operator and raising a family. All three of his deaf children attended MSD. (Courtesy of Arlyn and Hester Meyerson.)

Eight

Business Activities

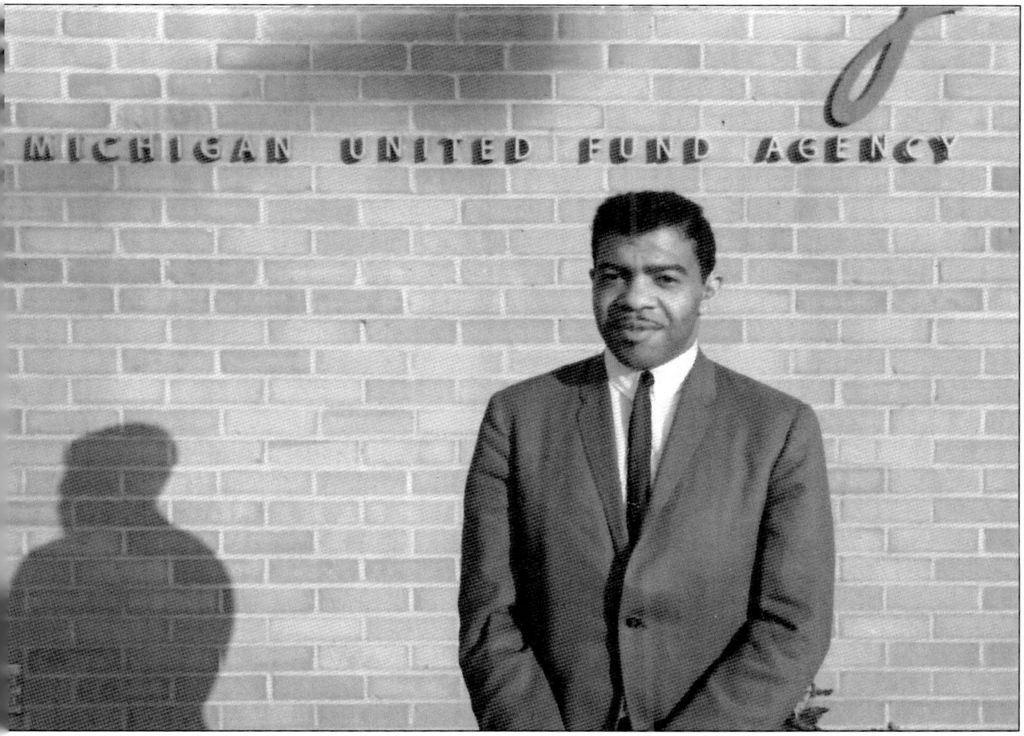

As a young adult, Ernest "Ernie" Hairston worked for the Michigan United Fund Agency in Lansing. Afterwards, he was sent to California State University Northridge to participate in a leadership training program for the deaf. (Courtesy of Ernest Hairston.)

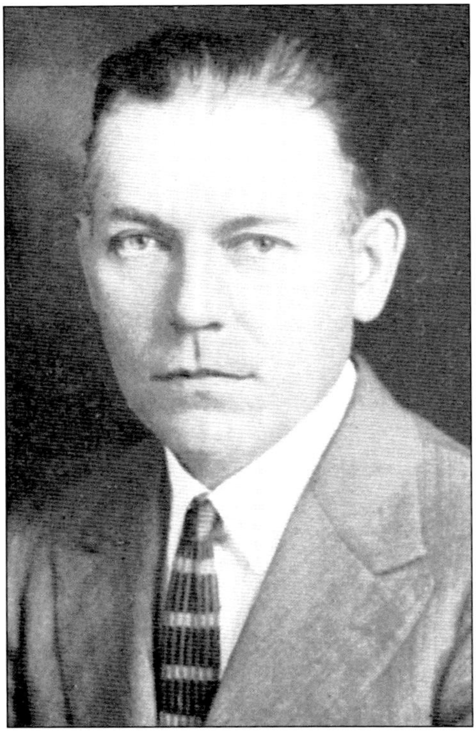

Henry Furman was one of the first DAD members in 1916. According to the *Silent Mute Journal*, he attended dental night school and worked for a dentist in the Detroit area. Furman placed a memorable classified ad in the October 1935 *Disc and Docket* newsletter: "Will the young lady who winked at me in Thompson's last Sat. night. Please meet me at the DAD next Sat. P.M. at nine? H. Furman." (Courtesy of DAD.)

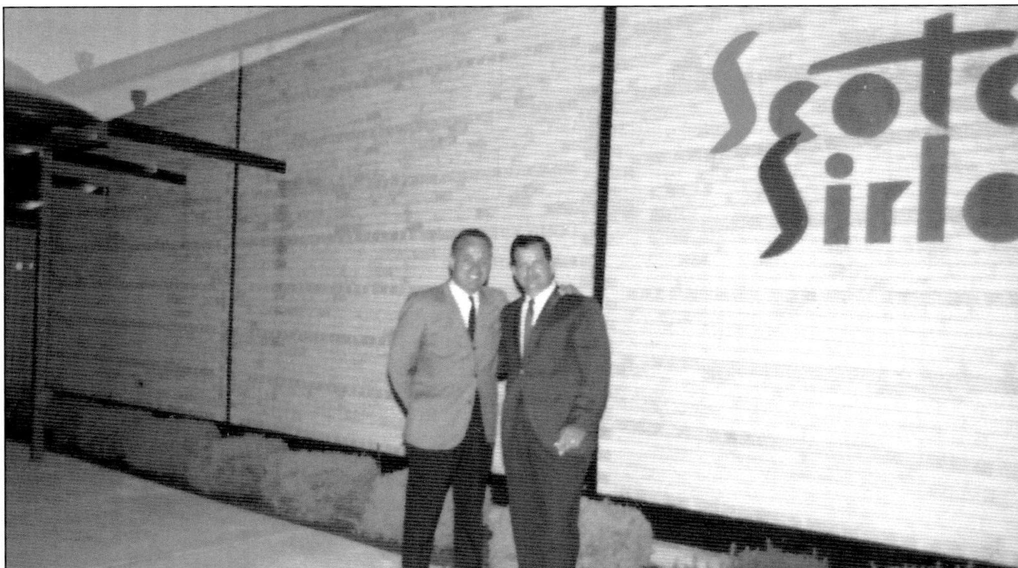

This photograph was taken in 1961 in front of the Scotch 'n' Sirloin restaurant, which Arlyn and his brother Jerry Meyerson ran. The restaurant carried 60 brands of Scotch whisky. The building was close to the Northland Playhouse, and actors and actresses often came by to eat after their performances. (Courtesy of Arlyn and Hester Meyerson.)

During the wintertime, beautiful snow covers Gladstone, Michigan. Pictured are John Wahowiak and his daughter Melvina Wahowiak McCall next to the family-owned Shoe Hospital building on the left. John ran the shoe repair shop before passing it down to his deaf son, Ray Wahowiak. The sign changed from Shoe Hospital to Electric Shoe Hospital with a nice quote: "We save your sole." Later, it was changed to Electric Shoe Shop. (Courtesy of Anson and Kathy McCall Mitchell.)

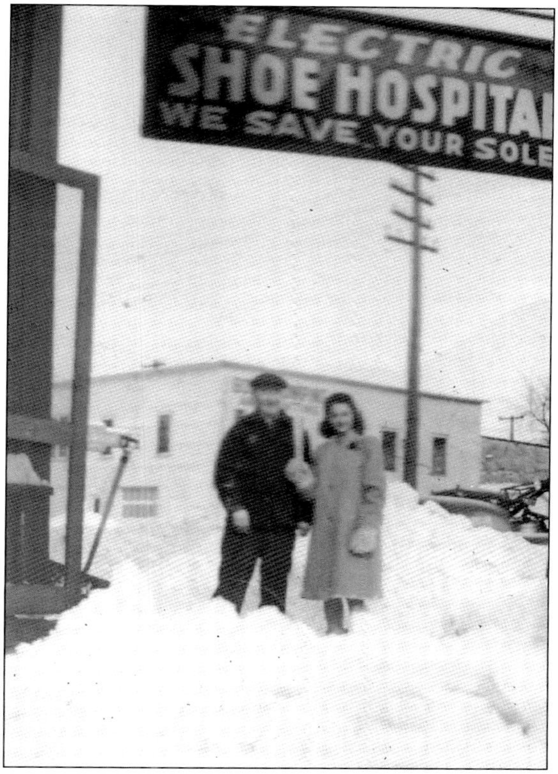

Some of the deaf residents of Gladstone, a nine-hour drive from the Detroit area, are heavily connected with DAD. From left to right are Mary Holberg, Georgianna Dumais Wahowiak, Melvina Wahowiak McCall (seated) John Wahowiak, and Ms. Holberg. Georgianna and John, Melvina's deaf parents, ran the shoe repair shop. (Courtesy of Anson and Kathy McCall Mitchell.)

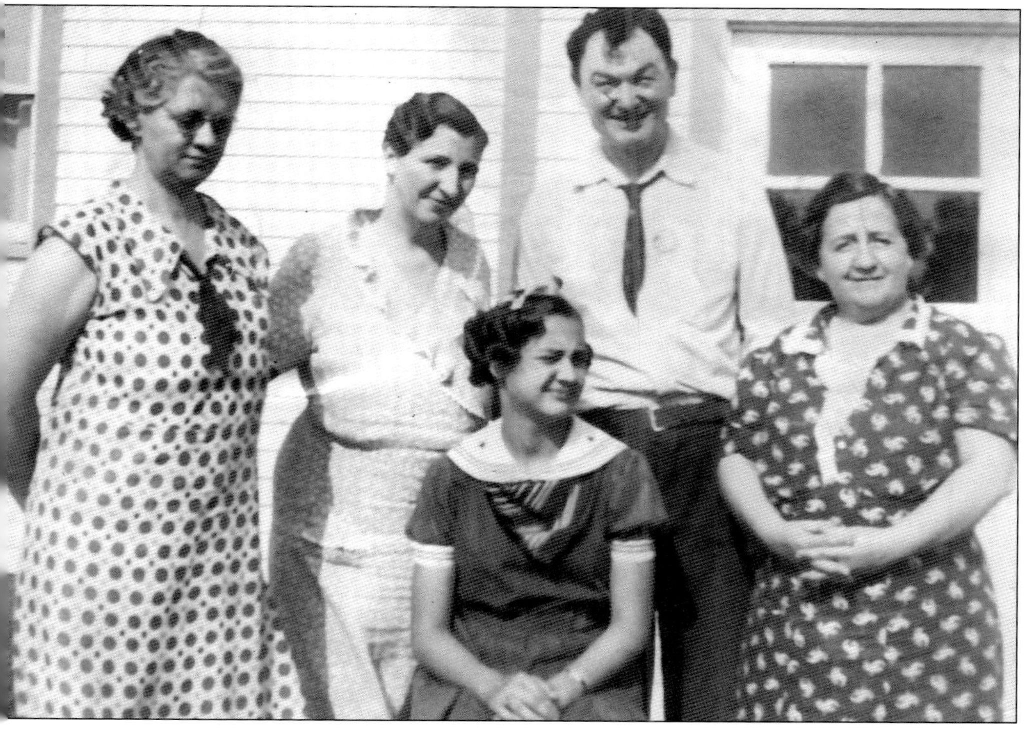

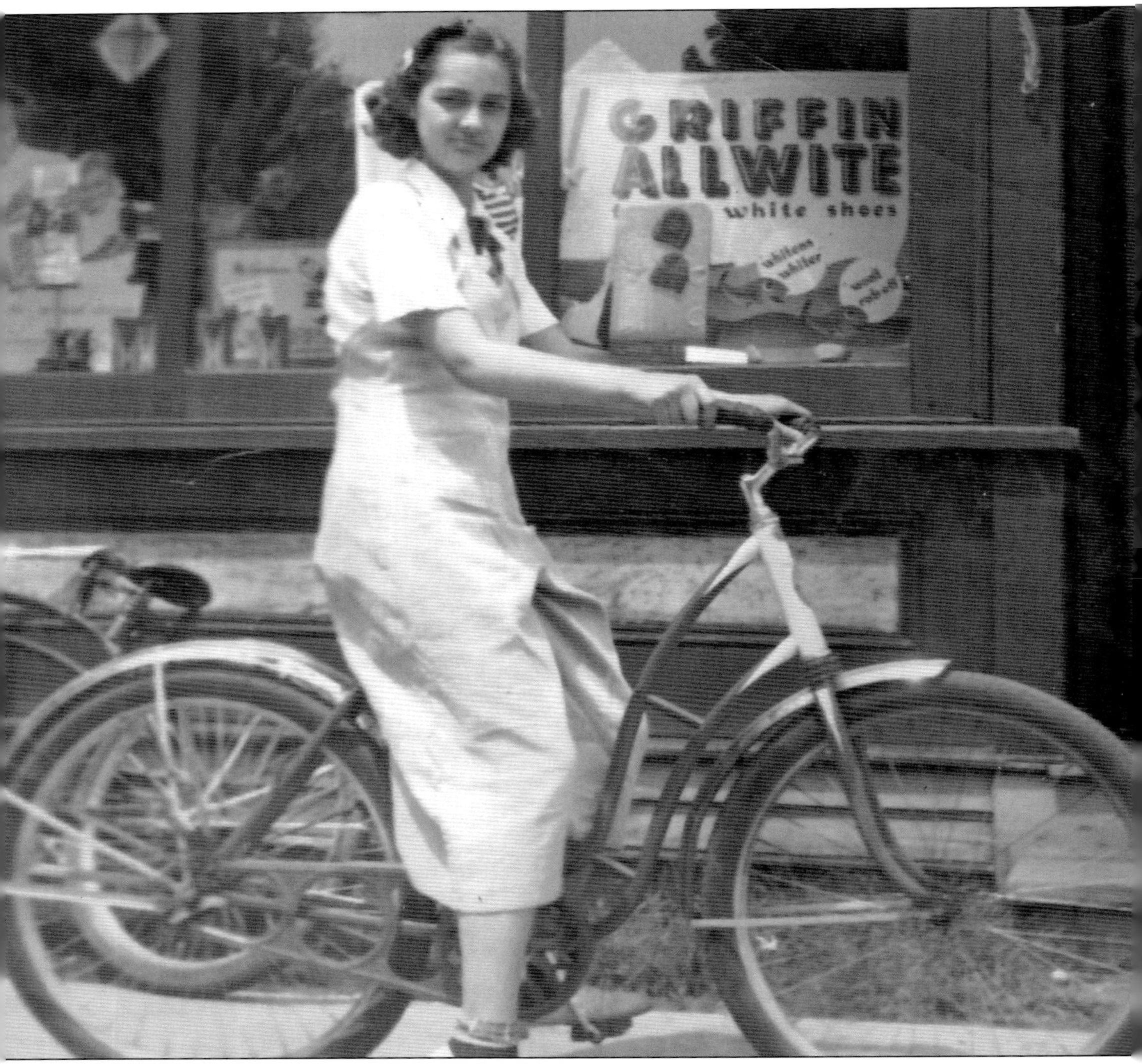

Melvina Wahowiak McCall sits on her bicycle in front of her deaf parents' shoe repair store. Later on, Melvina's brother, Ray, took over the business. It used to be located at 901 Minnesota Avenue in Gladstone. Today, the building has been converted into an apartment building with multiple units. Ray's hearing daughters recalled that the neighbors called them "dummy's daughters" and the store was called the "dummy shoe store." (Courtesy of Anson and Kathy McCall Mitchell.)

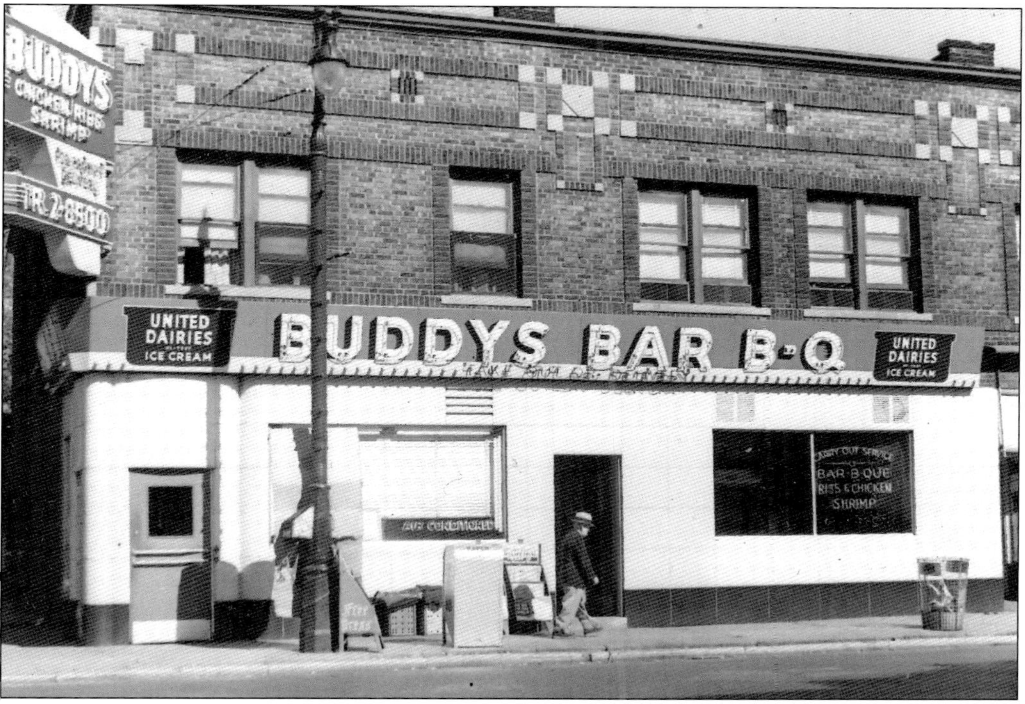

Shown in 1958, Arlyn Meyerson's father, Buddy, ran a restaurant, Buddy's BAR B-Q, at Twelfth Street and Clairmont Avenue from 1932 until 1961. Arlyn started to work there at 12 years old. Many deaf individuals from across the United States came to Detroit during World War II to work and lived near that restaurant. Arlyn quickly picked up sign language when he met a group of deaf New Yorkers who came to eat almost daily. (Courtesy of Arlyn and Hester Meyerson.)

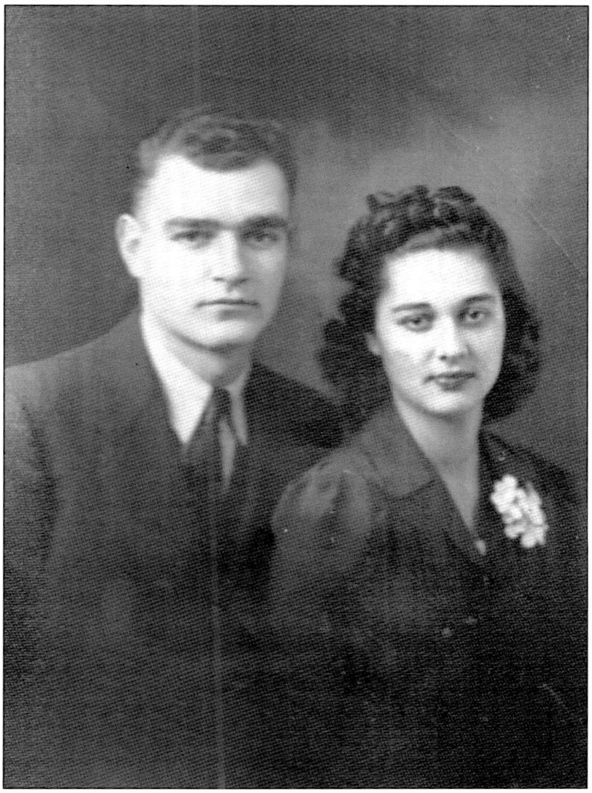

Shown here are Raymond "Ray" Wahowiak and his sister, Melvina Wahowiak McCall. Melvina graduated from MSD in 1941 as class valedictorian. Ray married "Joan" Germaine Oleniczak and took over his father's shoe shop in Gladstone. Ray and Joan gave birth to two hearing daughters. Melvina went on to marry Frederick "Fred" McCall and gave birth to four deaf children. (Courtesy of Anson and Kathy McCall Mitchell.)

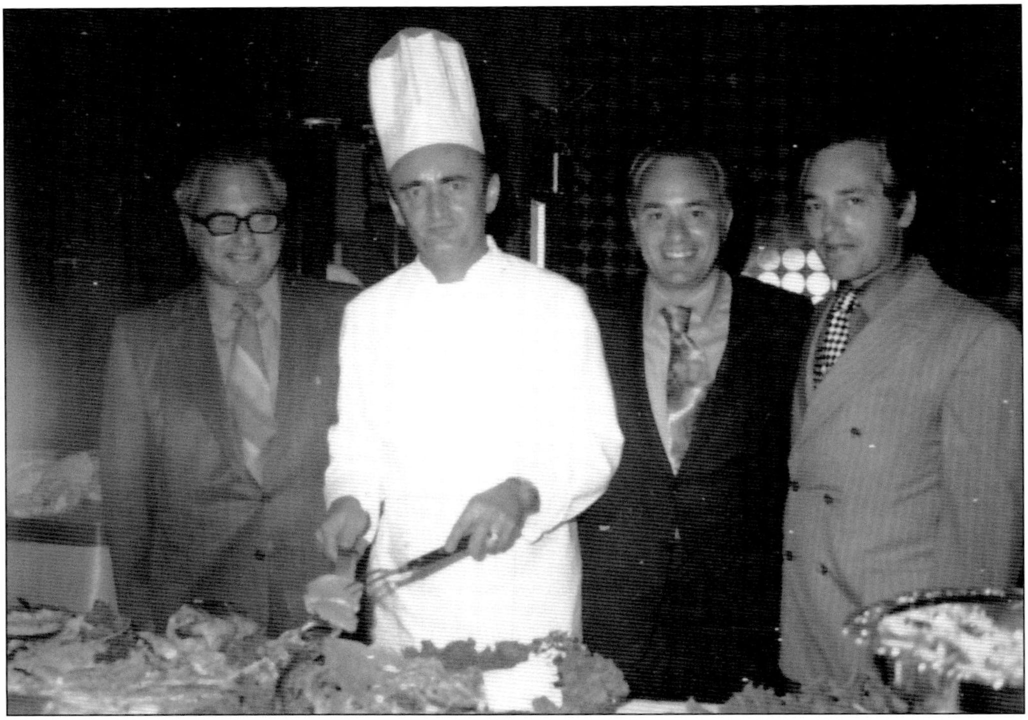

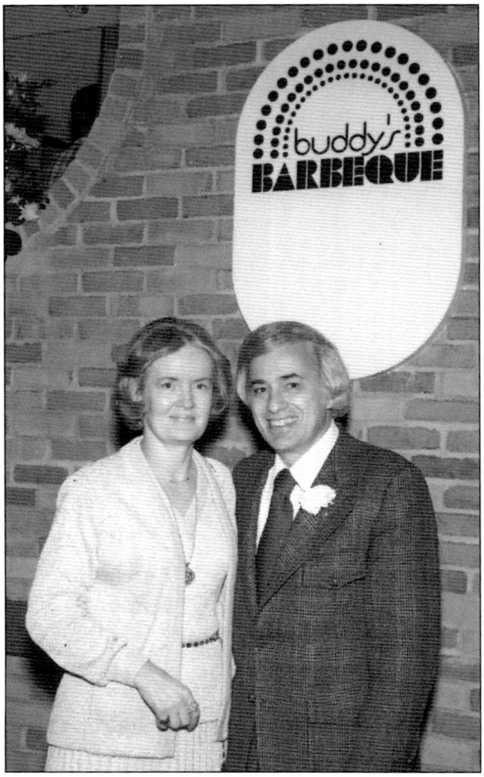

This c. 1965 photograph shows the Meyerson brothers with the chef at the Scotch 'n' Sirloin restaurant. From left to right are Jerry, the chef from Germany, Arlyn, and Aubrey. The brothers opened up the Trio at Franklin restaurant, which seated 400, in 1975 at 29200 Northwestern Highway in Southfield. Trio at Franklin was short-lived. (Courtesy of Arlyn and Hester Meyerson.)

After Trio at Franklin closed down, Arlyn became a salesman for World Book Encyclopedia and Kirby vacuums, and received a best salesman award in 1978. He and his wife, Hester, shown here, opened up Buddy's Barbeque in 1979, named after Arlyn's father. The restaurant seated 16 and offered carry-out orders. When Buddy's closed, Arlyn retired after 55 years in the restaurant business. (Courtesy of Arlyn and Hester Meyerson.)

Nine

Buildings

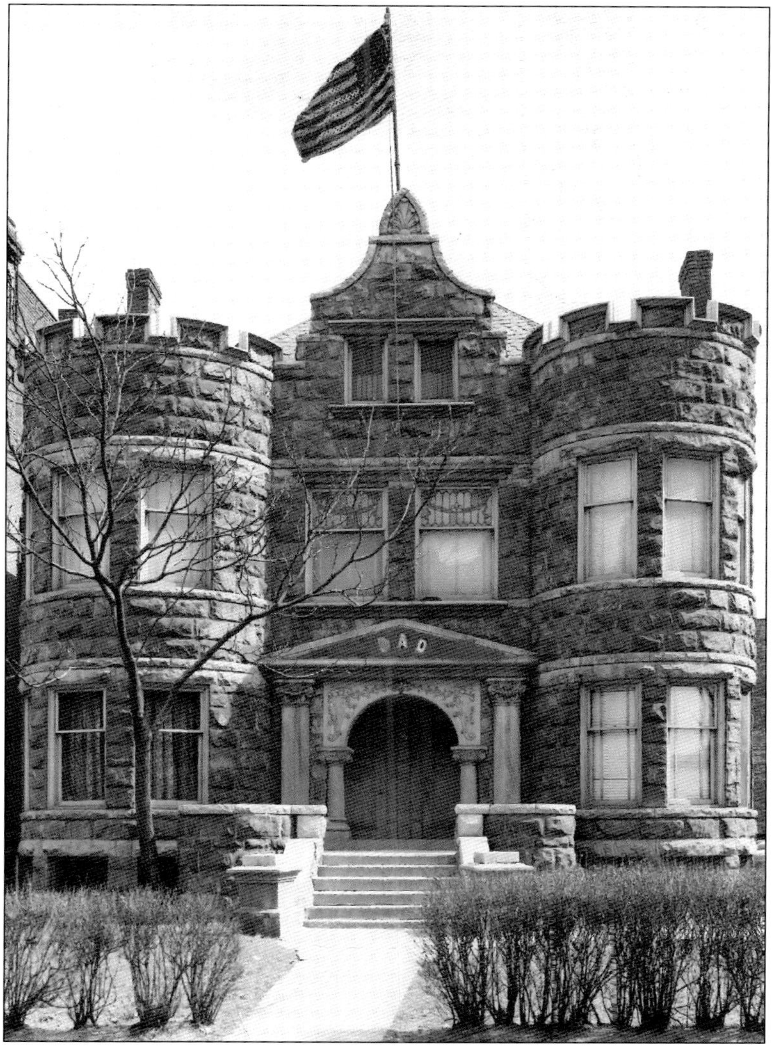

This beautiful building used to be owned by DAD. The stones over the front welcomed visitors with the letters "DAD." The building was located at 105 Davenport Street from 1950 to 1964. Its mortgage was paid off in 1955. After the club sold the building, it did not own another until 1968, as it rented various places. (Courtesy of DAD.)

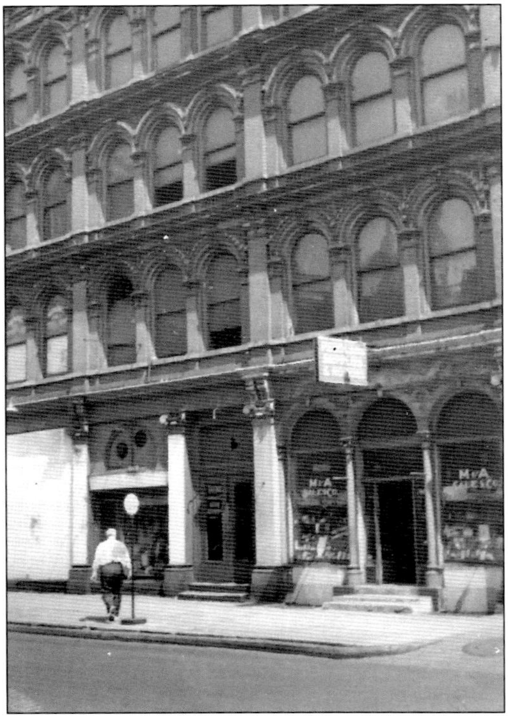

On October 16, 1916, the original "Rosedalers" started the Silent Athletic Club at 272 Rosedale Court, where Benjamin and Ralph Beaver lived with their mother. They later decided to establish DAD on Monroe Avenue. The only furnishing they had was the stove, and at business meetings, members stood in a circle. Emanuel M. Jacobs became the first president and is considered the founder. Ivor Friday encouraged the plan with other members, including Benjamin and Ralph Beaver. (Courtesy of DAD.)

When the membership grew, the group decided to move to Woodward Avenue between Jefferson and East Larnerd Streets. The club consisted of two small rooms with a card table and a few chairs. According to the 1929 program book for DAD, the members proudly escorted their lady visitors, showing off the nice little clubroom. When the club moved to Griswold Street, they added the pool table shown here. (Courtesy of DAD.)

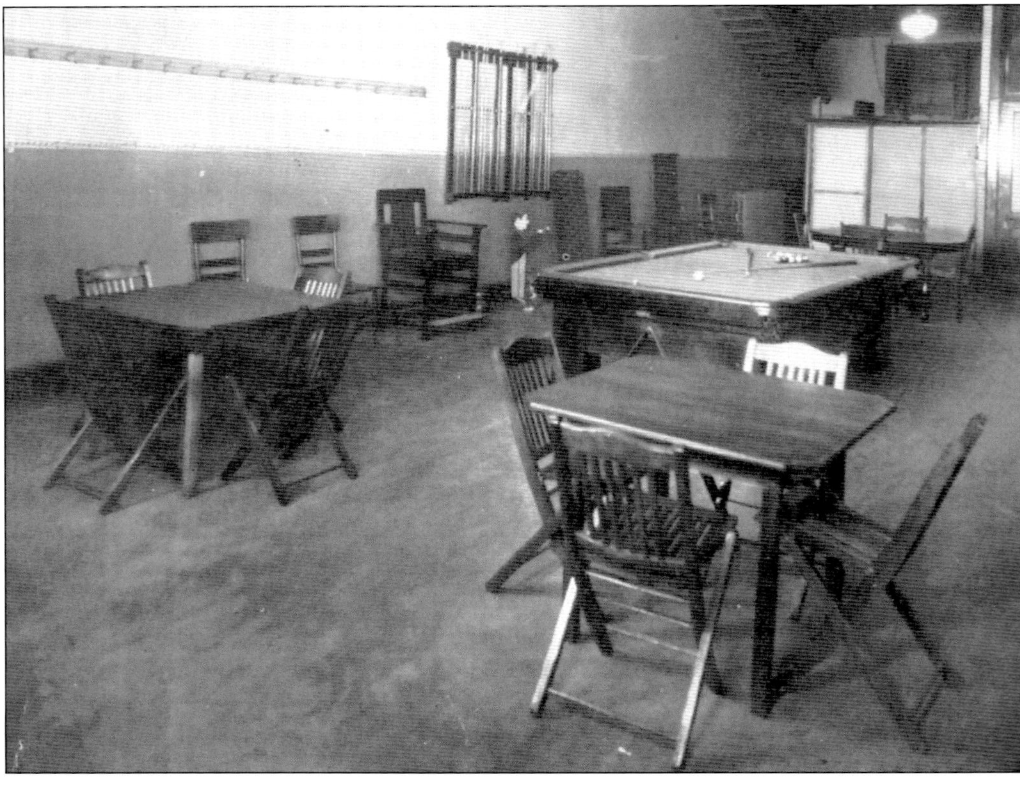

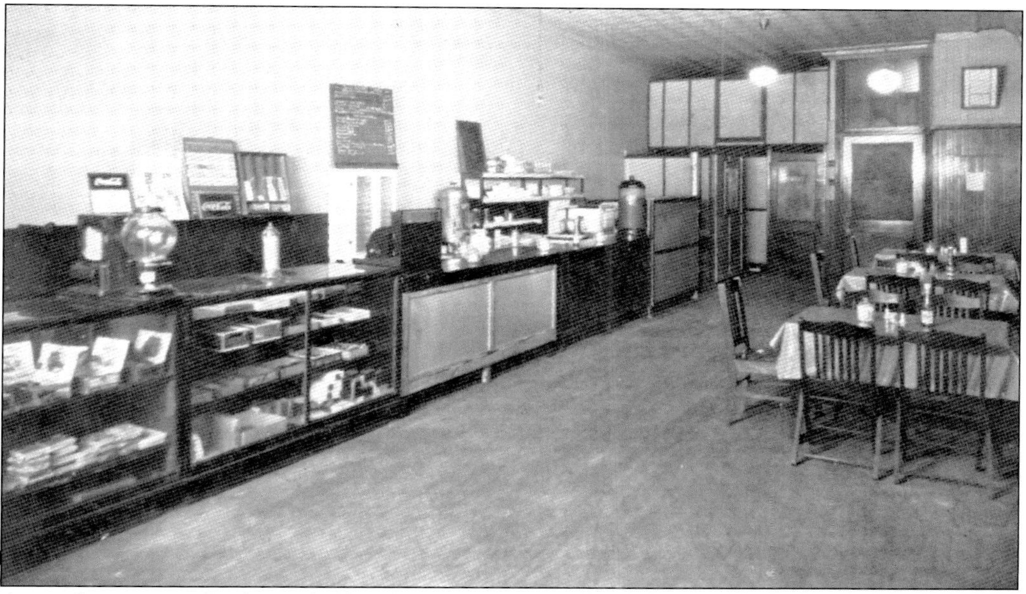

A new location with a larger hall and a separate poolroom was secured after the club outgrew its Farmer Street room. More furniture was added, and more public socials and lectures were given. Officially, DAD became incorporated at that location in 1918. (Courtesy of DAD.)

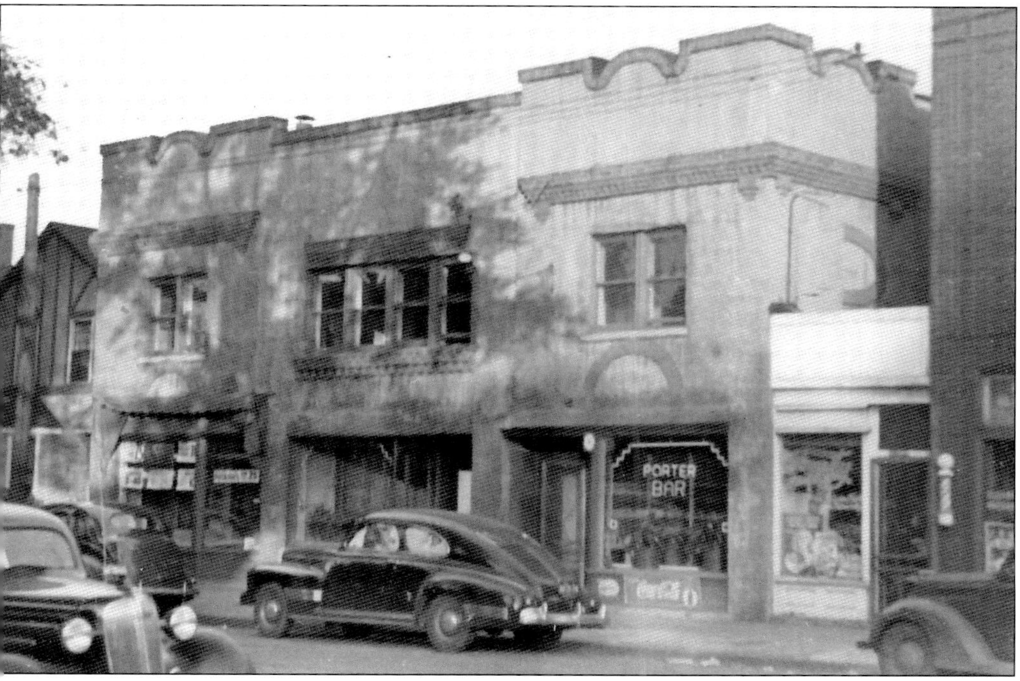

After the rooms at 8 East Jefferson Avenue were outgrown, the club moved to a bigger hall on Porter Street near Scotten Avenue with two floors. DAD also had great members devoted to carpentry, with S. Seppanen, Carl Frederick, and Tony Czubeck as the handymen. Frank Rocco was a comic stage star. All four were products of MSD. During that post–World War I time, many lost jobs, and the membership decreased. (Courtesy of DAD.)

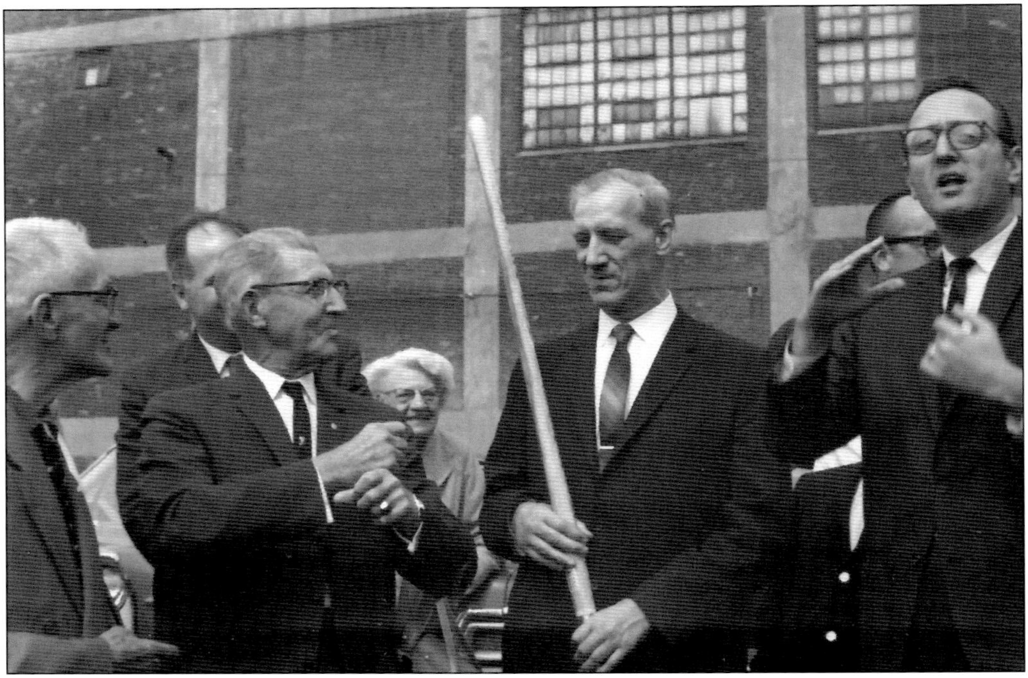

From left to right, unidentified; Benjamin Beaver; Harold M. Ryan, a former congressman and a lawyer; and Judge Joseph Pernick, child of a deaf parent, mingle on the land where the new DAD clubhouse was built in May 1966. The *Detroit News* stated, "Building for Deaf, groundbreaking ceremonies for a new social center for the DAD were held yesterday at Third and Abbott site." (Courtesy of DAD.)

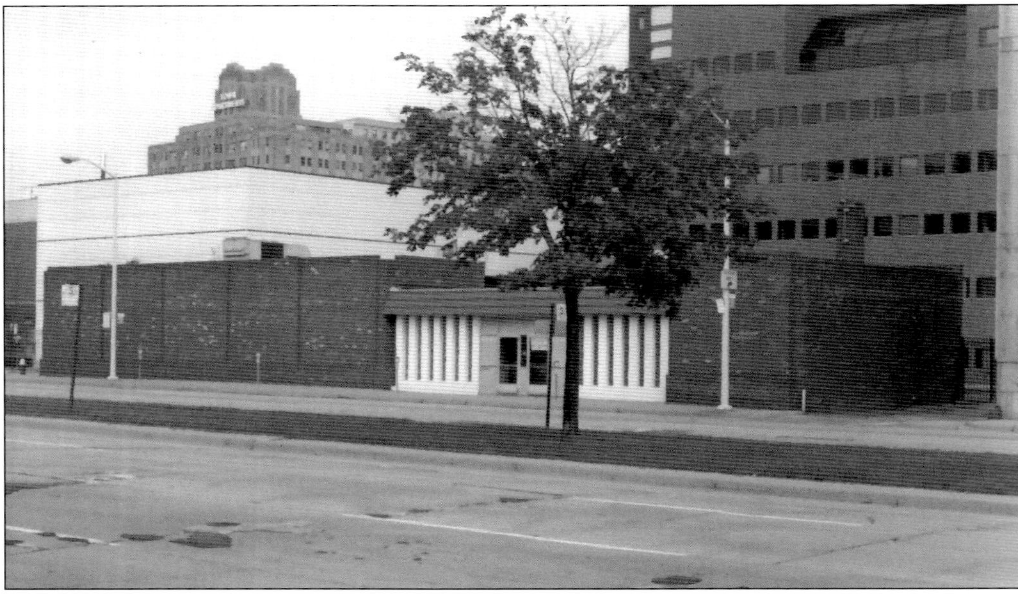

This popular clubhouse was at 1240 Third Boulevard, DAD's best location. However, it had to be sold due to financial difficulties. Today, the building stands next to the casino and nearby stadiums in downtown Detroit. (Courtesy of DAD.)

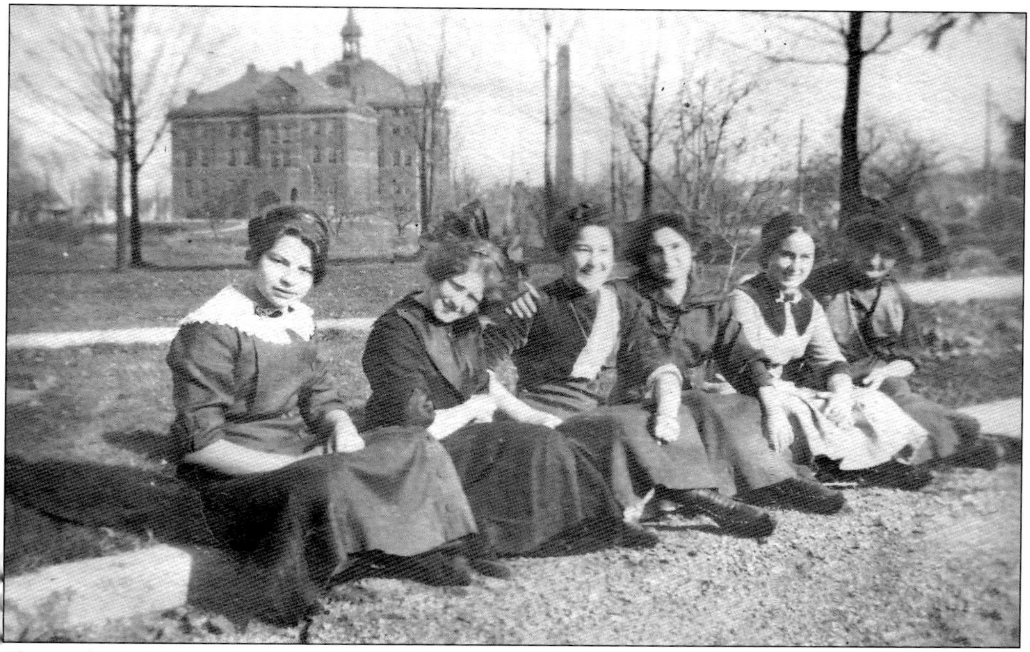

Shown here is one of the earliest MSD buildings, possibly Brown Hall, with a group of MSD girls sitting in front. Brown Hall was built in 1899 and opened in 1900. Georgianna Dumais Wahowiak attended MSD at that time along with other Dumais, Wahowiak, and McCall deaf families. (Courtesy of Anson and Kathy McCall Mitchell.)

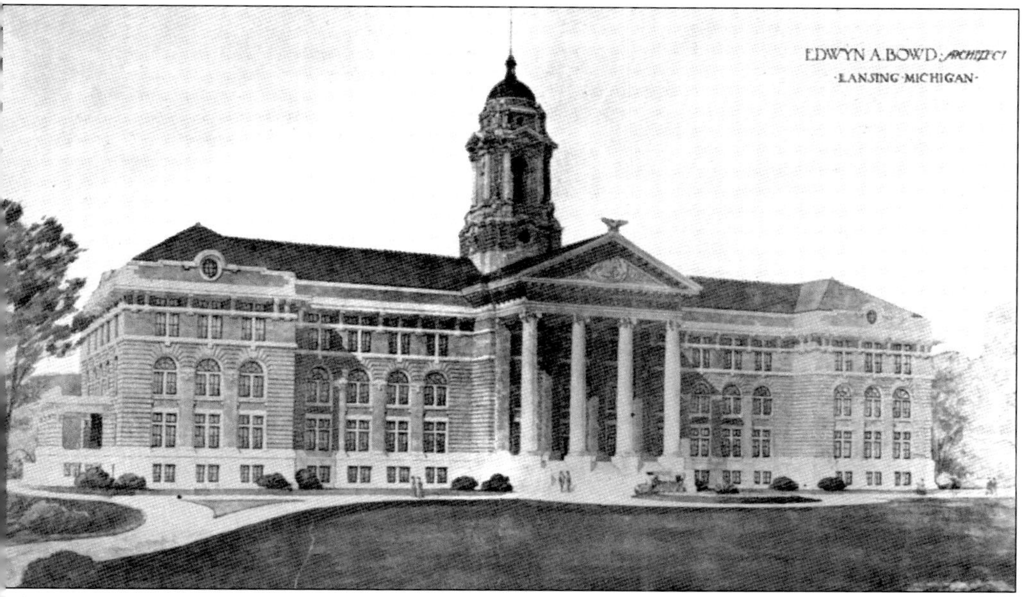

Edwyn A. Boyd, an architect in Lansing, designed the original MSD building. The superintendent, Francis Clarke, ran the school before the building burned down in 1912. The building was reconstructed in 1913 as close as possible to the original design without the top as Fay Hall, which still stands today. It was bought by a developer in 2011 along with the entire campus. Powers Catholic High School is now using the renovated building. (Courtesy of *MSD* magazine.)

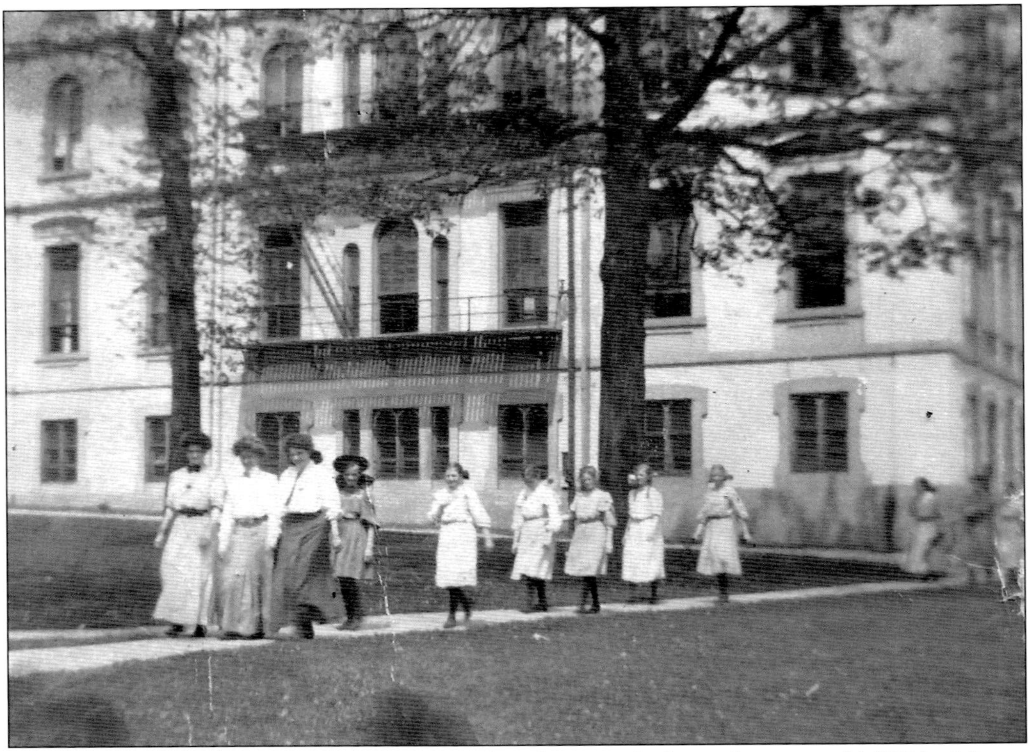

This photograph shows the original MSD building before the fire destroyed it in 1912. The new building opened its doors for classes in 1914. (Courtesy of Anson and Kathy McCall Mitchell.)

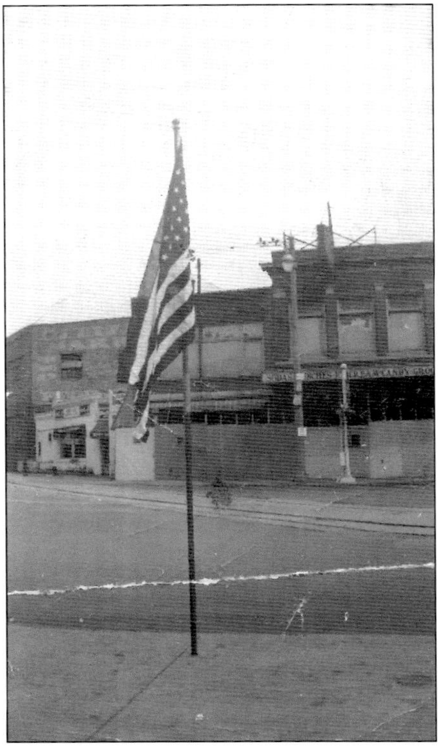

Shown is one of the earliest buildings rented by FAD at 100 1/2 South Saginaw Street, in the heart of Flint's business district. The club was established on February 19, 1919, by a group of deaf men. According to meeting minutes written in the fragile journal on September 19, 1923, the motion was approved to start welcoming ladies in October 1923. The separate Flint ladies auxiliary was founded in 1930 with Lillie Bristol as the first president. (Courtesy of FAD.)

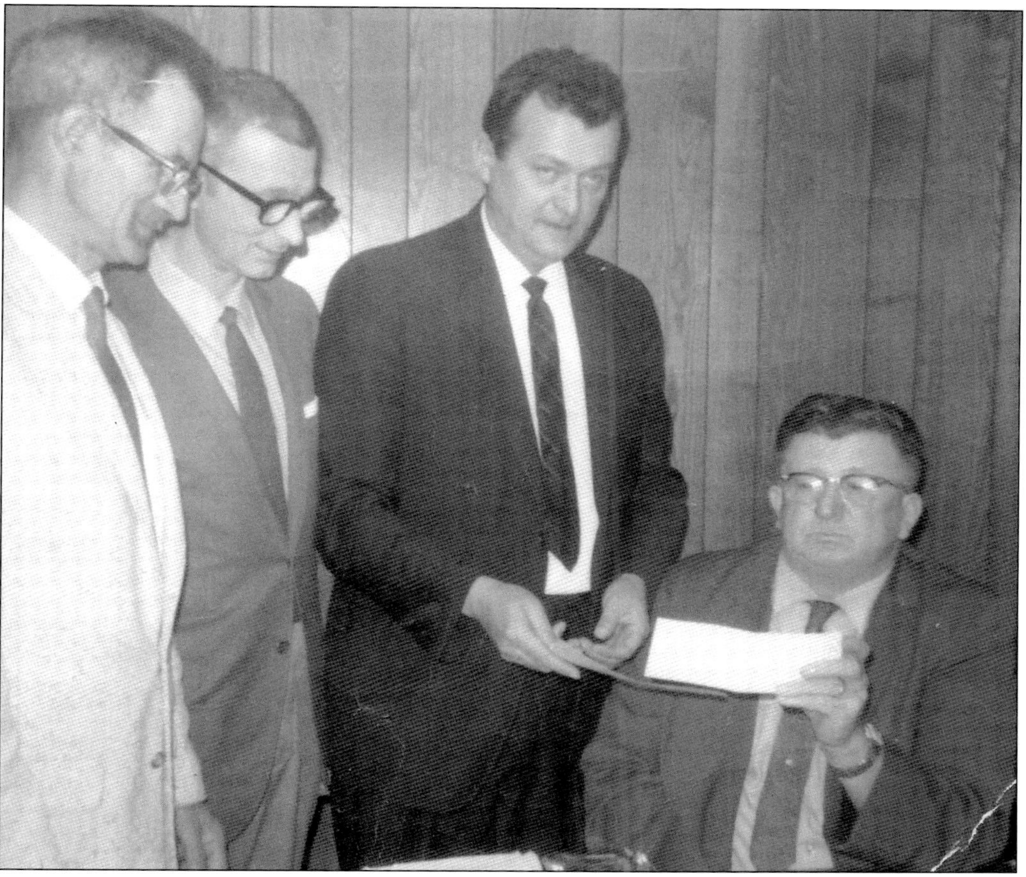

In April 1969, from left to right, Clayton Riechelt, Henry Dreuth, Gerald Mahoney (holding the check) and a realtor closed the sale of 4156 Holiday Drive for a new FAD building. The building below still stands as possibly one of the oldest deaf-owned club buildings in America. The property includes a nice pavilion and a big parking lot. Inside the building is a barroom, a stage, an office, and other rooms with televisions. This building is shared with the FAD Ladies Auxiliary and FAD members. (Both, courtesy of FAD.)

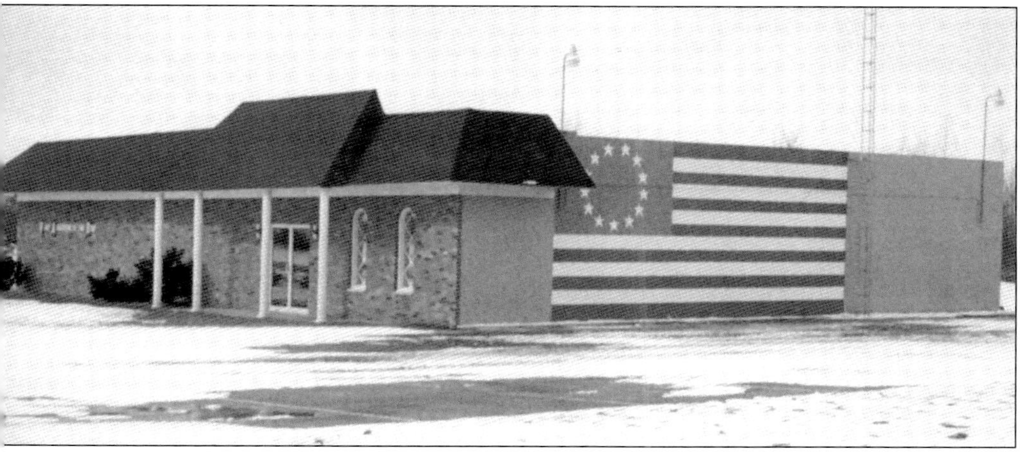

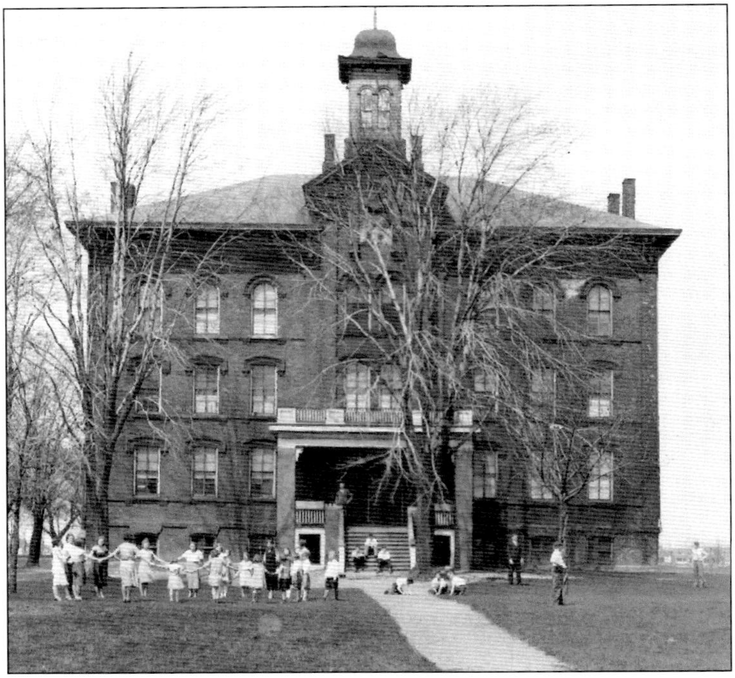

What was originally called the German Lutheran School for the Deaf Mutes was set up in 1873 with Pastor George Speckhard as the first superintendent. Speckhard took in two girl pupils as the first students, and the number grew to 17 in the first year. LSD stood on a 20-acre farm site approximately eight miles from downtown Detroit. In 1939, the old building was replaced with the present complex of buildings at 6861 Nevada Avenue in Detroit. (Courtesy of Judy and Larry Vardon.)

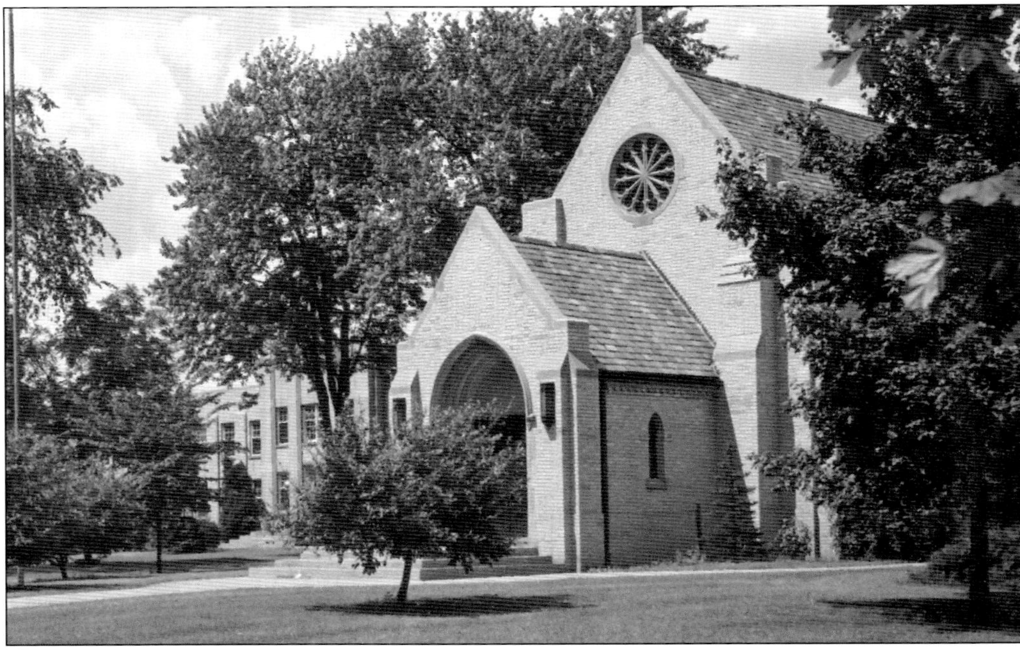

This beautifully designed Lutheran Church of the Deaf building was constructed in 1939 on the LSD campus somewhat in front of the school building. The building was called the Gloria Dei Clara Elizabeth Knudsen Chapel. William S. Knudsen donated $60,000 for the chapel, and it was officially opened in May 1940 with Gov. Luren Dickinson and Mayor Edward Jeffries present. Back then, there was a German-English service beginning at 10:30 a.m. and an English service later in the afternoon. (Courtesy of Judy and Larry Vardon.)

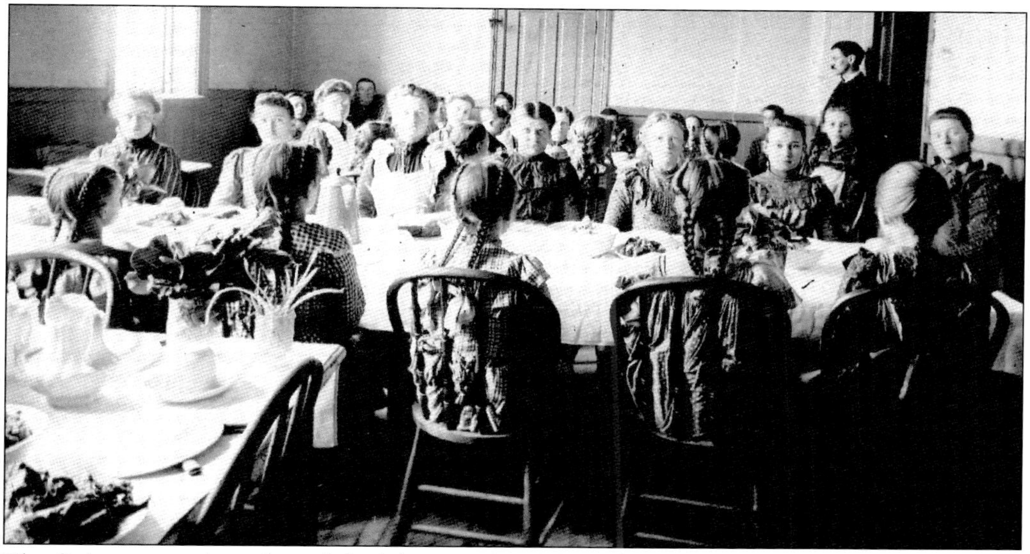

The dining room where the girls had their meals at LSD is shown here, possibly in the early 1880s. This image was taken during the first years of the school's existence. Limited finances made only the barest necessities possible. The pioneers had to work hard to get donations. Generous gifts made the school a modern institution that lasted for years until the doors were closed indefinitely. (Courtesy of Judy and Larry Vardon.)

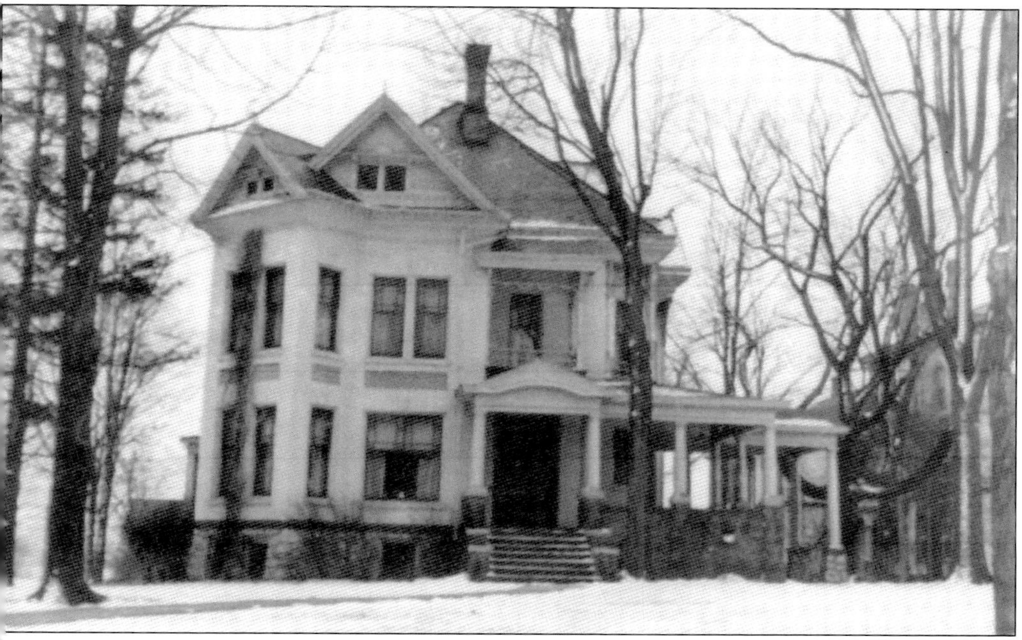

The superintendent's cottage at MSD was completed in 1890. Almost all the boys attending MSD helped to build the cottage by hand, including the exquisitely carved furniture. Francis Clarke was the first superintendent to live in that cottage, from 1892 to 1913. Today, the landmark belongs to a developer who purchased the land in 2011 under protest from the Deaf Community. One protester stated that this cottage really belongs to the Deaf Community. (Courtesy of John and Donna Delikta Klarr.)

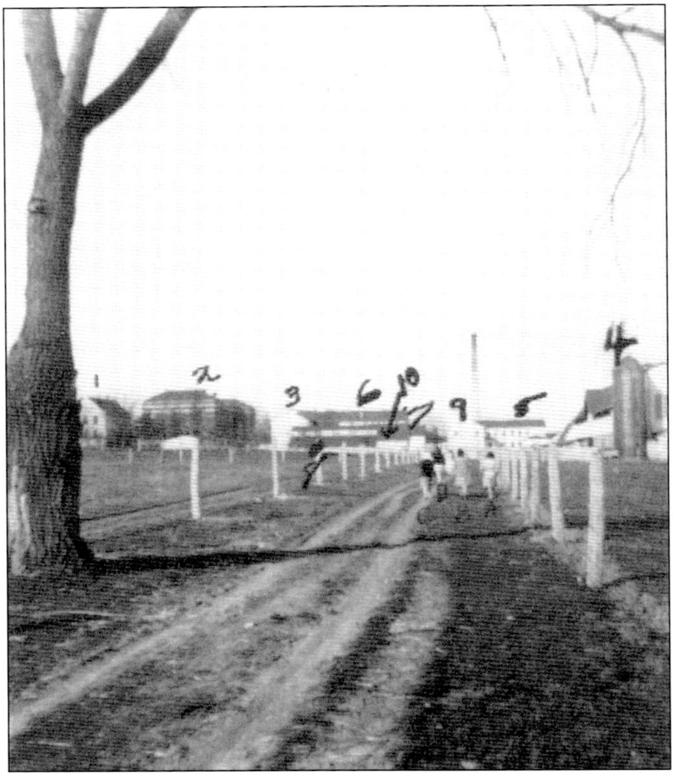

This photograph shows older buildings on the MSD campus in its earlier days. Numbers written on the photograph identify the buildings: 1. Gilbert Hall; 2. Fay Hall; 3. Orchard House; 4. Cow Barn Farm; 5. Power House; 6. Brown Hall; 7. unknown; 8. Steven Hall; 9. unknown; and 10. unknown. Many are gone today, and Fay Hall has been sold to a developer; Powers Catholic High School is currently using it. The MSD name is still carved on the sign topping Fay Hall's beautiful columns. (Courtesy of John and Donna Delikta Klarr.)

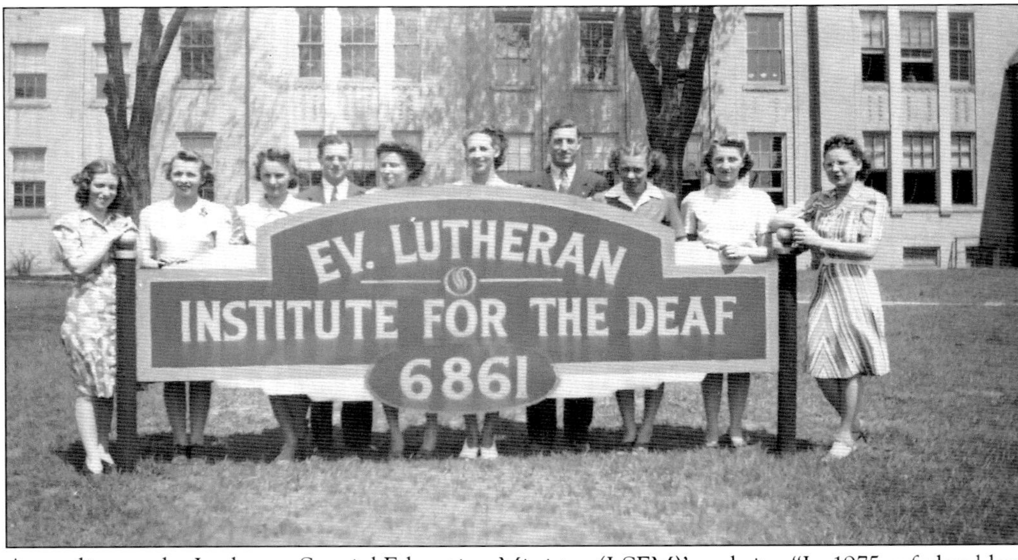

According to the Lutheran Special Education Ministry (LSEM)'s website, "In 1975, a federal law was passed mandating that public schools provide education for all handicapped children. This law and medical advances resulted in a dramatic decrease in the number of children attending the school. The ministry's focus shifted once again. Rather than close the doors, the board of trustees opened them wider." LSEM was relocated to Farmington Hills. (Courtesy of Judy and Larry Vardon.)

Ten

Special Memories

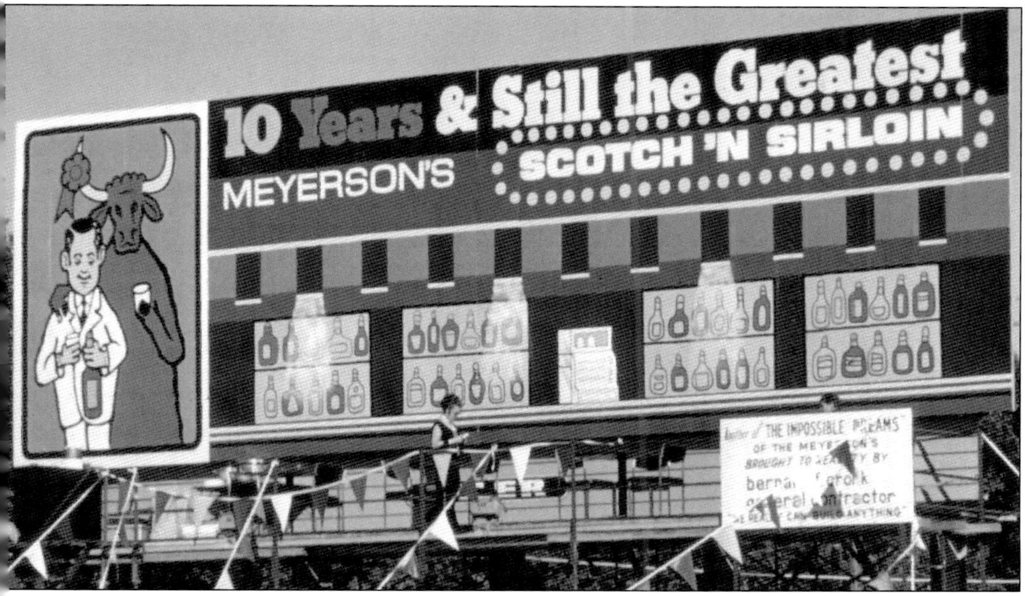

This unique billboard was set up in 1971 where the John Lodge Freeway connects to the Northwest Highway. The Meyerson brothers, owners of the Scotch 'n' Sirloin, celebrated 10 years in the restaurant business. Notice the platform with the tables and chairs set up in the front of the billboard. Waynette Hosteler was hired as a hostess for one day with a city permit to serve real drinks. Waynette is the daughter of deaf parents, Jayne and Wayne Hosteler. (Courtesy of Arlyn and Hester Meyerson.)

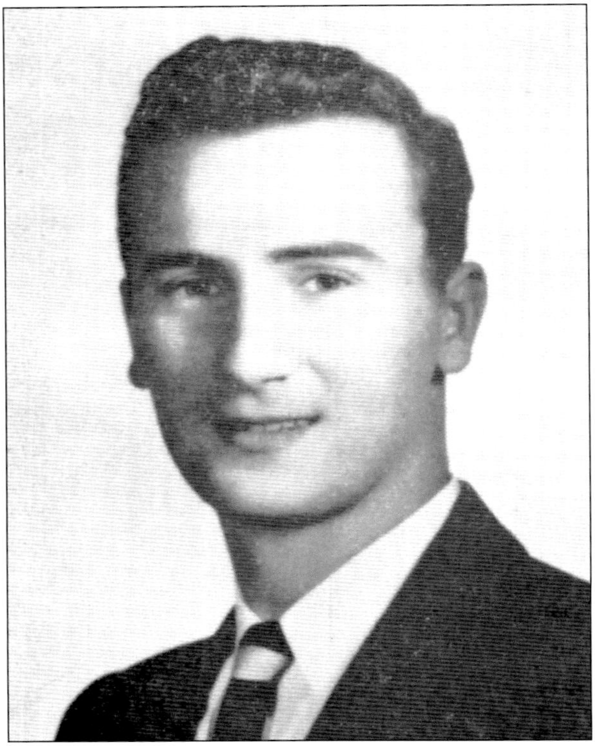

The four deaf gentlemen who died in a car accident during icy weather in 1962 will always be remembered. They were supposed to attend an invitational basketball tournament in Pittsburgh, a requirement to get an entry in the CAAD tournament. Valerio "Val" DiFalco, shown here, was the basketball coach for MCAD at the time of his death. He played softball and basketball until his knees gave out, then began managing and coaching. (Courtesy of William and Diane Knight.)

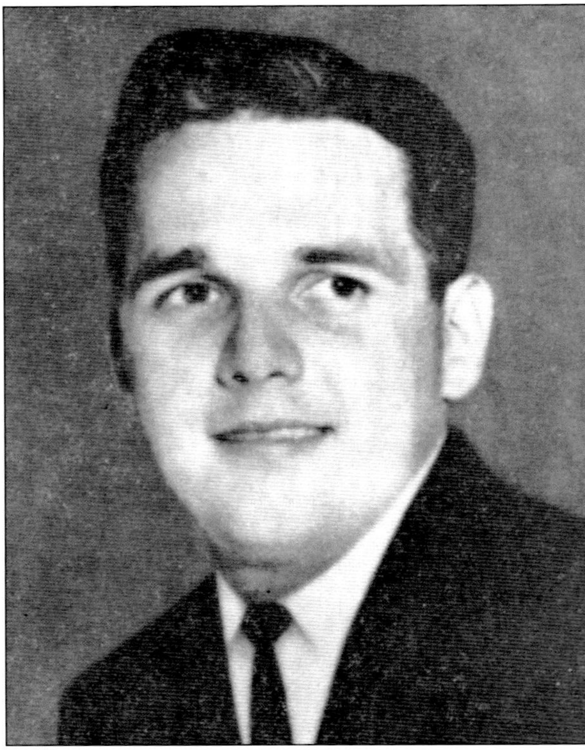

William "Bill" Knight III captained the MCAD basketball team for two years. He had played softball and was recognized for the all-tourney team as a short stop at a Chicago tournament in 1955. Golfing in the summers was his other activity. At the time of his death, he had lived in a new house for a couple of years with his wife, Diane, and their son, with a daughter on the way. (Courtesy of William and Diane Knight.)

Carroll C. Wood earned seven varsity letters in all sports at MSD. He was remembered for having once scored a record 53 points in one basketball game. A few relatives remembered him standing out in a crowd at six feet, three inches tall. At the time of his death, he was employed by the *Wayne Dispatch* as a linotype operator. His twin sister, Carole, was a student at Gallaudet at the time. (Courtesy of William and Diane Knight.)

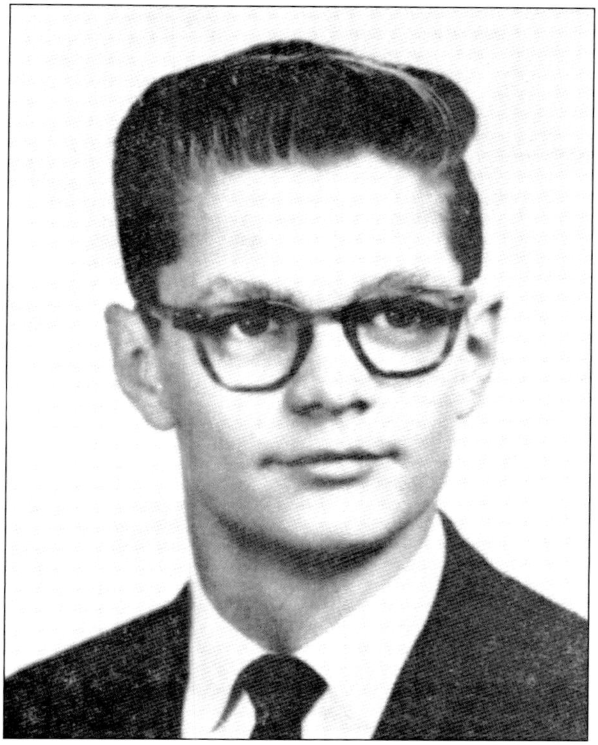

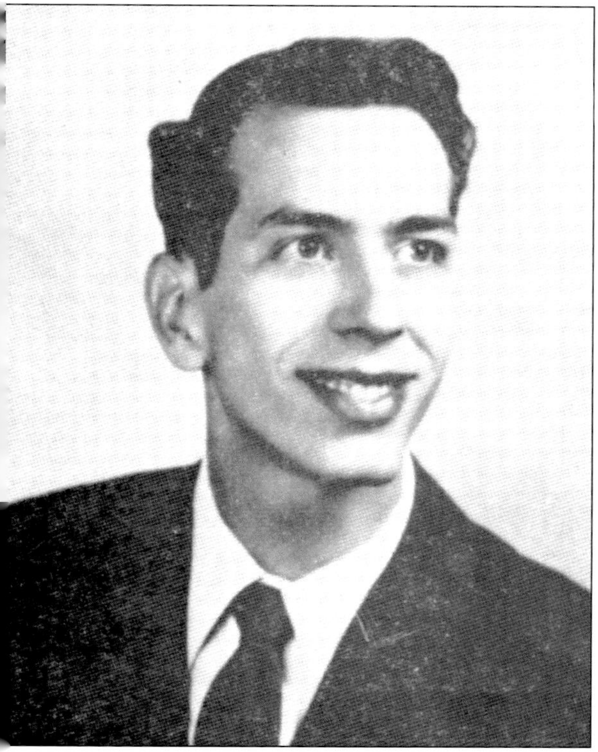

Marvin R. Pierce was well liked by everybody who attended Missouri School for the Deaf before he transferred to Michigan, and he graduated from MSD in 1955. He earned 10 varsity letters at school. He played for MCAD for a few years and performed well, scoring 17 points in one game before his death. (William and Diane Knight.)

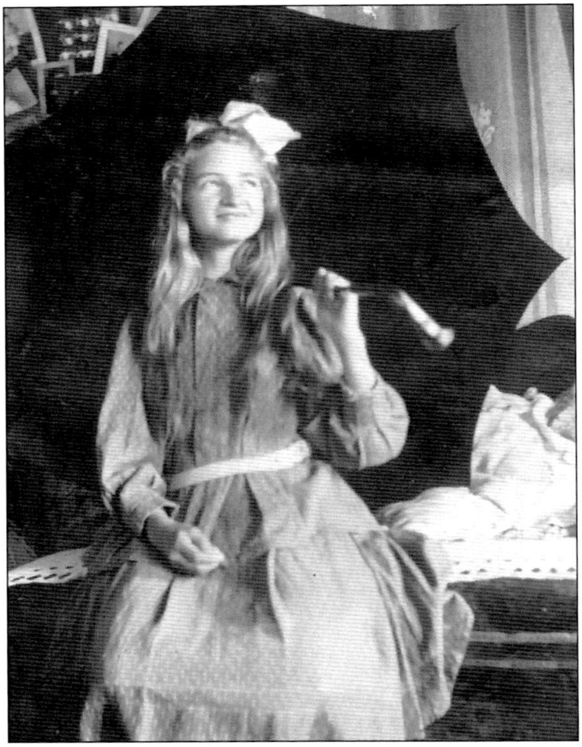

Mary Dumais, Melvina Wahowiak McCall's mother and Georgianna's deaf sister, died at 18 due to a ruptured appendix at home in the Upper Peninsula. She attended MSD with her sister. She is dressed up and looking happy in this photograph. (Courtesy of Anson and Kathy McCall Mitchell.)

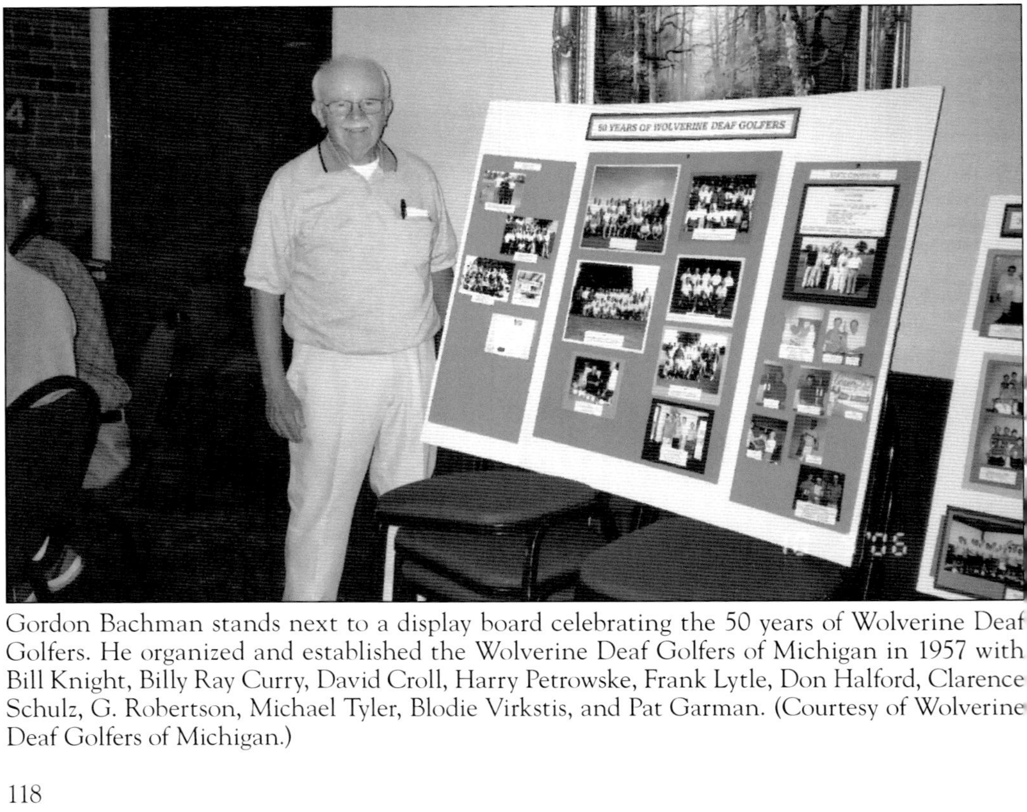

Gordon Bachman stands next to a display board celebrating the 50 years of Wolverine Deaf Golfers. He organized and established the Wolverine Deaf Golfers of Michigan in 1957 with Bill Knight, Billy Ray Curry, David Croll, Harry Petrowske, Frank Lytle, Don Halford, Clarence Schulz, G. Robertson, Michael Tyler, Blodie Virkstis, and Pat Garman. (Courtesy of Wolverine Deaf Golfers of Michigan.)

One of the most memorable events at LSD was the film *A New Life for Jennifer,* which was made during the school day in the classroom with Jennifer Freed as the star. The film was released in September 1964 after $30,000 had been spent on production. At the time, the deaf-oral students were doing the oral method, while the girls learned the signs in private lessons with their deaf houseparent, MSD alumna Sandra Evans. (Courtesy of Judy and Larry Vardon.)

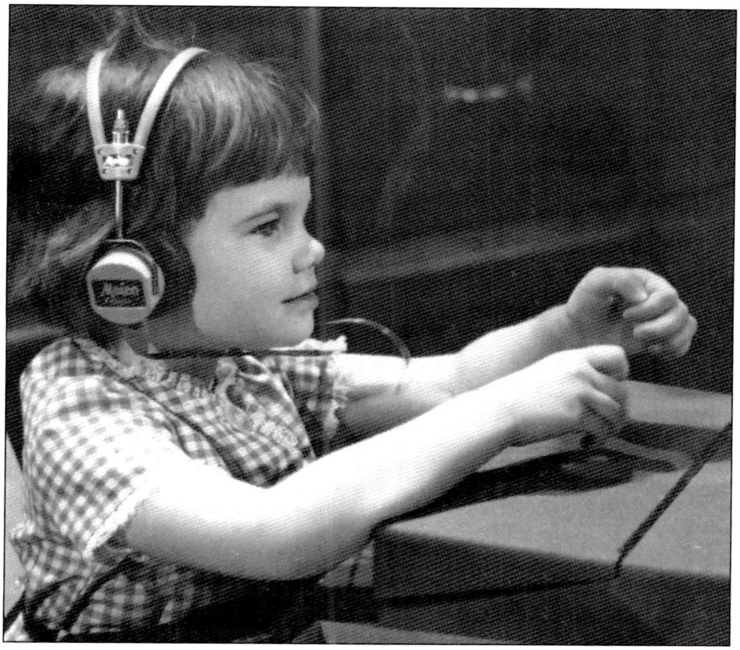

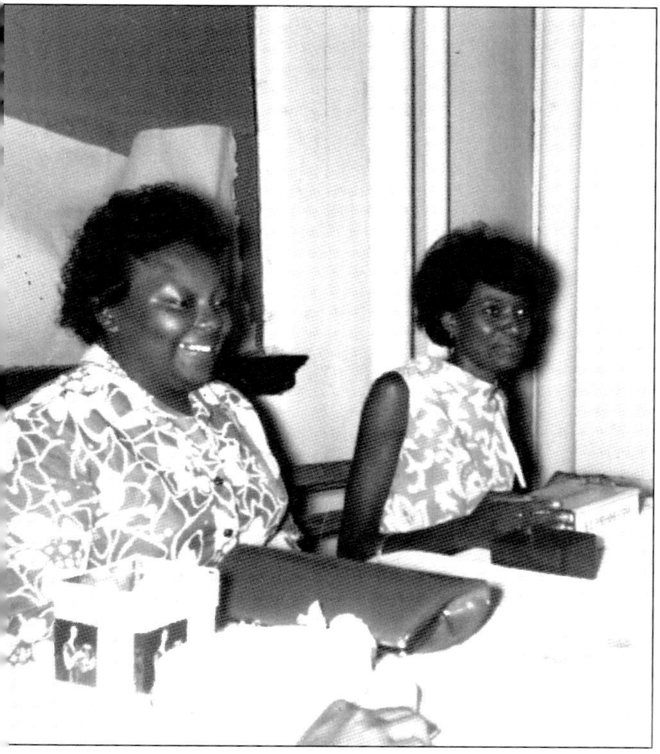

In the early Detroit Silent Club days, Ruby Tailson (left) and Rosa Ella Rollins (right) were activists among the black Deaf Community in the Detroit metro area. This photograph was taken in September 1968. (Courtesy of Glenn and Susan Stewart.)

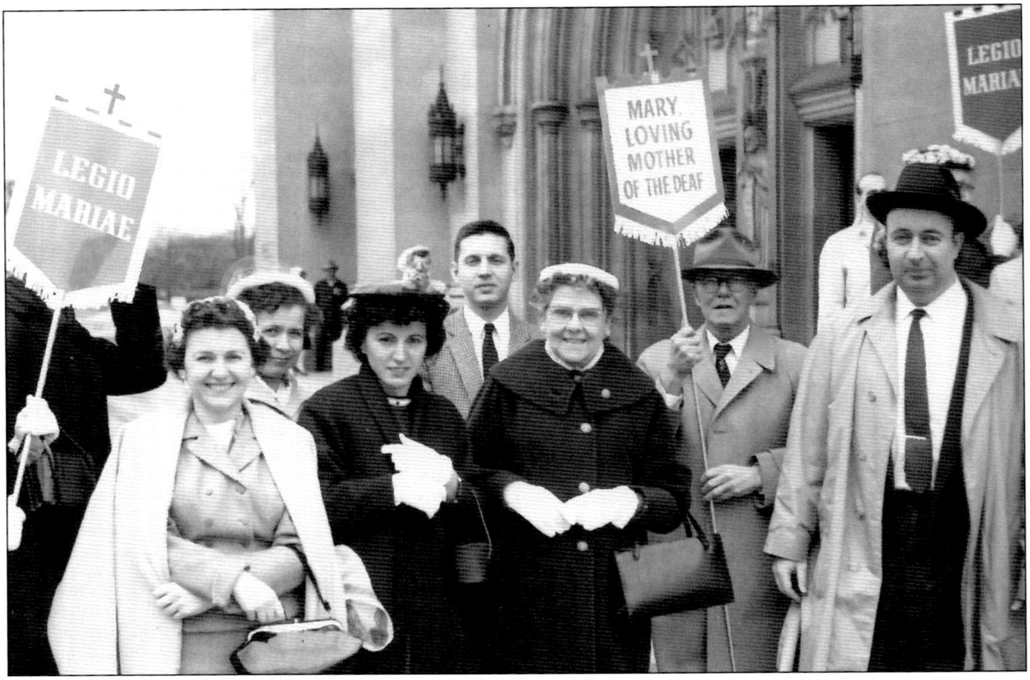

This photograph was taken around 1959. The two second and third from the right are believed to be Alexander and Anette Lobsinger, who were longtime Catholic deaf organization activists and DAD members since they came from Canada in 1920. (Courtesy of SJDC.)

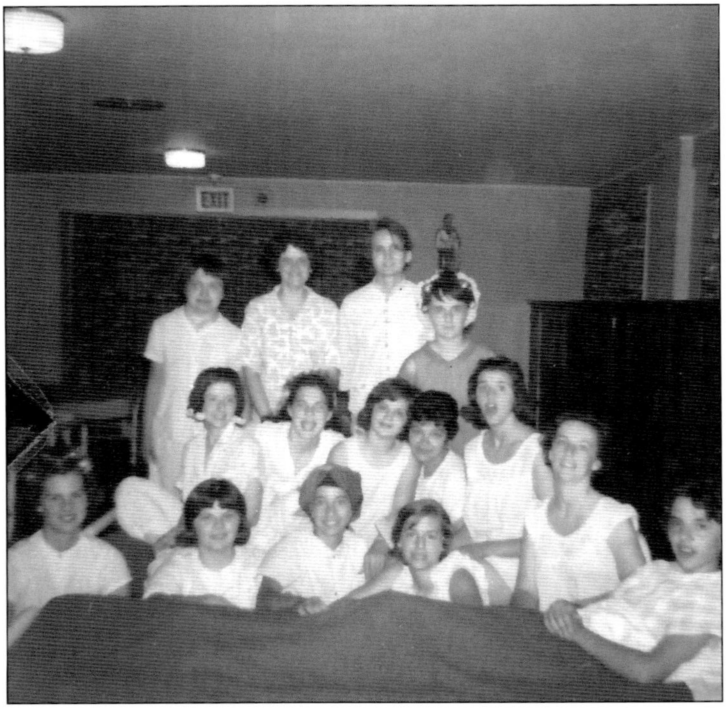

Picture in the dormitory at DDSD around the 1950s are, from left to right, (first row) Valerie Lerdahl, Joanne Wojnarowski, Susan Wilson, Arlene Lerdahl, Sue Flanagan, and Barbara Glenak; (second row) Linda Landino, Jean Scott, Janice Wojnarowski, Kathy Dunigan, and Ellen Davidson; (third row) Carol Telish, Kathy McElmeel, Mary Ann Melody, and Kathy Murphy. (Courtesy of John and Donna Delikta Klarr.)

Shown in August 2002 are Leon Fairfax (far right) and his wife, Leaner Fairfax (center). Leon was a passionate supporter of Detroit Black Deaf Advocates and a DDSD alumnus. He was also an active member of the Detroit Silent Club in the 1970s and 1980s, where he played softball. He was employed by the post office for over 30 years and passed away on May 19, 2015. (Courtesy of Glenn and Susan Stewart.)

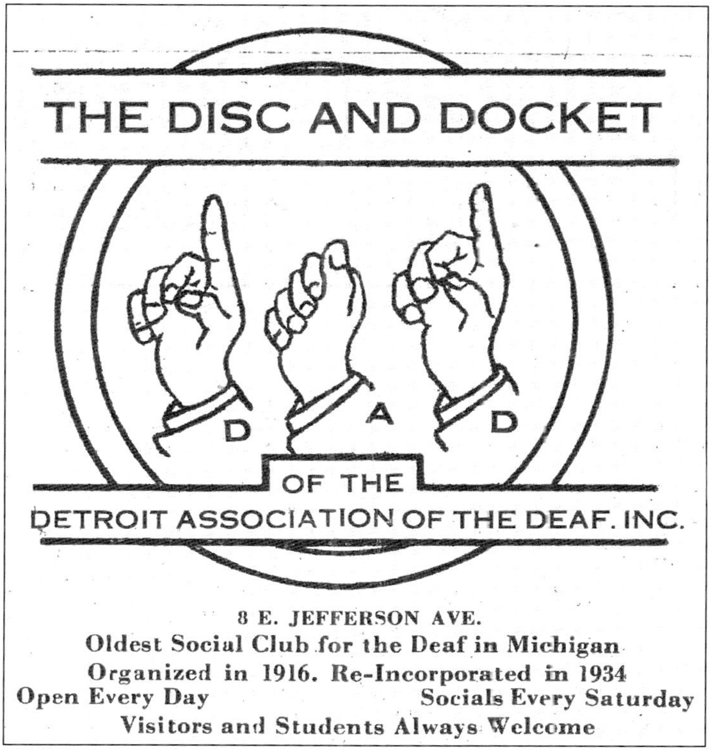

This is the earliest logo for the *Disc and Docket* newsletter, which later became the *Sign Post* newsletter, printed by Morris Purviance in typewriter setting and drawn by hand. Later in the 1930s, the drawing was similar, but the typewriter setting was replaced with a professional printed letter setting. Morris Purviance was called the "father of the *Sign Post*." (Courtesy of DAD.)

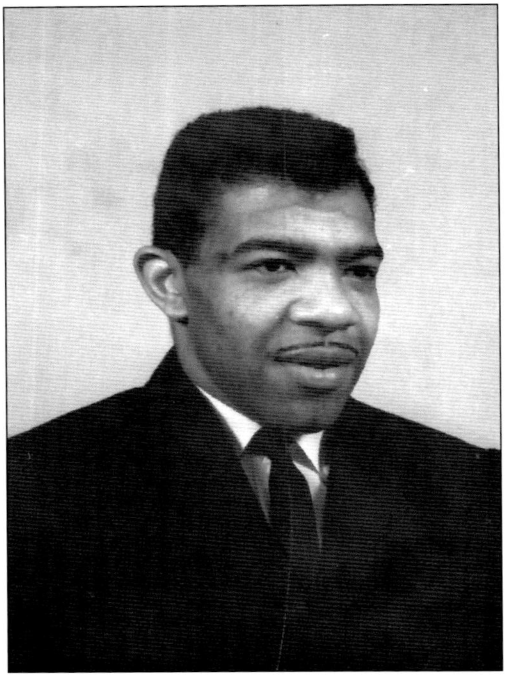

Ernest "Ernie" Hairston, a young adult in this photograph, worked for the Michigan United Fund Agency in Lansing, Michigan. Boyce Williams offered him a job when a grant was given for a limited time to train underprivileged deaf adults. Before he moved to Michigan, Hairston worked as the first black deaf teacher at the North Carolina School for the Deaf. He was also one of the coauthors of *Black and Deaf in America* with Linwood Smith. (Courtesy of Ernest Hairston.)

Eric Malzkuhn, often an entertainer in the early DAD days, participated in skits including *Setting Out*, a comedy film in color, in October 1945. On the same night was the first deaf full-length color production, called *Dog Trouble*, with Chester Beers, Marie Jansing, and Tippie the dog. MDA hosted the films at the DAD Hall at 105 Davenport Street in Detroit. Since then, *Dog Trouble* has been lost. (Courtesy of DAD.)

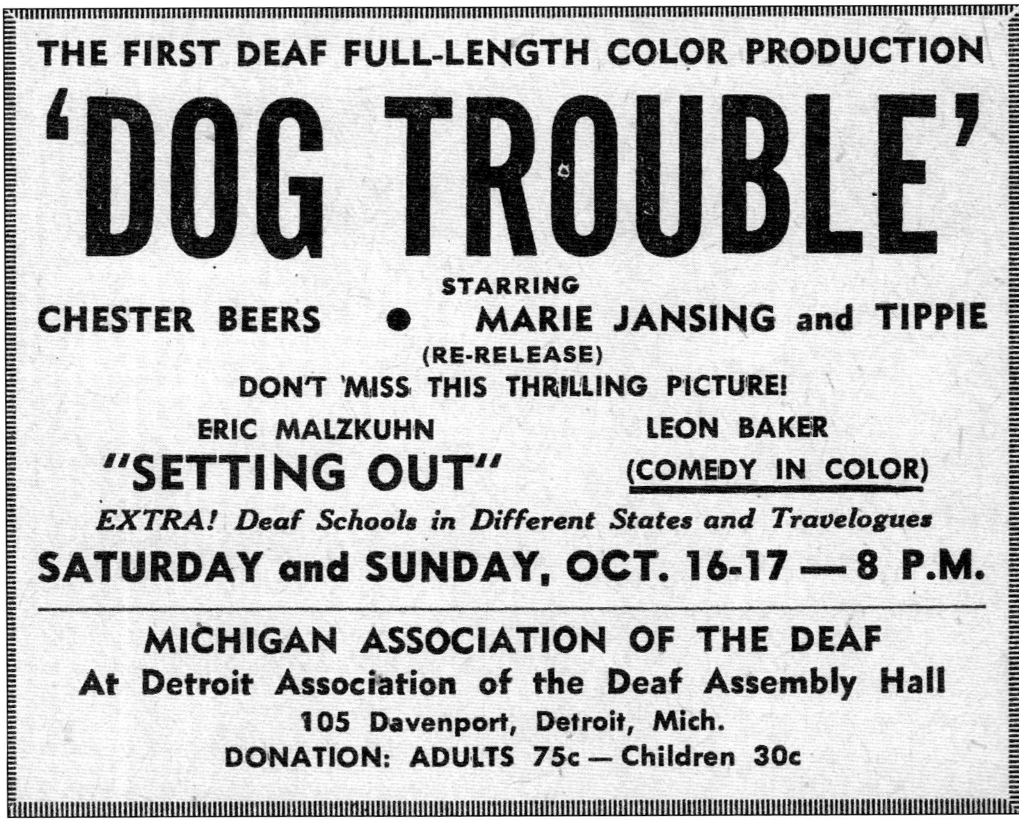

This original wooden announcement board is shown the year DAD officially started, 1916. It was removed from the wall at the last club-owned location on Third Avenue in Redford Township in January 2001. Today, it is stored in a safe resting place. (Courtesy of DAD.)

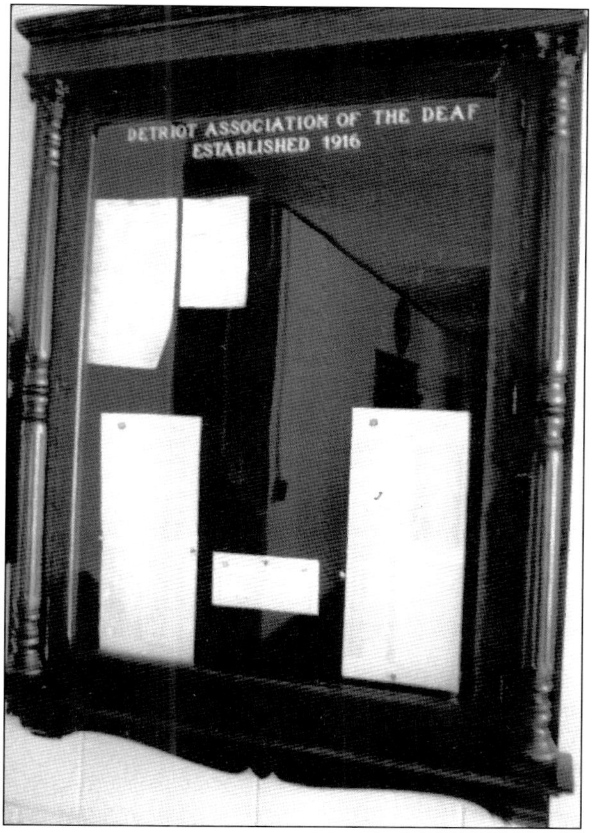

The DAD Ladies Auxiliary, pictured in the 1970s, shows their pride in making the quilt for the DAD Bazaar event. From left to right are Emma Rocco, Melvina McCall, and Jean Zito. (Courtesy of Dominic and Dorothy Etkie Zito.)

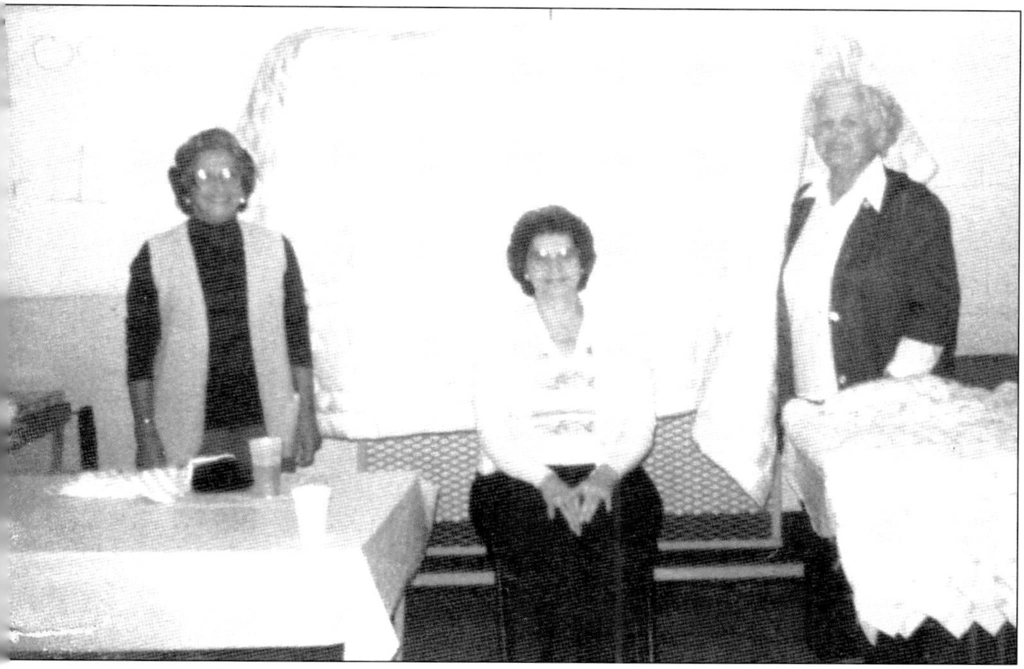

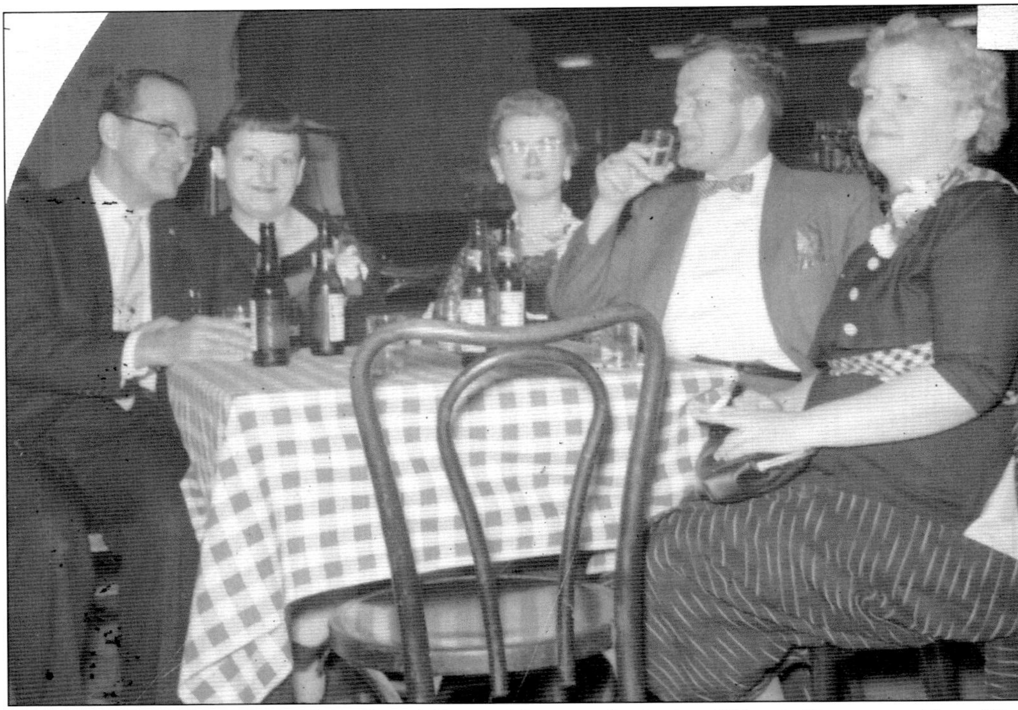

From left to right, DAD members David Ourso, Margaret Ludovico, Winnie Strang, and Jean Zito have a great time socializing. DAD offered many entertaining events, including drama club skits, movies, and themed parties. The best memory is having Dudley Cutshaw around to entertain the DAD members. Many miss him and his leadership and humor. Cutshaw kept DAD afloat by negotiating discounts from many businesses. (Courtesy of Dominic and Dorothy Etkie Zito.)

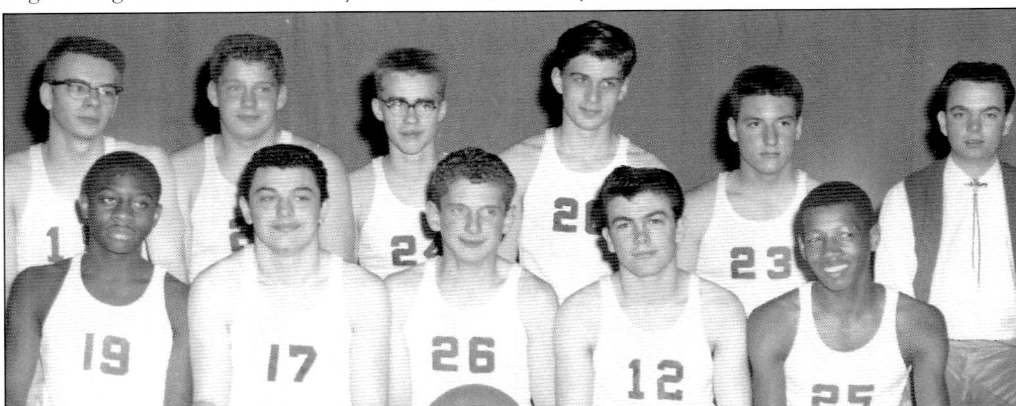

Pictured around 1961 at MSD are, from left to right, (seated) Fred McFadden, Istvan "Steve" Kovacs, Dominic Zito Jr., Anson Mitchell, and Abram Powell; (standing) Dennis Schenemenauer, Robert Beck, Stephen Gemmill, unidentified, David Takacs, and Ivan Harbough. Abram recalled that he started playing sports late in high school. He never realized he could play until he found his "crazy legs." (Courtesy of Dominic and Dorothy Etkie Zito.)

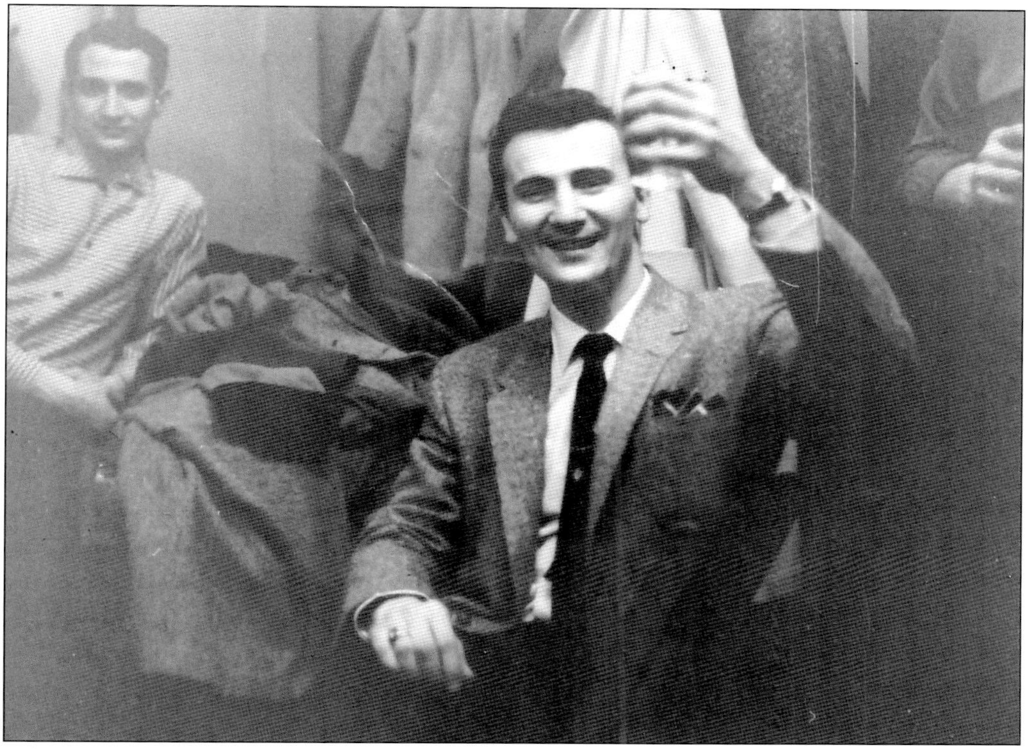

Valerio "Val" DiFalco cheers on his team with a drink at an MCAD event shortly before his death in 1962. He was an athletic director for the MCAD organization. He never played at MSD, despite his love for sports. After he left MSD, he went on to play a lot of sports before his knees gave out and he became a manager and a coach. (Courtesy of Arlyn and Hester Meyerson.)

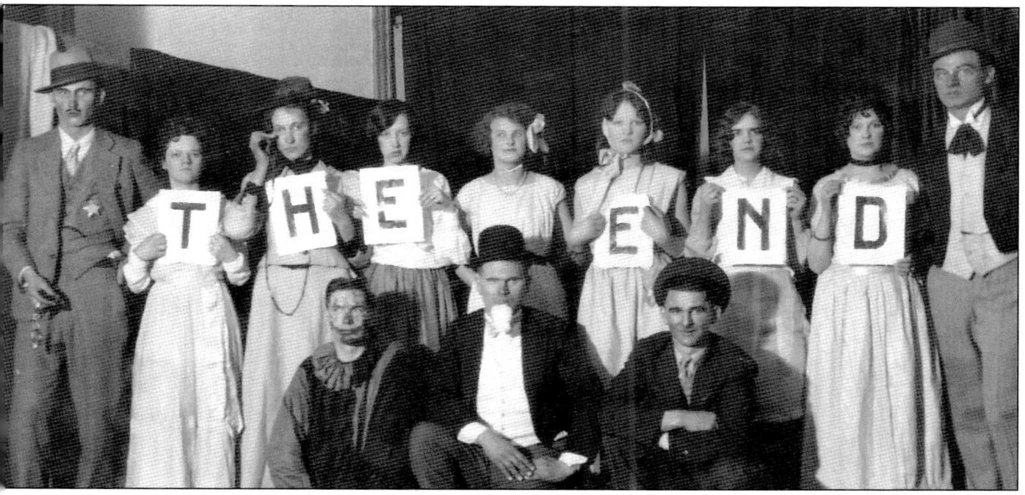

The Detroit Association of Catholic Deaf gave a show in sign language at 8:00 in the evening after the sermon on November 15, 1942. The play was open to the general public for 40¢ including tax, and proceeds went to the organization fund. According to *Our Silent Flock* newsletter, one of the plays included *God Bless America*. A deaf woman named Agnes Schrieber wrote the four one-act pantomime skits. (Courtesy of SJDC.)

Bibliography

"4 on Team of Deaf Killed in Collision." *Detroit News*. January 7, 1962, 1 and 4A.

1993 Second Alumni Reunion Celebration 120th Anniversary of the Ministry with Lutheran School for the Deaf 1873–1993. 1993.

Deaf-Mute Journal. August 8, 1922.

Chicago Livestock World. November 13, 1915.

Chilton's Motor Age. November 18, 1915 (volume 28, no. 21), 42.

Gannon, Jack. *Deaf Heritage: A Narrative History of Deaf America*. Silver Spring, MD: National Association of the Deaf, 1981.

The History of Lutheran School for the Deaf, 1873–1997. 1997.

Lythgoe, Darrin. Shetland Family History. Bayanne.info.

"Physician Politicians in Illinois Including Surgeons and Osteopaths." politicalgraveyard.com/geo/IL/physician.html.

Santa Ana Register. December 2, 1915, 12.

Sign Post. Detroit Association of the Deaf, 1920–1970.

About the Author

Kathleen Brockway, a deaf author, is an advocate for digital and historical preservation. She and Detroit Association of the Deaf were inspired by the stories of the deaf heritage in the Detroit area and were determined to share them with the public. The images were collected from living descendants of Detroit's earliest deaf families and deaf organizations to present this rich history. Brockway gives presentations on how to preserve deaf history better and is an advocate for establishing digital libraries across the United States. Currently, she is the chair of the Deaf Culture and History section with the National Association of the Deaf. One of her current projects is to help the Deaf Cultural Center in Olathe, Kansas, to expand into a bigger center with a digital library, museum, De'VIA (Deaf View/Image Art) and fine arts galleries, and more. The website for the center is www.deafculturalcenter.org. The center welcomes any donation to help it expand. For more information, please contact Kathleen through info@nad.org.

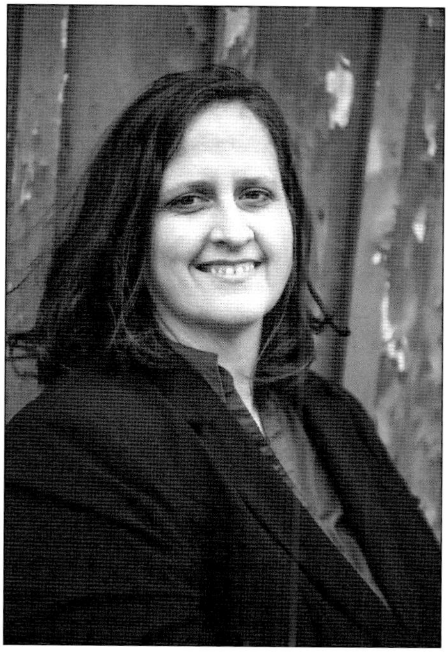